ESSEX
County Cricket Club
First-Class Records
1894-1994

Compiled by
Brian Heald

with

Mike Smith and Tony Debenham

Foreword by
Doug Insole

LIMLOW
BOOKS

First published in Great Britain by
Limlow Books Limited
St Peter's Hill, Litlington, Royston SG8 0QF
1995

British Library Cataloguing-in-Publication Data.
A catalogue record for this book is available from the British Library.

ISBN 1 874524 14 9

Printed by Peartree Printers, Derby

CONTENTS

SECTION 1 - TEAM RECORDS

SECTION 2 - INDIVIDUAL RECORDS - BATTING

SECTION 3 - PARTNERSHIP RECORDS

SECTION 4 - INDIVIDUAL RECORDS - BOWLING

SECTION 5 - INDIVIDUAL RECORDS - ALL-ROUND CRICKET

SECTION 6 - INDIVIDUAL RECORDS - WICKET-KEEPING

SECTION 7 - INDIVIDUAL RECORDS - FIELDING

SECTION 8 - MISCELLANEOUS

SECTION 9 - RECORDS AGAINST EACH OPPONENT

SECTION 10 - RECORDS ON EACH HOME GROUND

SECTION 11 - ESSEX C.C.C. FIRST-CLASS CAREER RECORDS

FOREWORD

The vital importance of statistics in the appreciation of the game of cricket and in assessing the prowess of those who play at the first-class level is beyond doubt. For many who are not active participants, the fascination of statistical data connected with the game is what makes them addicted to it.

And yet those with a close involvement in the game have always advised caution in the blind acceptance of averages as a true indication of the value of a player to his side. If he scored runs, who did he score them against, and in what circumstances? A big hundred on a bland pitch in a drawn match against ordinary bowling may be much less worthy than a hard earned and perhaps match winning 40 on a spiteful wicket against a strong attack. In writing about certain Essex players who have retired over the past decade or so I have often indicated that their value to our Club is not remotely calculable in terms of statistics alone. Nevertheless, I am happy to admit to an interest in facts and figures that has filled in many a winter's evening and which has helped me to respond sensibly to the welter of weird and wonderful questions dreamed up by cricketing nutcases the world over. Somebody somewhere is bound to know how many left-handed batsmen with gout have made their maiden centuries on a Thursday afternoon in September when the pavilion clock was an hour slow.

For Essex, it could be argued that the most vital statistic in the history of the Club was the loss of £3,559 in 1966 which brought to a head the financial crisis which required and which received the course of action that started us on the road to stability and comparative prosperity. It was clear that if the losses of previous years were not turned around, the Club would soon be bankrupt. It was decided that, in order to reduce expenditure to the absolute minimum, the professional playing staff would be reduced to 13 and that Second XI cricket would be given up, save for a few matches played by a team comprising club cricketers. As a result of those economies, total expenditure for the whole of the 1967 season was reduced to just over £32,000, from £40,000 in the previous year. From that point on, Essex began to make a profit every year, and the balance sheet has for some time been in a very healthy state. Even more noteworthy perhaps, back in the late 60's, was the remarkable performance of the young Essex team which, first under Brian Taylor and then under Keith Fletcher, over a decade or so developed into a Championship winning combination and provided the foundation for the side which was so consistently successful in all competitions in the 1980's.

It is almost an accepted truth these days that in order to achieve success there must be competition for places in a team. What those 13 Essex cricketers proved in the 1960's and demonstrated further as time progressed was that a small group of players, united by team spirit and determined to succeed, could not only achieve success but enjoy themselves thoroughly and, in the process, provide great entertainment for spectators throughout the country and especially for Essex members and supporters who had remained so loyal throughout.

For me, one of the greatest pleasures gained in a long association with Essex has been to hear at first hand of the exploits of the great players of the past, and, in fact, to meet many of them. Charles Kortright, "Sailor" Young and Walter Mead, for instance. Great characters all, whose value to the game cannot be reflected adequately by their statistical performances, but whose names and records form an essential part of the history of Essex cricket and of this book, which I hope you will enjoy.

DOUG INSOLE

INTRODUCTION

Although there are references to cricket in Essex during the eighteenth century, the present Essex County Cricket Club was formed in 1876 and the first official county match seems to have been played against Suffolk at Ipswich in June of that year. However, as far as this book is concerned, it is the doings of Essex as a first-class county that are recorded. Essex gained first-class status in 1894 and played friendly matches against Leicestershire, Surrey, Warwickshire and Yorkshire, as well as playing a match against Oxford University. Essex joined the County Championship in 1895 and have remained there ever since apart from the breaks caused by two World Wars.

Status
The matches covered in this book are those as listed in "British Isles First-Class Cricket Matches" published by the Association of Cricket Statisticians (ACS) in 1976. There are few matches played by Essex that are of doubtful status. I have therefore included games against Dublin University and Combined Services, both in 1922. Matches excluded are against Dublin University in 1905, Ireland in 1905 and Julien Cahn's XI in 1930.

Assumed Names
In the second edition of *Who's Who of Cricketers*, published by Hamlyn in association with the ACS, F.J.Cooper is stated as having possibly played two matches under the assumed name of "A.Brown". I have followed this line of thinking and grouped the "two" players together in the career records section at the end. If anyone has any information as to whether or not Cooper and Brown were the same person I should welcome it.

'Jack' Russell
During his career, and long after it was over, 'Jack' Russell was known by the initials 'A.C.' Later research confirmed that his given names were Charles Albert George. He signed his autograph using both sets of initials. I have used 'C.A.G.' in this book and to those readers who insist on 'A.C.', my apologies. I know that changes of name and/or initials can cause confusion, hence this note of explanation.

Grounds
Essex has used 12 grounds for home first-class matches. Performances in games played at the Garrison Ground, Colchester and at Hoffman's Ground, Chelmsford have been noted. Unless stated any reference to Colchester means Castle Park and to Chelmsford the County Ground. Recent research by Mike Smith and Tony Debenham has shown that matches at Colchester from 1920 to 1923 were played at Castle Park and not at the Garrison Ground as quoted previously.

Some counties have changed grounds, notably Glamorgan at Cardiff, Leicestershire at Leicester and Yorkshire at Sheffield. Dates of matches played at each venue can be found in the inter-county records in Section 9.

Acknowledgements
Most of the career records in this book have come from those compiled by the late Leslie Newnham, whose work has been continued by Kevin Montgomery and Mike Smith. To these gentlemen I am very grateful, especially to Mike Smith, the present Essex statistician, who has helped considerably. I should also like to thank Peter Griffiths for having the faith in me to write

this book; to Doug Insole, President of the County Club, for his Foreword, which is very perceptive, informative, and in parts witty; to Peter Edwards, Secretary-Manager of Essex County Cricket Club for his support; to David Baggett, for checking everything, a mammoth task; and to Philip Bailey, Robert Brooke, Brian Croudy and Tony Debenham for supplying information that was not readily to hand in my library.

Scorecards
I have been through every scorecard involving Essex, using Wisden Cricketer's Almanack, The Cricketer, First-Class Cricket Matches (ACS), Essex Handbooks and Yearbooks and First-Class Cricket, A Complete Record by Jim Ledbetter. Many other books have been consulted and a list follows this introduction.

Errors
In any work of reference errors can occur. Although I should like to claim infallibility, to do so would smack of arrogance and folly. If anyone finds any errors, please let me know so that they can be put right in any future edition of this book.

Symbols
* denotes not out or an unbroken partnership. The letter c after an innings denotes that the innings was closed after the requisite number of overs had been bowled in the first innings. This was restricted to 65 overs in 1966 and 100 overs from 1974 to 1980.

Brian Heald
Upminster
October 1994

LIST OF BOOKS CONSULTED

Bailey, Philip, Thorn, Philip and Wynne-Thomas, Peter. *Who's Who of Cricketers*. (Hamlyn) 1993

British Isles First-Class Cricket Matches. (Association of Cricket Statisticians) 1976

Brooke, Robert. *A History of the County Cricket Championship*. (Guinness) 1991

The Cricketer. Various issues

The Cricket Statistician. (Association of Cricket Statisticians) Various issues

Essex County Cricket Club Handbooks. Various years

First-Class Cricket Matches. (Association of Cricket Statisticians) Various years

Frindall, Bill. *The Wisden Book of Cricket Records*. (Headline) 1993

Green, Benny. *The Wisden Book of Obituaries*. (Macdonald Queen Anne Press) 1986

Ledbetter, Jim. *First-Class Cricket. A Complete Record*. (Breedon Books Sport and Limlow Books) Various years

Lemmon, David and Marshall, Mike. *Essex County Cricket Club. The Official History*. (The Kingswood Press) 1987

Martin-Jenkins, Christopher. *The Wisden Book of County Cricket*. (Queen Anne Press) 1981

Newnham, Leslie. *Essex County Cricket 1876-1975*. (Private) 1975

Newnham, Leslie. *Essex Cricketers 1876-1986*. (Association of Cricket Statisticians) 1987

Playfair Cricket Annual. Various years

Powell, William. *The Wisden Guide to Cricket Grounds*. (Stanley Paul) 1989

Wisden Cricketers' Almanack. Various years

Essex in 1979, the first County Championship

back: C.F.Driver *(Scorer)*, K.R.Pont, G.A.Gooch, N.Smith, N.Phillip, M.H.Denness, D.L.Acfield, P.J.Edwards *(Secretary-Manager)*

Front: K.S.McEwan, J.K.Lever, K.W.R.Fletcher *(Captain)*, T.N.Pearce *(President)*, R.E.East, S.Turner, B.R.Hardie

MATCH RESULTS SEASON BY SEASON

Year	_All_ P	W	L	D	T	A	_CC_ P	W	L	D	T	A	Pos
1894	9	1	6	2	-	-	-	-	-	-	-	-	-
1895	17	6	7	4	-	-	16	5	7	4	-	-	9th
1896	14	6	5	3	-	-	12	5	4	3	-	-	5th
1897	17	7	3	7	-	-	16	7	2	7	-	-	3rd
1898	21	11	6	4	-	-	20	10	6	4	-	-	5th
1899	21	7	6	8	-	-	20	6	6	8	-	-	6th
1900	22	4	6	12	-	-	22	4	6	12	-	-	10th
1901	21	4	5	12	-	1	21	4	5	12	-	1	10th
1902	22	2	5	15	-	-	20	2	5	13	-	-	13th
1903	20	7	6	7	-	2	20	7	6	7	-	2	8th
1904	20	3	10	7	-	-	20	3	10	7	-	-	14th
1905	22	4	10	8	-	-	20	3	10	7	-	-	12th
1906	23	10	6	7	-	-	22	9	6	7	-	-	7th
1907	24	10	9	5	-	-	22	10	7	5	-	-	7th
1908	22	5	7	10	-	-	22	5	7	10	-	-	11th
1909	20	2	7	11	-	2	18	2	7	9	-	2	14th
1910	19	6	8	5	-	-	17	5	8	4	-	-	11th
1911	18	8	5	5	-	-	18	8	5	5	-	-	6th
1912	20	1	9	10	-	1	17	1	8	8	-	1	15th
1913	18	2	9	7	-	-	18	2	9	7	-	-	15th
1914	24	9	9	6	-	-	24	9	9	6	-	-	8th
1919	20	2	6	12	-	-	18	2	4	12	-	-	14th
1920	26	9	10	7	-	-	24	9	9	6	-	-	9th
1921	28	5	15	8	-	-	26	5	13	8	-	-	15th
1922	29	8	4	17	-	-	26	7	4	15	-	-	8th
1923	28	7	12	9	-	-	26	6	11	9	-	-	13th
1924	27	2	13	12	-	2	26	2	12	12	-	2	15th
1925	29	9	7	13	-	-	28	9	7	12	-	-	7th
1926	32	7	9	15	1	-	30	6	9	14	1	-	9th
1927	32	9	8	15	-	-	30	8	8	14	-	-	8th
1928	32	2	3	17	-	-	30	2	13	15	-	-	16th
1929	32	6	12	14	-	-	28	6	9	13	-	-	12th
1930	29	7	6	16	-	-	28	7	5	16	-	-	6th
1931	30	7	12	11	-	-	28	7	11	10	-	-	10th
1932	31	4	16	11	-	-	28	4	14	10	-	-	14th
1933	30	13	10	7	-	-	28	13	8	7	-	-	4th
1934	30	9	5	16	-	-	28	9	4	15	-	-	8th
1935	30	12	13	5	-	-	28	11	12	5	-	-	9th
1936	28	10	8	10	-	-	26	8	8	10	-	-	9th
1937	30	14	12	4	-	-	28	13	11	4	-	-	6th
1938	30	13	12	5	-	-	28	12	11	5	-	-	6th
1939	30	13	11	6	-	-	28	12	10	6	-	-	4th
1946	27	8	10	9	-	-	26	8	9	9	-	-	8th
1947	29	6	11	11	1		26	6	9	10	1	-	11th
1948	28	5	9	14	-	-	26	5	8	13	-	-	13th
1949	29	7	10	12	-	-	26	7	9	10	-	-	9th
1950	31	4	13	14	-	-	28	4	12	12	-	-	17th
1951	31	6	2	23	-	-	28	6	2	20	-	-	8th
1952	31	8	5	17	1	-	28	8	4	15	1	-	10th
1953	29	7	8	14	-	1	27	6	7	14	-	1	12th
1954	31	4	11	16	-	-	28	3	11	14	-	-	15th
1955	30	6	15	9	-	-	28	6	15	7	-	-	14th
1956	30	6	11	13	-	-	28	6	10	12	-	-	11th
1957	31	12	7	12	-	-	28	11	6	11	-	-	5th
1958	30	9	8	13	-	-	28	9	7	12	-	-	6th
1959	31	13	7	10	1	-	28	11	7	9	1	-	9th
1960	31	9	5	17	-	1	27	9	3	15	-	1	6th
1961	31	11	10	10	-	-	28	10	8	10	-	-	6th
1962	31	9	6	16	-	-	28	8	6	14	-	-	9th
1963	30	7	4	19	-	-	28	6	4	18	-	-	12th
1964	31	8	11	12	-	-	28	7	11	10	-	-	10th
1965	31	6	7	18	-	-	28	4	7	17	-	-	15th
1966	32	7	10	15	-	-	28	4	10	14	-	-	16th
1967	30	3	9	18	-	-	28	3	9	16	-	-	15th
1968	28	5	7	16	-	2	27	5	6	16	-	1	14th
1969	26	8	6	12	-	-	24	6	6	12	-	-	6th
1970	27	5	6	16	-	-	24	4	6	14	-	-	12th
1971	25	7	5	13	-	-	24	6	5	13	-	-	10th
1972	22	7	4	11	-	-	20	6	4	10	-	-	5th
1973	22	6	6	10	-	-	20	6	5	9	-	-	8th
1974	21	4	3	13	1	-	20	4	3	12	1	-	12th
1975	22	7	7	8	-	-	20	7	6	7	-	-	7th
1976	22	7	5	10	-	-	20	7	4	9	-	-	6th
1977	23	7	5	11	-	1	21	7	5	9	-	1	6th
1978	24	12	1	11	-	-	22	12	1	9	-	-	2nd
1979	23	13	4	6	-	1	21	13	4	4	-	1	**1st**
1980	24	4	3	17	-	-	22	4	3	15	-	-	8th
1981	23	8	4	11	-	1	21	8	4	9	-	1	5th
1982	24	6	5	13	-	-	22	5	5	12	-	-	7th
1983	26	11	6	9	-	-	24	11	5	8	-	-	**1st**
1984	27	13	4	10	-	-	24	13	3	8	-	-	**1st**
1985	26	7	2	17	-	1	23	7	2	14	-	1	4th
1986	26	10	7	9	-	-	24	10	6	8	-	-	**1st**
1987	27	3	5	19	-	-	24	2	4	18	-	-	12th
1988	24	10	5	9	-	-	22	9	5	8	-	-	3rd
1989	24	14	3	7	-	-	22	13	2	7	-	-	2nd
1990	24	9	2	13	-	-	22	8	2	12	-	-	2nd
1991	25	12	5	8	-	-	22	11	5	6	-	-	**1st**
1992	25	11	7	7	-	-	22	11	6	5	-	-	**1st**
1993	20	5	6	9	-	-	17	4	6	7	-	-	11th
1994	19	7	5	7	-	-	17	7	5	5	-	-	6th
	2340	662	675	998	5	16	2152	618	618	911	5	15	

All first-class matches: P W L D T A — County Championship: P W L D T A Pos

11

ABANDONED MATCHES
(These are not included in the above table)

1901	v Leicestershire	Leyton	1953	v Derbyshire	Buxton
1903	v Middlesex	Lord's	1960	v Surrey	The Oval
	v Hampshire	Leyton	1968	v Oxford University	Oxford
1909	v Leicestershire	Leyton		v Glamorgan	Pontypridd
	v Middlesex	Leyton	1977	v Kent	Colchester
1912	v Lancashire	Manchester	1979	v Surrey	The Oval
1924	v Surrey	The Oval	1981	v Gloucestershire	Chelmsford
	v Somerset	Bath	1985	v Yorkshire	Sheffield

(The match against Surrey at The Oval in 1910 was abandoned after the second day's play because of the funeral of King Edward VII. The match did not count in the Championship and is listed as a first-class friendly)

RESULTS SEQUENCES

Most consecutive wins	5 in 1939-46, 1958-59 and 1978
Most consecutive defeats	5 in 1904, 1913, 1923, 1928, 1935, 1938 and 1964
Most consecutive matches without defeat	34 in 1978-79
Most consecutive matches without a win	26 in 1912-13
Most wins in a season (All matches)	14 in 1937 and 1989
Most wins in a season (Championship)	13 in 1937, 1979, 1984 and 1989
Most defeats in a season (All matches)	16 in 1932
Most defeats in a season (Championship)	15 in 1955
Most home wins in a season (All matches)	10 in 1957
Most home wins in a season (Championship)	9 in 1957 and 1979
Most home defeats in a season (All matches)	9 in 1924
Most home defeats in a season (Championship)	8 in 1924
Most away wins in a season (All matches)	7 in 1984 and 1991
Most away wins in a season (Championship)	7 in 1984
Most away defeats in a season (All matches)	10 in 1932
Most away defeats in a season (Championship)	9 in 1932
Fewest wins in a season (All matches)	1 in 1912
Fewest wins in a season (Championship)	1 in 1912
Fewest defeats in a season (All matches)	1 in 1978
Fewest defeats in a season (Championship)	1 in 1978
Fewest home wins in a season (All matches)	0 in 1987
Fewest home wins in a season (Championship)	0 in 1987
Fewest home defeats in a season (All matches)	0 in 1951, 1978 and 1985
Fewest home defeats in a season (Championship)	0 in 1896, 1951, 1957, 1978, 1985 and 1989
Fewest away wins in a season (All matches)	0 in 1912
Fewest away wins in a season (Championship)	0 in 1912
Fewest away defeats in a season (All matches)	0 in 1960
Fewest away defeats in a season (Championship)	0 in 1960

RESULTS AGAINST EACH TEAM

County Championship

	Seasons	P	W	L	D	T	A
v Derbyshire	1895-1994	152	62	28	62	-	1
v Durham	1992-1994	3	2	1	0	-	-
v Glamorgan	1925-1994	105	36	18	51	-	1
v Gloucestershire	1898-1994	116	37	43	35	1	1
v Hampshire	1895-1994	126	41	32	53	-	1
v Kent	1898-1994	163	43	54	66	-	1
v Lancashire	1897-1994	135	28	43	63	1	1
v Leicestershire	1895-1994	138	39	32	67	-	2
v Middlesex	1895-1994	150	31	51	68	-	2
v Northamptonshire	1906-1994	144	45	35	63	1	-

County Championship

	Seasons	P	W	L	D	T	A
v Nottinghamshire	1901-1994	113	28	25	60	-	-
v Somerset	1895-1994	123	50	28	44	1	1
v Surrey	1895-1994	166	36	64	66	-	3
v Sussex	1897-1994	144	47	35	61	1	-
v Warwickshire	1895-1994	102	32	26	44	-	-
v Worcestershire	1910-1994	127	38	27	62	-	-
v Yorkshire	1895-1994	145	23	76	46	-	1
TOTALS		2152	618	618	911	5	15

Other Matches

	Seasons	P	W	L	D	T	A
v Australian Imperial Forces	1919	2	0	2	0	-	-
v Australians	1896-1993	29	3	14	12	-	-
v Cambridge Univ	1910-1994	56	21	3	32	-	-
v Canadians	1954	1	0	0	1	-	-
v Combined Services	1922-1950	2	1	0	1	-	-
v Commonwealth XI	1953	1	1	0	0	-	-
v Dublin University	1922	1	0	0	1	-	-
v England A	1992-1993	2	1	0	1	-	-
v Indians	1932-1982	9	2	1	6	-	-
v Jamaica	1970	1	0	0	1	-	-
v Leicestershire	1894	2	0	1	1	-	-
v M.C.C.	1895-1987	10	2	3	5	-	-
v New Zealanders	1927-1994	12	2	6	4	-	-
v Nottinghamshire	1929	2	0	2	0	-	-

Other Matches

	Seasons	P	W	L	D	T	A
v Oxford Univ	1894-1972	16	8	3	5	-	1
v Pakistanis	1954-1992	6	1	2	3	-	-
v T.N.Pearce's XI	1952	1	0	1	0	-	-
v South Africans	1907-1965	11	1	6	4	-	-
v South African Fezela XI	1961	1	0	1	0	-	-
v Surrey	1894-1947	4	0	3	1	-	-
v Victoria	1991	1	0	0	1	-	-
v Warwickshire	1894	2	0	1	1	-	-
v West Indians	1906-1991	14	1	6	7	-	-
v Yorkshire	1894	2	0	2	0	-	-
TOTALS		188	44	57	87	-	1
GRAND TOTALS		2340	662	675	998	5	16

HOME RECORD BY GROUNDS

	Seasons	P	W	L	D	T	A
Brentwood	1922-1969	58	21	15	21	1	-
Chelmsford (County Ground)	1925-1994	208	70	50	87	1	1
Chelmsford (Hoffman's Ground)	1959-1961	3	0	2	1	-	-
Clacton	1931-1966	60	26	15	19	-	-
Colchester (Castle Park)	1914-1994	101	35	20	46	-	1

	Seasons	P	W	L	D	T	A
Colchester (Garrison Ground)	1924-1972	25	8	10	7	-	-
Harlow	1970	2	1	1	0	-	-
Ilford	1923-1994	108	34	25	48	1	-
Leyton	1894-1977	407	111	128	167	1	4
Romford	1950-1968	34	14	8	12	-	-
Southend	1906-1994	120	43	38	39	-	-
Westcliff	1934-1976	69	21	24	24	-	-

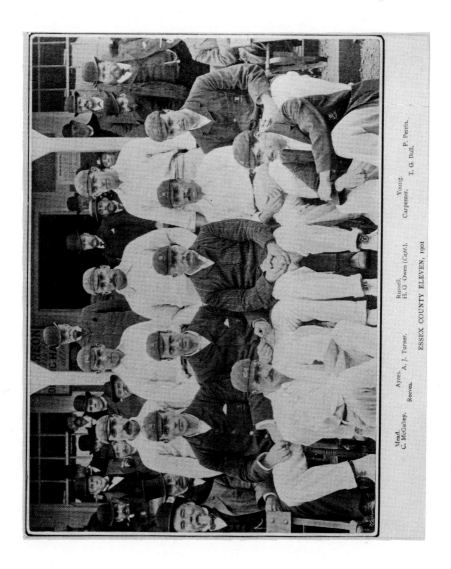

Mead.   Ayres.   Russell.   Young.
C. McGahey.   A. J. Turner.   H. G. Owen (*Capt.*).   Carpenter.   P. Perrin.
Reeves.   T. G. Bull.

ESSEX COUNTY ELEVEN, 1901

14

HIGHEST INNINGS TOTALS

For Essex

761-6d	v Leicestershire	Chelmsford	1990
692	v Somerset	Taunton	1895
673	v Leicestershire	Leicester	1899
621	v Leicestershire	Leicester	1991
616-5d	v Surrey	The Oval	1904
616	v Kent	Chelmsford	1988
609-4d	v Derbyshire	Leyton	1912
604-7d	v Northamptonshire	Northampton	1921
597	v Derbyshire	Chesterfield	1904
597	v Surrey	The Oval	1946
593-7	v Nottinghamshire	Clacton	1951
592-8d	v Leicestershire	Chelmsford	1988
590	v Nottinghamshire	Leyton	1904
588-9d	v Northamptonshire	Colchester	1937
584-9d	v Hampshire	Southampton	1927
578-6d	v Gloucestershire	Bristol (Packer)	1927
573-9d	v Northamptonshire	Northampton	1908
570-8d	v Surrey	Brentwood	1934
566-6d	v Middlesex	Chelmsford	1991
564-8d	v Hampshire	Bournemouth	1933
560-5d	v Worcestershire	Leyton	1921
560-9d	v Sussex	Leyton	1933
559-9	v Lancashire	Leyton	1904
553	v Gloucestershire	Gloucester	1938
551	v Kent	Leyton	1900
545-9d	v Northamptonshire	Leyton	1921
544	v Kent	Folkestone	1991
543-8d	v Derbyshire	Chelmsford	1991
541-5d	v Kent	Chelmsford	1994
541-7d	v Northamptonshire	Northampton	1922
539	v Surrey	The Oval	1990
535-6d	v Sussex	Colchester	1938
532-7d	v Hampshire	Bournemouth	1947
531-7d	v Nottinghamshire	Nottingham	1939
530	v Somerset	Taunton	1926
526	v Kent	Chelmsford	1992
524-7d	v Yorkshire	Leeds	1984
522-3d	v Derbyshire	Chelmsford	1989
522-8d	v Warwickshire	Leyton	1930
522	v Sussex	Leyton	1906
521-9d	v Sussex	Hove	1936
521	v Yorkshire	Leyton	1905
521	v Worcestershire	Leyton	1922
516	v Kent	Leyton	1901
516	v Kent	Leyton	1908
515	v Leicestershire	Leicester	1898
514	v Northamptonshire	Clacton	1948
510-2d	v Lancashire	Ilford	1992
508-9d	v Kent	Chelmsford	1990
507-9d	v Derbyshire	Leyton	1905
507	v Hampshire	Leyton	1913
507	v Gloucestershire	Leyton	1919
505-7d	v Hampshire	Leyton	1929
505	v Worcestershire	Stourbridge	1911
503	v Hampshire	Southend	1936
502	v Kent	Maidstone	1947

502	v Warwickshire	Colchester	1982
501	v Worcestershire	Leyton	1920
500	v Worcestershire	Worcester	1920
500	v Worcestershire	Leyton	1933

Against Essex

803-4d	by Kent	Brentwood	1934
721	by Australians	Southend	1948
662-8d	by Nottinghamshire	Nottingham	1947
636-6d	by Northamptonshire	Chelmsford	1990
634-7d	by Middlesex	Chelmsford	1983
621-6d	by Kent	Tonbridge	1922
614-8d	by Warwickshire	Birmingham	1904
613-6d	by Surrey	The Oval	1990
611	by Sussex	Leyton	1905
609-6d	by Australians	Leyton	1909
595-4d	by Nottinghamshire	Leyton	1926
592-6d	by Northamptonshire	Northampton	1990
591	by Sussex	Hove	1993
586-5d	by Glamorgan	Brentwood	1948
580-6d	by Kent	Maidstone	1947
579	by Middlesex	Leyton	1919
576-9d	by Nottinghamshire	Clacton	1951
564-3d	by Australians	Leyton	1912
560-6d	by Kent	Blackheath	1959
558-8d	by Nottinghamshire	Leyton	1921
555-1d	by Yorkshire	Leyton	1932
552-9d	by Nottinghamshire	Leyton	1905
552	by Derbyshire	Chesterfield	1928
548	by Derbyshire	Chesterfield	1904
548	by Kent	Gravesend	1938
543	by Kent	Leyton	1911
539	by Northamptonshire	Kettering	1933
538-9d	by Australians	Leyton	1926
538	by Sussex	Leyton	1928
534-7d	by Hampshire	Leyton	1913
532-6d	by Northamptonshire	Northampton	1952
532	by Kent	Maidstone	1950
528-6d	by Surrey	The Oval	1947
528	by Middlesex	Lord's	1905
525-7d	by Middlesex	Uxbridge	1994
525	by Warwickshire	Leyton	1901
524-9d	by Surrey	Leyton	1926
523	by Sussex	Leyton	1919
523	by Gloucestershire	Chelmsford	1928
521	by Leicestershire	Leyton	1914
520	by Sussex	Leyton	1902
520	by Leicestershire	Chelmsford	1990
515	by Worcestershire	Chelmsford	1934
514-6d	by Yorkshire	Leyton	1928
512-9d	by Yorkshire	Bradford	1913
512-9d	by Yorkshire	Sheffield	1928
510	by Lancashire	Clacton	1947
508-8d	by Nottinghamshire	Nottingham	1905
508	by Derbyshire	Leyton	1900
506-4d	by Surrey	Leyton	1928
505-6d	by Lancashire	Leyton	1904
505	by Warwickshire	Leyton	1900
504	by Yorkshire	Bradford	1902

| 503-4d | by South Africans | Colchester | 1955 |
| 501-6d | by Warwickshire | Birmingham | 1930 |

HIGHEST FOURTH INNINGS TOTALS

For Essex

442-6 (won)	v Derbyshire	Derby	1992
412-3 (won)	v Sussex	Hove	1993
405-6 (won)	v Worcestershire	Worcester	1994
385-8 (won)	v Somerset	Taunton	1946
352-7 (drawn, set 464)	v Kent	Gravesend	1924
351-4 (won)	v Lancashire	Colchester	1990
341-3 (won)	v Middlesex	Leyton	1906
340 (lost by 31 runs)	v Cambridge University	Chelmsford	1933
339-6 (won)	v Lancashire	Manchester	1898
335-6 (won)	v Gloucestershire	Southend	1992
331 (lost by 48 runs)	v Gloucestershire	Bristol	1908
327-8 (drawn, set 328)	v Nottinghamshire	Southend	1948
325-8 (drawn, set 333)	v Glamorgan	Southend	1990
315 (lost by 3 runs)	v Yorkshire	Colchester	1991
314-3 (won)	v Derbyshire	Clacton	1959
313-8 (won)	v Gloucestershire	Gloucester	1978
312 (lost by 276 runs)	v Northamptonshire	Chelmsford	1990
311-2 (won)	v Gloucestershire	Clacton	1953
311-9 (drawn, set 341)	v Kent	Maidstone	1993
309-6 (won)	v Kent	Maidstone	1990
(after the Essex 1st innings and the Kent 2nd innings had been forfeited)			
308-7 (drawn, set 351)	v Kent	Maidstone	1961
307-8 (won)	v Glamorgan	Clacton	1934
305-8 (won)	v Nottinghamshire	Ilford	1969
303-7 (drawn, set 319)	v Sussex	Eastbourne	1986
301-5 (won)	v Gloucestershire	Clacton	1962

Against Essex

410-6 (won)	by Hampshire	Southend	1983
374 (lost by 35 runs)	by Warwickshire	Ilford	1984
370-9 (won)	by Indians	Southend	1946
348 (lost by 8 runs)	by Warwickshire	Birmingham	1977
348-8 (won)	by Middlesex	Lord's	1982
346-7 (drawn, set 370)	by Gloucestershire	Leyton	1909
343-6 (won)	by Kent	Tunbridge Wells	1992
(reduced to a single innings match because of rain)			
342 (lost by 81 runs)	by Glamorgan	Cardiff	1932
340-5 (drawn, set 514)	by Surrey	The Oval	1911
340-8 (won)	by Surrey	Chelmsford	1947
337-6 (won)	by Leicestershire	Ilford	1956
335-6 (won)	by Middlesex	Leyton	1928
334-3 (won)	by Northamptonshire	Wellingborough	1955
327-8 (drawn, set 358)	by Worcestershire	Worcester	1946
327-3 (won)	by Surrey	The Oval	1985
321-4 (won)	by Kent	Chelmsford	1983
320-7 (won)	by Cambridge University	Cambridge	1932
319 (lost by 104 runs)	by Worcestershire	Worcester	1923
314 (lost by 32 runs)	by Surrey	Westcliff	1938
314-8 (won)	by Nottinghamshire	Southend	1955
311-5 (won)	by Glamorgan	Cardiff	1948
311 (lost by 87 runs)	by Kent	Clacton	1957
311 (lost by 13 runs)	by Glamorgan	Colchester	1981

308	(lost by 85 runs)	by Derbyshire	Southend	1982
306	(lost by 131 runs)	by Sussex	Leyton	1913
302-3	(drawn set 432)	by Sussex	Hove	1930
302-7	(drawn, set 344)	by Nottinghamshire	Nottingham	1985
302-6	(won)	by Somerset	Taunton	1992

HIGHEST MATCH AGGREGATES

1808 for 20 wickets	Essex v Sussex	Hove	1993
(The record aggregate for a first-class match in Britain)			
1570 for 29 wickets	Essex v Kent	Chelmsford	1988
1531 for 31 wickets	Essex v Kent	Maidstone	1993
1531 for 23 wickets	Essex v Middlesex	Uxbridge	1994
1530 for 19 wickets	Essex v Leicestershire	Chelmsford	1990
1422 for 34 wickets	Essex v Kent	Gravesend	1938
1414 for 24 wickets	Essex v Kent	Brentwood	1934

LOWEST INNINGS TOTALS

For Essex

30	v Yorkshire	Leyton	1901
34	v Kent	Brentwood	1969
37	v Surrey	Leyton	1899
41	v Yorkshire	Leyton	1901
44	v Nottinghamshire	Nottingham	1910
44	v Northamptonshire	Colchester	1986
46	v Surrey	The Oval	1912
47	v Warwickshire	Leyton	1968
50	v Nottinghamshire	Nottingham	1908

Against Essex

14	by Surrey	Chelmsford	1983
31	by Derbyshire	Derby	1914
31	by Yorkshire	Huddersfield	1935
37	by Cambridge University	Cambridge	1965
41	by M.C.C.	Lord's	1896
43	by Kent	Southend	1925
43	by Glamorgan	Neath	1935
45	by Northamptonshire	Southend	1923
45	by Leicestershire	Brentwood	1957
46	by Leicestershire	Leicester	1894
47	by Sussex	Southend	1914
47	by Cambridge University	Harlow	1970
48	by Somerset	Bath	1951
48	by Somerset	Westcliff	1961
49	by Worcestershire	Leyton	1922
50	by Glamorgan	Chelmsford	1946

LOWEST MATCH AGGREGATES
(Completed matches only)

175 for 29 wickets	Essex v Yorkshire	Leyton	1901
240 for 16 wickets	Essex v Glamorgan	Ilford	1939
265 for 30 wickets	Essex v Yorkshire	Dewsbury	1933
267 for 31 wickets	Essex v Warwickshire	Birmingham	1894
286 for 14 wickets	Essex v Leicestershire	Leyton	1968
292 for 32 wickets	Essex v Kent	Westcliff	1966

LARGEST INNINGS VICTORIES

Innings and 317 runs	v Somerset	Taunton	1895
Innings and 297 runs	v Worcestershire	Leyton	1922
Innings and 295 runs	v Worcestershire	Chelmsford	1939
Innings and 293 runs	v Northamptonshire	Colchester	1937
Innings and 275 runs	v Gloucestershire	Leyton	1908

LARGEST VICTORIES BY RUNS MARGIN

350 runs	v Cambridge University	Cambridge	1991
345 runs	v Surrey	Southend	1933
323 runs	v Surrey	The Oval	1914
322 runs	v Kent	Gravesend	1937
302 runs	v Lancashire	Clacton	1937

LARGEST INNINGS DEFEATS

Innings and 451 runs	by Australians	Southend	1948
Innings and 373 runs	by Yorkshire	Leyton	1932
Innings and 261 runs	by Surrey	The Oval	1894

LARGEST DEFEATS BY RUNS MARGIN

371 runs	by Somerset	Ilford	1924
352 runs	by Surrey	Southend	1907
327 runs	by South Africans	Leyton	1929
317 runs	by Gloucestershire	Bristol	1947
309 runs	by Australian Imperial Forces	Southend	1919
307 runs	by Middlesex	Chelmsford	1937
302 runs	by Kent	Tunbridge Wells	1930
301 runs	by Nottinghamshire	Nottingham	1910

VICTORY AFTER FOLLOWING-ON

Essex (114 and 374) beat Warwickshire (334 and 119) by 35 runs
Ilford 1984
Essex (149 and 310) beat Hampshire (300-8d and 80) by 79 runs
Bournemouth 1992

DEFEAT AFTER OPPONENTS FOLLOWED-ON

Gloucestershire (120 and 321) beat Essex (314 and 67) by 60 runs
Gloucester 1921

TIED MATCHES

Essex (178 & 137-9)	Somerset (208 & 107)	Chelmsford	1926

(Under the laws of the game at the time the match was ruled a tie with the scores level and Essex having one wicket to fall)

Essex (267 & 239)	Northamptonshire (215 & 291)	Ilford	1947
Essex (261 & 231)	Lancashire (266 & 226-7d)	Brentwood	1952
Essex (364-6d & 176-8d)	Gloucestershire (329 & 211)	Leyton	1959
Essex (200-8d & 218)	Sussex (245 & 173-5d)	Hove	1974

NARROWEST MARGINS OF VICTORY

1 wicket	v Sussex	Leyton	1899
1 wicket	v Worcestershire	Worcester	1947
1 wicket	v Glamorgan	Westcliff	1952
1 wicket	v Kent	Romford	1961
1 wicket	v Middlesex	Westcliff	1964
1 run	v Yorkshire	Huddersfield	1897
2 runs	v Northamptonshire	Ilford	1959
4 runs	v Kent	Dartford	1966
5 runs	v Surrey	The Oval	1900

NARROWEST MARGINS OF DEFEAT

1 wicket	by Gloucestershire	Leyton	1898
1 wicket	by South Africans	Colchester	1924
1 wicket	by Somerset	Weston-super-Mare	1932
1 wicket	by Middlesex	Chelmsford	1938
1 wicket	by Glamorgan	Cardiff	1956
1 wicket	by Kent	Folkestone	1977
1 wicket	by Yorkshire	Scarborough	1979
1 run	by Glamorgan	Swansea	1969
3 runs	by Yorkshire	Colchester	1991
5 runs	by Middlesex	Southend	1939

MOST RUNS IN A DAY'S PLAY

By One Team

721 for 10 wickets	by Australians	Southend	1948
623 for 2 wickets	by Kent	Brentwood	1934

By Both Teams

622 for 12 wickets	Sussex (523) v Essex (99-2)	Leyton	1919
610 for 13 wickets	Kent (548) v Essex (62-3)	Gravesend	1938
602 for 13 wickets	Lancashire (408) v		
	Essex (194-3)	Manchester	1919

(In 1919 matches were of two days duration and playing hours were extended)

THREE HUNDREDS IN AN INNINGS

Essex (692)	v Somerset	Taunton	1895
H.A.Carpenter 153, C.P.McGahey 147, A.P.Lucas 135			
Essex (616-5d)	v Surrey	The Oval	1904
H.A.Carpenter 199, C.P.McGahey 173, E.H.D.Sewell 106			
Essex (590)	v Nottinghamshire	Leyton	1904
F.L.Fane 126, C.P.McGahey 225, C.P.Buckenham 100			
Essex (516)	v Kent	Leyton	1908
F.L.Fane 108, J.W.H.T.Douglas 115, F.H.Gillingham 100			
Essex (507)	v Hampshire	Leyton	1913
C.D.McIver 134, C.A.G.Russell 102, F.H.Gillingham 105			
Essex (541-7d)	v Northamptonshire	Northampton	1922
*C.A.G.Russell 172, P.A.Perrin 114, J.O'Connor 102**			
Essex (436)	v Middlesex	Leyton	1928
J.O'Connor 123, C.A.G.Russell 108, C.Bray 108*			

20

Essex (521-9d)   v Sussex   Hove   1936
   J.R.Sheffield 105, J.O'Connor 127, T.N.Pearce 102
Essex (588-9d)   v Northamptonshire   Colchester   1937
   R.M.Taylor 129, J.O'Connor 192, M.S.Nichols 109*
Essex (597)   v Surrey   The Oval   1946
   A.V.Avery 210, T.C.Dodds 103, T.N.Pearce 116*
Essex (761-6d)   v Leicestershire   Chelmsford   1990
   G.A.Gooch 215, P.J.Prichard 245, N.A.Foster 101*
Essex (621)   v Leicestershire   Leicester   1991
   J.P.Stephenson 113, N.Hussain 196, M.A.Garnham 123

FOUR HUNDREDS IN AN INNINGS AGAINST

Australians (721)   v Essex   Southend   1948
   W.A.Brown 153, D.G.Bradman 187, S.J.E.Loxton 120, R.A.Saggers 104*

THREE HUNDREDS IN AN INNINGS AGAINST

Kent (621-6d)   v Essex   Tonbridge   1922
   A.F.Bickmore 120, James Seymour 159, C.S.Hurst 110
Gloucestershire (405-2)   v Essex   Bristol (Packer) 1927
   A.E.Dipper 185*, W.L.Neale 100, W.R.Hammond 105*
Yorkshire (514-6d)   v Essex   Leyton   1928
   P.Holmes 136, H.Sutcliffe 129, M.Leyland 133*
Kent (803-4d)   v Essex   Brentwood   1934
   W.H.Ashdown 332, F.E.Woolley 172, L.E.G.Ames 202*
Kent (532)   v Essex   Maidstone   1950
   L.E.G.Ames 130, P.Hearn 112, H.A.Pawson 137
Kent (560-6d)   v Essex   Blackheath   1959
   A.H.Phebey 130, M.C.Cowdrey 250, J.F.Pretlove 102
Middlesex (634-7d)   v Essex   Chelmsford   1983
   G.D.Barlow 132, M.W.Gatting 160, J.E.Emburey 133
Sussex (591)   v Essex   Hove   1993
   K.Greenfield 107, A.P.Wells 106, J.A.North 114

SIX FIFTIES IN AN INNINGS

Essex (498-6d)   v Hampshire   Portsmouth   1926
   J.R.Freeman 52, J.A.Cutmore 53, J.O'Connor 64,C.A.G.Russell 156, M.S.Nichols 81,
J.W.H.T.Douglas 54**
Essex (560-9d)   v Sussex   Leyton   1933
   J.A.Cutmore 88, J.O'Connor 93, L.C.Eastman 67, D.R.Wilcox 74, D.F.Pope 55,
T.P.B.Smith 54*

FIVE FIFTIES IN AN INNINGS

Essex (673)   v Leicestershire   Leicester   1899
   F.L.Fane 207, P.A.Perrin 132, C.P.McGahey 99, F.Street 76, G.W.Ayres 83
Essex (559-9)   v Lancashire   Leyton   1904
   H.A.Carpenter 67, P.A.Perrin 143, A.J.Turner 72, R.P.Keigwin 75, W.Reeves 57*
Essex (521)   v Yorkshire   Leyton   1905
   F.L.Fane 106, H.A.Carpenter 69, F.H.Gillingham 82, C.P.McGahey 105, W.Reeves 71
Essex (522)   v Sussex   Leyton   1906
   F.L.Fane 68, J.W.H.T.Douglas 66, W.M.F.Turner 76, W.Reeves 104, C.P.Buckenham 68.

Essex (363-4d)　　　v Sussex　　　　　Hastings　　　　1906
F.L.Fane 82, P.A.Perrin 60, C.P.McGahey 68, F.H.Gillingham 66*, W.M.F.Turner 54*
Essex (560-5d)　　　v Worcestershire　　Leyton　　　　　1921
F.H.Gillingham 53, C.A.G.Russell 151, J.R.Freeman 93, J.W.H.T.Douglas 123,
H.M.Morris 74*
Essex (441-8d)　　　v Yorkshire　　　　Southend　　　　1934
D.F.Pope 60, D.R.Wilcox 109, C.T.Ashton 51, T.P.B.Smith 54*, A.G.Powell 62*
Essex (503)　　　　v Sussex　　　　　Southend　　　　1936
*L.G.Crawley 63, M.S.Nichols 110, J.O'Connor 100, N.Vere Hodge 77,
J.W.A.Stephenson 65*
Essex (502)　　　　v Kent　　　　　　Maidstone　　　　1947
T.C.Dodds 83, S.J.Cray 114, F.H.Vigar 68, T.N.Pearce 92, T.P.B.Smith 67
Essex (514)　　　　v Northamptonshire　Clacton　　　　　1948
A.V.Avery 100, S.J.Cray 139, R.Horsfall 51, T.N.Pearce 62, R.Smith 60
Essex (499-8c)　　　v Worcestershire　　Westcliff　　　　1976
B.E.A.Edmeades 65, K.S.McEwan 55, G.A.Gooch 136, K.W.R.Fletcher 68, K.D.Boyce 75
Essex (502)　　　　v Warwickshire　　Colchester　　　　1982
G.A.Gooch 72, B.R.Hardie 86, K.S.McEwan 128, D.R.Pringle 54, S.Turner 83
Essex (592-8d)　　　v Leicestershire　　Chelmsford　　　1988
J.P.Stephenson 99, M.E.Waugh 86, P.J.Prichard 59, N.Hussain 165*, D.E.East 66
Essex (522-3d)　　　v Derbyshire　　　Chelmsford　　　1989
G.A.Gooch 148, J.P.Stephenson 94, A.W.Lilley 113*, M.E.Waugh 77, P.J.Prichard 54*
Essex (440-9d)　　　v Kent　　　　　　Maidstone　　　　1993
P.J.Prichard 104, J.J.B.Lewis 67, N.Shahid 60, M.A.Garnham 66, D.R.Pringle 76

SIX FIFTIES IN AN INNINGS AGAINST

Middlesex (579)　　　v Essex　　　　　Leyton　　　　　1919
*E.L.Kidd 92, E.H.Hendren 128, P.F.Warner 58, C.H.Gunasekera 58, E.Martin 64,
H.R.Murrell 96**
Surrey (524-9d)　　　v Essex　　　　　Leyton　　　　　1926
*J.B.Hobbs 69, A.Sandham 67, A.Jeacocke 51, T.F.Shepherd 93, D.R.Jardine 60,
P.G.H.Fender 104*
Nottinghamshire (662-8d)　v Essex　　　Nottingham　　　1947
*W.W.Keeton 188, R.T.Simpson 63, J.Hardstaff, jun 164, F.H.Winrow 73, W.Voce 57,
H.J.Butler 51**
Surrey (469)　　　　v Essex　　　　　Ilford　　　　　1948
*L.B.Fishlock 51, D.G.W.Fletcher 70, H.S.Squires 74, J.F.Parker 67, A.J.W.McIntyre 68,
J.C.Laker 56**

FIVE FIFTIES IN AN INNINGS AGAINST

Warwickshire (525)　　v Essex　　　　　Leyton　　　　　1901
J.H.G.Devey 111, J.F.Byrne 63, T.S.Fishwick 86, A.F.A.Lilley 121, C.Charlesworth 60
Middlesex (433-7d)　　v Essex　　　　　Lord's　　　　　1904
P.F.Warner 75, E.A.Beldam 67, J.T.Rawlin 52, B.J.T.Bosanquet 71, J.H.Stogdon 96
Leicestershire (493)　　v Essex　　　　　Leyton　　　　　1905
C.E.de Trafford 103, C.J.B.Wood 97, H.Whitehead 83, A.E.Knight 74, S.Coe 83
Yorkshire (423-6d)　　v Essex　　　　　Huddersfield　　　1905
J.W.Rothery 53, D.Denton 134, G.H.Hirst 80, W.Rhodes 66, S.Haigh 65*
Lancashire (412-5d)　　v Essex　　　　　Leyton　　　　　1911
R.H.Spooner 78, A.Hartley 57, J.T.Tyldesley 55, H.Makepeace 100*, K.G.McLeod 92*
Yorkshire (512-9d)　　v Essex　　　　　Bradford　　　　1913
R.Kilner 85, G.H.Hirst 77, S.Haigh 69, M.W.Booth 56, E.R.Wilson 104*
Nottinghamshire (558-8d) v Essex　　　　Leyton　　　　　1921
G.M.Lee 51, G.Gunn 58, A.W.Carr 204, J.Hardstaff,sen 63, W.R.D.Payton 62

Kent (450)   v Essex   Leyton   1921
   James Seymour 85, A.P.Day 101, G.N.Foster 71, W.H.Ashdown 79*, C.H.Knott 80
Kent (621-6d)   v Essex   Tonbridge   1922
   A.F.Bickmore 120, James Seymour 159, F.E.Woolley 77, W.H.Ashdown 82, C.S.Hurst 110
Nottinghamshire (595-4d) v Essex   Leyton   1926
   G.Gunn 86, W.W.Whysall 209, A.W.Carr 53, W.R.D.Payton 87*, B.Lilley 86*
Yorkshire (512-9d)   v Essex   Sheffield   1928
   P.Holmes 53, A.Mitchell 80, E.Oldroyd 112, W.Rhodes 50, G.G.Macaulay 67*
South Africans (389-7d) v Essex   Leyton   1929
   I.J.Siedle 51, R.H.Catterall 61, H.W.Taylor 95, H.G.Owen-Smith 64, H.G.Deane 58*
Warwickshire (501-6d)   v Essex   Birmingham   1930
   E.J.Smith 124, A.J.Croom 83, L.A.Bates 110, R.E.S.Wyatt 78, J.H.Parsons 52
Northamptonshire (539)   v Essex   Kettering   1933
   A.H.Bakewell 123, J.E.Timms 60, V.W.C.Jupp 95, E.F.Towell 66, A.L.Cox 52
Hampshire (483)   v Essex   Portsmouth   1934
   J.Arnold 68, W.G.L.F.Lowndes 102, A.S.Kennedy 99, G.S.Boyes 66, G.Hill 59*
Sussex (461-6d)   v Essex   Colchester   1934
   J.H.Parks 93, A.Melville 95, T.E.R.Cook 89, James Langridge 86, H.W.Parks 53
Lancashire (412-5d)   v Essex   Manchester   1935
   J.L.Hopwood 101, E.Paynter 66, N.Oldfield 50, C.Washbrook 107*, W.E.Phillipson 51*
Kent (580-6d)   v Essex   Maidstone   1947
   L.J.Todd 136, A.E.Fagg 65, L.E.G.Ames 152, B.H.Valentine 65, H.A.Pawson 65*
Australians (721)   v Essex   Southend   1948
   S.G.Barnes 79, W.A.Brown 153, D.G.Bradman 187, S.J.E.Loxton 120, R.A.Saggers 104*
South Africans (503-4d) v Essex   Colchester   1955
   D.J.McGlew 118, W.R.Endean 64, H.J.Keith 94, P.N.F.Mansell 99, R.A.McLean 101*
Middlesex (634-7d)   v Essex   Chelmsford   1982
   G.D.Barlow 132, C.T.Radley 67, M.W.Gatting 160, J.E.Emburey 133, P.R.Downton 67*
Northamptonshire (636-6d) v Essex   Chelmsford   1990
   A.Fordham 159, N.A.Felton 56, R.J.Bailey 107, A.J.Lamb 165, A.L.Penberthy 83
Surrey (613-6d)   v Essex   The Oval   1990
   D.J.Bicknell 50, R.I.Alikhan 148, D.M.Ward 208, A.J.Stewart 51, I.A.Greig 57*
Kent (380)   v Essex   Southend   1991
   T.R.Ward 53, N.R.Taylor 50, G.R.Cowdrey 67, S.A.Marsh 83, C.Penn 52
Sussex (591)   v Essex   Hove   1993
   N.J.Lenham 52, K.Greenfield 107, A.P.Wells 106, M.P.Speight 95, J.A.North 114

EIGHT FIFTIES IN A MATCH

Essex (493-4d & 412-3)   v Sussex   Hove   1993
   1st inns P.J.Prichard 225*, Salim Malik 73, M.C.Ilott 51, N.Hussain 70*
   2nd inns J.P.Stephenson 122, Salim Malik 63, N.Hussain 118, G.A.Gooch 74*

SEVEN FIFTIES IN A MATCH

Essex (499-8c & 200-2d) v Worcestershire   Westcliff   1976
   1st inns B.E.A.Edmeades 65, K.S.McEwan 55, G.A.Gooch 136, K.W.R.Fletcher 68,
     K.D.Boyce 75
   2nd inns B.E.A.Edmeades 59, B.R.Hardie 61*
Essex (463-4d & 259-3d) v Cambridge University Cambridge   1984
   1st inns G.A.Gooch 89, C.Gladwin 162, K.W.R.Fletcher 59, K.S.McEwan 69
   2nd inns B.R.Hardie 68, D.R.Pringle 96, S.Turner 50
Essex (440-9d & 311-9)   v Kent   Maidstone   1993
   1st inns P.J.Prichard 104, J.J.B.Lewis 67, N.Shahid 60, M.A.Garnham 66, D.R.Pringle 76
   2nd inns P.J.Prichard 106, J.P.Stephenson 83

EIGHT FIFTIES IN A MATCH AGAINST

Sussex (591 & 312-3d)   v Essex   Hove   1993
1st inns N.J.Lenham 52, K.Greenfield 107, A.P.Wells 106, M.P.Speight 95, J.A.North 114
2ns inns N.J.Lenham 149, C.W.J.Athey 96, K.Greenfield 50

SEVEN FIFTIES IN A MATCH AGAINST

Kent (450 & 188-2d)   v Essex   Leyton   1921
1st inns James Seymour 85, A.P.Day 101, G.N.Foster 71, W.H.Ashdown 79*, C.H.Knott 80
2nd inns G.C.Collins 78*, James Seymour 106
South Africans (389-7d & 281-8d) v Essex   Leyton   1929
1st inns I.J.Siedle 51, R.H.Catterall 61, H.W.Taylor 95, H.G.O.Owen-Smith 64,
*   H.G.Deane 58**
2nd inns H.W.Taylor 67, H.G.Owen-Smith 90
Sussex (461-6d & 215-3d) v Essex   Colchester   1934
1st inns J.H.Parks 93, A.Melville 95, T.E.R.Cook 89, James Langridge 86, H.W.Parks 53
2nd inns John G.Langridge 94, T.E.R.Cook 54*
Surrey (469 & 155-6)   v Essex   Ilford   1948
1st inns L.B.Fishlock 51, D.G.W.Fletcher 70, H.S.Squires 74, J.F.Parker 67,
*   A.J.W.McIntyre 68, J.C.Laker 56**
2nd inns J.F.Parker 53
Northamptonshire (404-9d & 368-7) v Essex   Clacton   1949
1st inns D.Brookes 76, N.Oldfield 71, W.Barron 102, R.G.Garlick 51
2nd inns N.Oldfield 82, F.R.Brown 94, P.C.Davis 72
Kent (380 & 183-0d)   v Essex   Southend   1991
1st inns T.R.Ward 53, N.R.Taylor 50, G.R.Cowdrey 67, S.A.Marsh 83, C.Penn 52
2nd inns T.R.Ward 88*, M.R.Benson 92*

MOST EXTRAS IN AN INNINGS

For Essex

57 (b10, lb15, w8, nb24)   v Worcestershire   Westcliff   1976

Against Essex

67 (b2, lb8, w5, nb52)   by Middlesex   Uxbridge   1994
(Before this, when no balls only conceded one run, the highest was 57 (b39, lb4, w8, nb6)
by Yorkshire at Southend in 1947)

SECTION 2 - INDIVIDUAL RECORDS - BATTING

HIGHEST INDIVIDUAL INNINGS

For Essex

343*	P.A.Perrin	v Derbyshire	Chesterfield	1904
286	J.R.Freeman	v Northamptonshire	Northampton	1921
277	C.P.McGahey	v Derbyshire	Leyton	1905
275	G.A.Gooch	v Kent	Chelmsford	1988
273	C.A.G.Russell	v Northamptonshire	Leyton	1921
259	G.A.Gooch	v Middlesex	Chelmsford	1991
248	J.O'Connor	v Surrey	Brentwood	1934
245	P.A.Perrin	v Derbyshire	Leyton	1912
245	P.J.Prichard	v Leicestershire	Chelmsford	1990
238*	J.A.Cutmore	v Gloucestershire	Bristol (Packer)	1927
237	J.O'Connor	v Somerset	Leyton	1933
236	G.A.Gooch	v Kent	Chelmsford	1994
230	C.P.McGahey	v Northamptonshire	Northampton	1908
228*	K.W.R.Fletcher	v Sussex	Hastings	1968
227	G.A.Gooch	v Derbyshire	Chesterfield	1984
225*	P.J.Prichard	v Sussex	Hove	1993
225	C.P.McGahey	v Nottinghamshire	Leyton	1904
224	A.V.Avery	v Northamptonshire	Northampton	1952
222	L.G.Crawley	v Glamorgan	Swansea	1928
220	G.A.Gooch	v Hampshire	Southampton	1989
219*	D.J.Insole	v Yorkshire	Colchester	1949
219*	M.E.Waugh	v Lancashire	Ilford	1992
218	K.S.McEwan	v Sussex	Chelmsford	1977
217	F.L.Fane	v Surrey	The Oval	1911
215	G.A.Gooch	v Leicestershire	Chelmsford	1990
215	Salim Malik	v Leicestershire	Ilford	1991
214*	A.V.Avery	v Worcestershire	Clacton	1948
211*	T.N.Pearce	v Leicestershire	Westcliff	1948
210*	J.W.H.T.Douglas	v Derbyshire	Leyton	1921
210	A.V.Avery	v Surrey	The Oval	1946
208*	A.V.Avery	v Glamorgan	Westcliff	1953
208*	K.S.McEwan	v Warwickshire	Birmingham	1979
207*	M.E.Waugh	v Yorkshire	Middlesbrough	1990
207	F.L.Fane	v Leicestershire	Leicester	1899
206	R.Horsfall	v Kent	Blackheath	1951
205	P.A.Perrin	v Kent	Leyton	1900
205	M.S.Nichols	v Hampshire	Southend	1936
205	T.E.Bailey	v Sussex	Eastbourne	1947
205	G.A.Gooch	v Cambridge University	Cambridge	1980
205	G.A.Gooch	v Worcestershire	Worcester	1994
204	M.E.Waugh	v Gloucestershire	Ilford	1990
202*	J.P.Stephenson	v Somerset	Bath	1990
202	G.A.Gooch	v Nottinghamshire	Nottingham	1985
201	F.H.Gillingham	v Middlesex	Lord's	1904

Against Essex

332	W.H.Ashdown	for Kent	Brentwood	1934
313	H.Sutcliffe	for Yorkshire	Leyton	1932
290*	A.Ducat	for Surrey	Leyton	1921
285*	J.W.Hearne	for Middlesex	Leyton	1929
274	A.O.Jones	for Nottinghamshire	Leyton	1905
266	E.Paynter	for Lancashire	Manchester	1937
263	M.Leyland	for Yorkshire	Hull	1936

260*	G.Boycott	for Yorkshire	Colchester (Garrison) 1970
258*	F.Jakeman	for Northamptonshire	Northampton 1951
255*	H.Sutcliffe	for Yorkshire	Southend 1924
250*	F.A.Tarrant	for Middlesex	Leyton 1914
250	M.C.Cowdrey	for Kent	Blackheath 1959
244	W.R.Hammond	for Gloucestershire	Chelmsford 1928
244	A.E.Fagg	for Kent	Colchester 1938
243	B.Sutcliffe	for New Zealanders	Southend 1949
239	J.Iremonger	for Nottinghamshire	Nottingham 1905
233	G.Boycott	for Yorkshire	Colchester (Garrison) 1971
232	H.Storer	for Derbyshire	Derby 1933
231*	Nawab of Pataudi,sen	for Worcestershire	Worcester 1933
231	R.Abel	for Surrey	The Oval 1896
230*	W.H.Denton	for Northamptonshire	Leyton 1913
230	K.S.Ranjitsinhji	for Sussex	Leyton 1902
230	G.Brown	for Hampshire	Bournemouth 1920
230	A.Sandham	for Surrey	The Oval 1927
229	C.A.Ollivierre	for Derbyshire	Chesterfield 1904
224*	C.L.Townsend	for Gloucestershire	Clifton 1899
224*	P.Holmes	for Yorkshire	Leyton 1932
223*	W.G.Quaife	for Warwickshire	Leyton 1900
222*	E.H.Hendren	for Middlesex	Leyton 1933
221	T.E.Jesty	for Surrey	The Oval 1986
220*	D.L.Haynes	for Middlesex	Ilford 1990
220	R.A.Young	for Sussex	Leyton 1905
219*	G.H.G.Doggart	for Cambridge University	Cambridge 1949
219	K.S.Ranjitsinhji	for Sussex	Hove 1901
219	W.Bardsley	for Australians	Leyton 1909
218*	James Seymour	for Kent	Leyton 1911
217	R.Abel	for Surrey	The Oval 1895
215*	J.B.Hobbs	for Surrey	Leyton 1914
215	R.H.Spooner	for Lancashire	Leyton 1904
215	D.E.Davies	for Glamorgan	Brentwood 1948
215	P.W.G.Parker	for Cambridge University	Cambridge 1976
214	James Seymour	for Kent	Tunbridge Wells 1914
213	D.M.Smith	for Sussex	Southend 1992
212*	W.E.Jones	for Glamorgan	Brentwood 1948
212	C.S.Dempster	for New Zealanders	Leyton 1931
212	R.T.Simpson	for Nottinghamshire	Nottingham 1952
212	M.J.Horton	for Worcestershire	Leyton 1959
211	D.W.Barrick	for Northamptonshire	Northampton 1952
211	W.J.Edrich	for Middlesex	Lord's 1953
209*	R.A.Smith	for Hampshire	Southend 1987
209	W.W.Whysall	for Nottinghamshire	Leyton 1926
209	H.Storer	for Derbyshire	Derby 1929
208	C.G.Macartney	for Australians	Leyton 1912
208	A.Ducat	for Surrey	Leyton 1928
208	D.M.Ward	for Surrey	The Oval 1990
207	C.P.Mead	for Hampshire	Leyton 1919
207	W.R.Hammond	for Gloucestershire	Westcliff 1939
207	W.Larkins	for Northamptonshire	Northampton 1990
206*	A.J.Stewart	for Surrey	The Oval 1989
204*	J.G.Dewes	for Cambridge University	Cambridge 1949
204	A.W.Carr	for Nottinghamshire	Leyton 1921
203	C.Milburn	for Northamptonshire	Clacton 1966
203	M.J.Procter	for Gloucestershire	Gloucester 1978
202*	L.E.G.Ames	for Kent	Brentwood 1934
202*	A.E.Fagg	for Kent	Colchester 1938
202*	P.N.Kirsten	for Derbyshire	Chesterfield 1980
202	K.S.Duleepsinhji	for Sussex	Leyton 1929

201*	E.H.Hendren	for Middlesex	Leyton	1927
201*	J.D.B.Robertson	for Middlesex	Lord's	1957
201	W.M.Woodfull	for Australians	Leyton	1926
201	E.T.Killick	for Cambridge University	Cambridge	1929
200*	W.G.Quaife	for Warwickshire	Birmingham	1904
200*	E.H.Hendren	for Middlesex	Leyton	1923
200*	C.P.Mead	for Hampshire	Southampton	1927
200*	H.W.Parks	for Sussex	Chelmsford	1931
200*	Javed Miandad	for Glamorgan	Colchester	1981
200	A.Sandham	for Surrey	Leyton	1923
200	M.J.Stewart	for Surrey	The Oval	1962
200	M.D.Moxon	for Yorkshire	Colchester	1991

HUNDRED ON FIRST-CLASS DEBUT

For Essex

107*	G.Barker	v Canadians	Clacton	1954
100*	A.W.Lilley	v Nottinghamshire	Nottingham	1978
116*	J.J.B.Lewis	v Surrey	The Oval	1990

Against Essex

118	A.P.F.Chapman	for Cambridge University	Cambridge	1920
103*	A.L.Hilder	for Kent	Gravesend	1924
123	H.Gimblett	for Somerset	Frome	1935
116	M.D.Moxon	for Yorkshire	Leeds	1981

HIGHEST MAIDEN HUNDREDS

207	F.L.Fane	v Leicestershire	Leicester	1899
205*	T.E.Bailey	v Sussex	Eastbourne	1947
195	M.H.Denness	v Leicestershire	Leicester	1977
176*	L.G.Crawley	v Sussex	Leyton	1927
173	Salim Malik	v Kent	Folkestone	1991
170	R.Horsfall	v Hampshire	Bournemouth	1947
165*	N.Hussain	v Leicestershire	Chelmsford	1988
162	N.G.Wykes	v Kent	Leyton	1927
162	C.Gladwin	v Cambridge University	Cambridge	1984
157	A.C.H.Seymour	v Glamorgan	Cardiff	1991
152	T.N.Pearce	v Lancashire	Clacton	1931

YOUNGEST BATSMEN TO SCORE A HUNDRED

19y 44d	A.J.Turner	111	v Yorkshire	Huddersfield	1897
19y 123d	A.W.Lilley	100	v Nottinghamshire	Nottingham	1978
19y 247d	P.J.Prichard	100	v Lancashire	Manchester	1984
20y 43d	K.W.R.Fletcher	103	v Lancashire	Manchester	1964
20y 51d	P.A.Perrin	139	v Warwickshire	Birmingham	1896
20y 90d	J.J.B.Lewis	116	v Surrey	The Oval	1990
20y 168d	K.R.Pont	113	v Warwickshire	Birmingham	1973
20y 342d	L.A.Savill	100	v Somerset	Brentwood	1956

OLDEST BATSMEN TO SCORE A HUNDRED

49y 39d	P.A.Perrin	102	v Northamptonshire	Kettering	1925
45y 273d	F.H.Gillingham	100	v Surrey	Leyton	1921
45y 183d	A.P.Lucas	103	v Derbyshire	Leyton	1902
45y 31d	H.A.Carpenter	126	v Worcestershire	Worcester	1914
43y 356d	J.W.H.T.Douglas	103	v Nottinghamshire	Leyton	1926

43y 239d	T.N.Pearce	111	v Derbyshire	Westcliff	1949
43y 14d	K.W.R.Fletcher	121	v Middlesex	Lord's	1987
42y 356d	J.R.Freeman	123	v Nottinghamshire	Leyton	1926
42y 31d	H.G.P.Owen	106	v Derbyshire	Leyton	1901

HUNDRED IN EACH INNINGS OF A MATCH

For Essex

114	&	145*	C.P.McGahey	v Gloucestershire	Leyton	1901
127	&	104	H.Carpenter	v Kent	Leyton	1901
170	&	102*	P.A.Perrin	v Nottinghamshire	Nottingham	1903
140	&	103*	P.A.Perrin	v Middlesex	Lord's	1905
112	&	100*	P.A.Perrin	v Nottinghamshire	Nottingham	1911
126	&	101*	P.A.Perrin	v Kent	Leyton	1919
115	&	118	C.A.G.Russell	v Surrey	The Oval	1922
131	&	104	C.A.G.Russell	v Lancashire	Liverpool	1928
138	&	120	J.O'Connor	v Gloucestershire	Bristol	1930
104	&	129	D.R.Wilcox	v Kent	Westcliff	1937
119	&	100	A.V.Avery	v Glamorgan	Ebbw Vale	1949
111	&	118	D.J.Insole	v Kent	Gillingham	1955
111	&	102*	K.W.R.Fletcher	v Nottinghamshire	Nottingham	1976
102	&	116	K.S.McEwan	v Warwickshire	Birmingham	1977
174	&	126	G.A.Gooch	v Northamptonshire	Northampton	1990
113*	&	159*	J.P.Stephenson	v Somerset	Taunton	1992
102	&	108*	G.A.Gooch	v Sussex	Southend	1992
104	&	106	P.J.Prichard	v Kent	Maidstone	1993
109	&	114	G.A.Gooch	v Hampshire	Chelmsford	1993
101	&	205	G.A.Gooch	v Worcestershire	Worcester	1994

Against Essex

109	&	119	V.T.Trumper	for Australians	Leyton	1902
107*	&	104	E.Needham	for Derbyshire	Leyton	1908
153	&	126	H.T.W.Hardinge	for Kent	Leyton	1908
165	&	123*	E.Tyldesley	for Lancashire	Leyton	1921
143	&	105*	James Seymour	for Kent	Leyton	1923
174*	&	108	J.Daniell	for Somerset	Taunton	1925
105	&	111	W.E.Bates	for Glamorgan	Leyton	1927
115	&	101*	B.H.Lyon	for Gloucestershire	Bristol	1930
113	&	119*	J.B.Hobbs	for Surrey	The Oval	1932
114*	&	105*	H.W.Parks	for Sussex	Leyton	1933
130	&	107	L.Amarnath	for Indians	Brentwood	1936
244	&	202*	A.E.Fagg	for Kent	Colchester	1938

(The only instance of a batsman scoring two double centuries in a match. This occurred while four Essex bowlers were playing in the Gentlemen v Players match at Lord's.)

165	&	111*	L.G.Berry	for Leicestershire	Clacton	1947
197	&	104	L.Hutton	for Yorkshire	Southend	1947
136	&	117*	A.E.Fagg	for Kent	Maidstone	1948
243	&	100*	B.Sutcliffe	for New Zealanders	Southend	1949
113	&	101*	F.C.Gardner	for Warwickshire	Ilford	1950
167	&	103*	P.B.H.May	for Surrey	Southend	1951
115*	&	103*	M.C.Cowdrey	for Kent	Gillingham	1955
144*	&	109*	Javed Burki	for Oxford University	Brentwood	1960
107	&	131*	M.J.Harris	for Nottinghamshire	Chelmsford	1971
111	&	118*	I.V.A.Richards	for Glamorgan	Southend	1990

HUNDRED BY A NUMBER ELEVEN BATSMAN

163	T.P.B.Smith	v Derbyshire	Chesterfield	1947
	(The World Record)			

FOUR HUNDREDS IN CONSECUTIVE INNINGS

K.S.McEwan	218	v Sussex	Chelmsford	1977
	102 & 116	v Warwickshire	Birmingham	
	106*	v Gloucestershire	Southend	

THREE HUNDREDS IN CONSECUTIVE INNINGS

P.A.Perrin	170 & 102*	v Nottinghamshire	Nottingham	1903
	102 retired hurt	v Derbyshire	Leyton	

CARRYING BAT THROUGH A COMPLETED INNINGS

For Essex

C.A.G.Russell	89*	(161)	v Northamptonshire	Northampton	1913
J.R.Freeman	67*	(206)	v Lancashire	Colchester	1922
J.R.Freeman	113*	(283)	v Oxford University	Chelmsford	1926
D.F.Pope	87*	(216)	v Glamorgan	Colchester	1930
J.A.Cutmore	31*	(64)	v Yorkshire	Dewsbury	1933
A.V.Avery	84*	(180)	v Derbyshire	Southend	1939
A.V.Avery	83*	(165)	v Gloucestershire	Brentwood	1946
A.V.Avery	92*	(154)	v Nottinghamshire	Nottingham	1954
G.Barker	36*	(80)	v Kent	Westcliff	1966
B.R.Hardie	88*	(254)	v Australians	Chelmsford	1975
(In this innings one batsman was absent ill)					
B.R.Hardie	59*	(172)	v Leicestershire	Leicester	1979
J.P.Stephenson	113*	(259)	v Somerset	Taunton	1992

Against Essex

L.G.Wright	59*	(112)	for Derbyshire	Leyton	1899
R.W.Rice	58*	(147)	for Gloucestershire	Clifton	1901
L.G.Wright	58*	(136)	for Derbyshire	Leyton	1903
L.J.Moon	62*	(136)	for Middlesex	Leyton	1903
C.J.B.Wood	105*	(303)	for Leicestershire	Southend	1906
J.Vine	67*	(186)	for Sussex	Hove	1907
E.Needham	107*	(195)	for Derbyshire	Leyton	1908
W.Rhodes	85*	(152)	for Yorkshire	Leyton	1910
W.H.Denton	230*	(476)	for Northamptonshire	Leyton	1913
H.W.Lee	80*	(212)	for Middlesex	Leyton	1920
H.Sutcliffe	125*	(307)	for Yorkshire	Southend	1920
H.W.Lee	52*	(132)	for Middlesex	Lord's	1924
J.Daniell	174*	(318)	for Somerset	Taunton	1925
E.W.Dawson	126*	(256)	for Leicestershire	Leyton	1928
W.W.Whysall	111*	(238)	for Nottinghamshire	Nottingham	1929
A.E.Fagg	117*	(230)	for Kent	Maidstone	1948
B.Dudleston	101*	(178)	for Leicestershire	Leyton	1971
J.A.Ormrod	66*	(187)	for Worcestershire	Chelmsford	1975
D.L.Amiss	122*	(273)	for Warwickshire	Colchester	1978
J.H.Edrich	61*	(108)	for Surrey	Southend	1978
K.D.Smith	120*	(230)	for Warwickshire	Southend	1980
P.D.Bowler	159*	(340)	for Derbyshire	Chesterfield	1988

FASTEST FIFTY

mins					
15	R.Smith	(78)	v Nottinghamshire	Brentwood	1949

FASTEST HUNDREDS

mins					
44	R.N.S.Hobbs	(100)	v Australians	Chelmsford	1975
58	K.D.Boyce	(113)	v Leicestershire	Chelmsford	1975

FIFTY WITH FEWEST SCORING STROKES

THIRTEEN STROKES

	B.Taylor	(58)	v Warwickshire	Westcliff	1954

(Scored with 12 fours and 1 six)

HUNDRED BEFORE LUNCH

Hundred Before Lunch on First Day

	Final Score	Lunch Score			
E.H.D.Sewell	107	107	v Warwickshire	Birmingham	1904
C.D.McIver	134	117*	v Hampshire	Leyton	1913
C.A.G.Russell	108	108*	v Northamptonshire	Northampton	1921
G.Barker	181*	100*	v Kent	Colchester	1961
K.S.McEwan	156	104*	v Nottinghamshire	Nottingham	1976
K.S.McEwan	128	112*	v Lancashire	Southport	1978
G.A.Gooch	164	102*	v Leicestershire	Leicester	1981
G.A.Gooch	174	102*	v Cambridge University	Cambridge	1983
G.A.Gooch	139	103	v Surrey	Chelmsford	1988

Hundred Before Lunch After First Day

	Final Score	Lunch Score	Day			
E.H.D.Sewell	106*	106*	2	v Surrey	The Oval	1904
J.G.Dixon	108	101*	2	v Gloucestershire	Leyton	1919
K.S.McEwan	218	103*	2	v Sussex	Chelmsford	1977
S.Turner	102	102	2	v Kent	Chelmsford	1979
K.S.McEwan	185	120*	2	v Derbyshire	Chelmsford	1979
K.S.McEwan	132	103*	2	v Lancashire	Manchester	1984
K.S.McEwan	110	110	2	v Cambridge University	Cambridge	1985

(the last two in consecutive matches)

Hundred Added to Overnight Score Before Lunch

	Final Score	Session Scores	Day			
S.P.Meston	130	25*-130	2	v Lancashire	Leyton	1907
F.H.Gillingham	194	60*-194*	2	v Gloucestershire	Leyton	1908
T.N.Pearce	111*	4*-111*	3	v Kent	Ilford	1949
T.E.Bailey	114*	12*-114*	3	v Nottinghamshire	Southend	1955
D.J.Insole	114	9*-114*	3	v Nottinghamshire	Southend	1955
(both in same innings)						
B.R.Knight	165	16*-122*	2	v Middlesex	Brentwood	1962
K.S.McEwan	112	4*-106*	3	v Northamptonshire	Northampton	1976
K.S.McEwan	186	41*-146*	2	v Northamptonshire	Ilford	1978
G.A.Gooch	205	62*-162*	2	v Cambridge Univ	Cambridge	1980
N.Hussain	165*	35*-138*	2	v Leicestershire	Chelmsford	1988
G.A.Gooch	160	0*-105*	2	v Leicestershire	Chelmsford	1992

30

MOST RUNS OFF ONE OVER

30 off a six ball over G.A.Gooch off S.R.Gorman (662664)
v Cambridge University Cambridge 1985

MOST SIXES IN AN INNINGS

For Essex

8	K.D.Boyce (113)	v Leicestershire	Chelmsford	1975
7	R.N.S.Hobbs (100)	v Australians	Chelmsford	1975
7	N.Phillip (134)	v Gloucestershire	Gloucester	1978
7	G.A.Gooch (88)	v Cambridge Univ	Cambridge	1985

Against Essex

9	C.L.Hooper (160)	for Kent	Chelmsford	1994
7	J.E.Walsh (106)	for Leicestershire	Loughborough	1948

MOST FOURS IN AN INNINGS

68 P.A.Perrin (343*) v Derbyshire Chesterfield 1904
(record for an English batsman)

FEWEST BOUNDARIES IN AN INNINGS

NO BOUNDARIES
Runs
84* A.V.Avery v Derbyshire Southend 1939

ONE BOUNDARY
Runs
97* T.N.Pearce v Northamptonshire Colchester 1935

SLOW SCORING

AN HOUR BEFORE SCORING FIRST RUN
Min
72 F.H.Vigar v Hampshire Portsmouth 1946

MONOPOLISING THE SCORING
(OVER 70% OF AN INNINGS TOTAL)

75.8%	G.Barker (85)	Essex (112) v Yorkshire	Sheffield	1962
74.3%	G.A.Gooch (84)	Essex (113) v Kent	Canterbury	1984

HUNDREDS SCORED FOR ESSEX

Ashton, C.T.	(3)	110*	v Middlesex	Leyton	1922
		118	v Surrey	Brentwood	1934
		100	v Gloucestershire	Bristol	1936
Avery, A.V.	(25)	109	v Nottinghamshire	Nottingham	1937
		136	v Nottinghamshire	Worksop	1938
		138	v Gloucestershire	Gloucester	1938
		121	v Middlesex	Lord's	1939
		161	v Glamorgan	Cardiff	1939
		102	v Northamptonshire	Brentwood	1946
		210	v Surrey	The Oval	1946
		115	v Warwickshire	Birmingham	1946
		108	v Surrey	The Oval	1948
		118	v Derbyshire	Colchester	1948
		146	v Lancashire	Blackpool	1948
		103	v Derbyshire	Derby	1948
		214*	v Worcestershire	Clacton	1948
		100	v Northamptonshire	Clacton	1948
		143	v M.C.C.	Lord's	1949
		117	v Glamorgan	Ebbw Vale	1949
		100	v Glamorgan	Ebbw Vale	1949
		141	v Nottinghamshire	Nottingham	1950
		100	v Nottinghamshire	Nottingham	1951
		106	v Sussex	Hove	1951
		154	v Middlesex	Colchester	1951
		166*	v Worcestershire	Southend	1951
		153	v Hampshire	Southampton	1952
		224	v Northamptonshire	Northampton	1952
		208*	v Glamorgan	Westcliff	1953
Bailey, T.E.	(22)	205*	v Sussex	Eastbourne	1947
		104*	v Surrey	Southend	1951
		155*	v Kent	Tunbridge Wells	1952
		108*	v Somerset	Weston-s-Mare	1954
		107	v South Africans	Colchester	1955
		152*	v Kent	Clacton	1955
		114*	v Nottinghamshire	Southend	1955
		111*	v Somerset	Taunton	1956
		108	v Kent	Dartford	1956
		141*	v Hampshire	Westcliff	1956
		102*	v Glamorgan	Ilford	1957
		132	v Worcestershire	Leyton	1957
		118	v Cambridge Univ	Cambridge	1959
		119	v Northamptonshire	Ilford	1959
		146	v Hampshire	Bournemouth	1959
		102*	v Kent	Blackheath	1959
		104*	v Northamptonshire	Northampton	1959
		138	v Warwickshire	Clacton	1959
		118	v Oxford University	Brentwood	1960
		117*	v Warwickshire	Birmingham	1961
		124*	v Sussex	Ilford	1962
		122	v Warwickshire	Birmingham	1963
Barker, G.	(30)	107*	v Canadians	Clacton	1954
		104	v Nottinghamshire	Nottingham	1955
		106	v Warwickshire	Birmingham	1955
		157	v Leicestershire	Ilford	1956
		107	v Sussex	Colchester	1957
		117	v Middlesex	Leyton	1957
		100	v Nottinghamshire	Southend	1957

Barker, G. (contd)		157	v Nottinghamshire	Nottingham	1958
		105	v Kent	Westcliff	1959
		157*	v Leicestershire	Leicester	1959
		128*	v Derbyshire	Clacton	1959
		110	v Northamptonshire	Leyton	1960
		146	v Sussex	Eastbourne	1960
		103	v Hampshire	Bournemouth	1960
		181*	v Kent	Colchester	1961
		147	v Cambridge Univ	Cambridge	1962
		131	v Sussex	Worthing	1962
		116	v Surrey	The Oval	1963
		118	v Lancashire	Blackpool	1963
		121*	v Derbyshire	Derby	1964
		123	v Australians	Southend	1964
		146	v Leicestershire	Leicester	1964
		119	v Nottinghamshire	Nottingham	1965
		124*	v Warwickshire	Birmingham	1967
		148	v Worcestershire	Worcester	1967
		126	v Kent	Romford	1968
		118	v Sussex	Colchester (Gar)	1969
		116	v Surrey	The Oval	1969
		124	v Worcestershire	Worcester	1970
		105	v Northamptonshire	Northampton	1970
Bear, M.J.	(9)	123	v Gloucestershire	Romford	1957
		117	v Middlesex	Lord's	1962
		107	v Kent	Romford	1962
		132	v Worcestershire	Worcester	1963
		135	v Warwickshire	Ilford	1964
		105	v Warwickshire	Birmingham	1966
		137	v Glamorgan	Cardiff	1967
		124	v Warwickshire	Westcliff	1967
		107*	v Warwickshire	Birmingham	1968
Border, A.R.	(10)	110	v Derbyshire	Derby	1986
		150	v Glamorgan	Swansea	1986
		138	v Surrey	The Oval	1986
		108*	v Sussex	Eastbourne	1986
		169*	v Derbyshire	Chesterfield	1988
		112	v Warwickshire	Birmingham	1988
		161	v Sussex	Ilford	1988
		168	v Kent	Canterbury	1988
		110*	v Northamptonshire	Northampton	1988
		130*	v Nottinghamshire	Colchester	1988
Boyce, K.D.	(3)	147*	v Hampshire	Ilford	1969
		100	v Glamorgan	Chelmsford	1969
		113	v Leicestershire	Chelmsford	1975
Bray, C.	(5)	108	v Middlesex	Leyton	1928
		100	v Northamptonshire	Leyton	1931
		122	v Glamorgan	Chelmsford	1931
		129	v New Zealanders	Southend	1931
		111*	v Gloucestershire	Southend	1932
Buckenham, C.P.	(2)	100	v Nottinghamshire	Nottingham	1904
		124	v Lancashire	Leyton	1907
Burns, J.		114	v Warwickshire	Birmingham	1895
Carpenter, H.A.	(22)	145	v Surrey	The Oval	1895
		153	v Somerset	Taunton	1895
		141	v Warwickshire	Birmingham	1897
		133	v Leicestershire	Leicester	1898
		103	v Kent	Tonbridge	1898
		135	v Gloucestershire	Leyton	1900
		140	v Sussex	Leyton	1900

Carpenter, H.A. (contd)		112	v Derbyshire	Leyton	1900
		151	v Derbyshire	Derby	1900
		136	v Gloucestershire	Leyton	1901
		127	v Kent	Leyton	1901
		104	v Kent	Leyton	1901
		119	v Lancashire	Leyton	1901
		118	v Nottinghamshire	Leyton	1901
		144	v Derbyshire	Chesterfield	1901
		199	v Surrey	The Oval	1904
		108*	v Leicestershire	Leicester	1904
		104	v Nottinghamshire	Nottingham	1905
		138*	v Sussex	Leyton	1905
		100	v Nottinghamshire	Leyton	1905
		177	v Middlesex	Lord's	1906
		126*	v Worcestershire	Worcester	1914
Cass, G.R.		104*	v Warwickshire	Birmingham	1967
Cooke, R.M.O.	(2)	139	v Sussex	Ilford	1973
		100	v Warwickshire	Chelmsford	1974
Crabtree, H.P.	(4)	101	v Worcestershire	Worcester	1946
		146	v Nottinghamshire	Clacton	1946
		118	v Indians	Southend	1946
		117	v South Africans	Southend	1947
Crawley, L.G.	(6)	176*	v Sussex	Leyton	1927
		222	v Glamorgan	Swansea	1928
		155	v Warwickshire	Chelmsford	1932
		138	v Derbyshire	Leyton	1932
		108	v Northamptonshire	Southend	1933
		118	v Glamorgan	Pontypridd	1936
Cray, S.J.	(7)	100	v Northamptonshire	Ilford	1947
		105	v Nottinghamshire	Nottingham	1947
		114	v Kent	Maidstone	1947
		139	v Northamptonshire	Clacton	1948
		119	v Northamptonshire	Northampton	1949
		129	v Worcestershire	Southend	1949
		163	v Nottinghamshire	Ilford	1950
Cutmore, J.A.	(15)	134*	v Lancashire	Leyton	1925
		119	v Somerset	Taunton	1926
		238*	v Gloucestershire	Bristol (Packer)	1927
		101	v Sussex	Hastings	1928
		180	v Worcestershire	Leyton	1930
		117	v Somerset	Colchester (Gar)	1930
		122	v Derbyshire	Derby	1930
		106	v Sussex	Chelmsford	1931
		106	v Surrey	Leyton	1932
		117	v Sussex	Horsham	1933
		101	v Northamptonshire	Kettering	1933
		104	v Hampshire	Chelmsford	1934
		135*	v Northamptonshire	Clacton	1934
		100*	v Northamptonshire	Northampton	1935
		137	v Indians	Brentwood	1936
Davies, G.B.	(2)	100	v Northamptonshire	Leyton	1914
		118	v Somerset	Weston-s-Mare	1914
Denness, M.H.	(6)	195	v Leicestershire	Leicester	1977
		122	v Somerset	Taunton	1977
		124*	v Northamptonshire	Chelmsford	1977
		126	v Warwickshire	Colchester	1978
		122	v Leicestershire	Chelmsford	1979
		136	v Surrey	Southend	1979

34

Dixon, J.G.	(3)	108	v Gloucestershire	Leyton	1919
		120	v Hampshire	Colchester (Gar)	1921
		173	v Worcestershire	Leyton	1922
Dodds, T.C.	(17)	103	v Surrey	The Oval	1946
		111	v Hampshire	Westcliff	1946
		157	v Leicestershire	Leicester	1947
		152	v Glamorgan	Cardiff	1948
		104	v Surrey	Ilford	1948
		124	v Derbyshire	Derby	1948
		102	v Northamptonshire	Westcliff	1949
		123	v Northamptonshire	Northampton	1949
		106	v West Indians	Southend	1950
		138	v South Africans	Ilford	1951
		100	v Worcestershire	Southend	1951
		146	v Somerset	Westcliff	1952
		150	v Somerset	Taunton	1952
		100	v Middlesex	Lord's	1952
		117	v Northamptonshire	Ilford	1953
		121	v Kent	Ilford	1954
		128	v Warwickshire	Colchester	1956
Douglas, J.W.H.T.	(18)	102*	v Sussex	Leyton	1908
		115	v Kent	Leyton	1908
		176	v Nottinghamshire	Nottingham	1911
		129	v Australians	Leyton	1912
		109	v Lancashire	Leyton	1912
		118*	v Somerset	Leyton	1914
		146	v Lancashire	Leyton	1914
		116	v Hampshire	Leyton	1919
		144	v Gloucestershire	Leyton	1919
		128	v Worcestershire	Leyton	1920
		147	v Worcestershire	Worcester	1920
		123*	v Worcestershire	Leyton	1921
		210*	v Derbyshire	Leyton	1921
		123*	v Middlesex	Leyton	1921
		110*	v Derbyshire	Leyton	1923
		147*	v Gloucestershire	Cheltenham	1923
		102	v Nottinghamshire	Leyton	1924
		103	v Nottinghamshire	Leyton	1926
East, D.E.	(4)	131	v Gloucestershire	Southend	1985
		100	v Middlesex	Lord's	1985
		100*	v Gloucestershire	Colchester	1986
		134	v Gloucestershire	Ilford	1988
East, R.E.		113	v Hampshire	Chelmsford	1976
Eastman, L.C.	(7)	101	v Surrey	Southend	1924
		161	v Derbyshire	Derby	1929
		129	v Glamorgan	Chelmsford	1931
		122	v Leicestershire	Chelmsford	1932
		113*	v Lancashire	Leyton	1933
		100	v Worcestershire	Worcester	1933
		157*	v Hampshire	Bournemouth	1933
Edmeades, B.E.A.	(14)	135	v Lancashire	Manchester	1964
		100	v Northamptonshire	Northampton	1967
		107	v Leicestershire	Leicester	1968
		121	v Cambridge Univ	Cambridge	1969
		148	v Somerset	Taunton	1969
		114*	v Leicestershire	Leicester	1969
		102	v Warwickshire	Birmingham	1970
		120*	v Leicestershire	Chelmsford	1970
		115	v Middlesex	Lord's	1970
		106	v Gloucestershire	Chelmsford	1970

Edmeades, B.E.A. (contd)		102	v Hampshire	Chelmsford	1972
		163	v Leicestershire	Leyton	1972
		110	v Lancashire	Leyton	1973
		155	v Leicestershire	Colchester	1976
Eve, S.C.		120	v Warwickshire	Brentwood	1949
Fane, F.L.	(18)	207	v Leicestershire	Leicester	1899
		116	v Sussex	Hove	1899
		120*	v Nottinghamshire	Leyton	1901
		105*	v Nottinghamshire	Nottingham	1902
		106	v Yorkshire	Bradford	1902
		126	v Nottinghamshire	Leyton	1904
		100	v Sussex	Leyton	1905
		106	v Yorkshire	Leyton	1905
		102	v Northamptonshire	Leyton	1906
		130	v Middlesex	Leyton	1906
		108	v Kent	Leyton	1908
		115	v Australians	Leyton	1909
		217	v Surrey	The Oval	1911
		162	v Sussex	Eastbourne	1911
		125	v Lancashire	Leyton	1911
		115	v Middlesex	Leyton	1913
		105	v Northamptonshire	Leyton	1913
		130	v Yorkshire	Bradford	1913
Fletcher, K.W.R.	(45)	103*	v Lancashire	Manchester	1964
		125	v Australians	Southend	1964
		101*	v Nottinghamshire	Nottingham	1965
		106	v West Indians	Southend	1966
		101*	v Leicestershire	Clacton	1966
		118*	v Gloucestershire	Bristol	1967
		131*	v Somerset	Bath	1968
		228*	v Sussex	Hastings	1968
		134*	v Northamptonshire	Northampton	1969
		110*	v Glamorgan	Chelmsford	1969
		117	v Cambridge Univ	Cambridge	1970
		102*	v Nottinghamshire	Nottingham	1970
		103	v Lancashire	Ilford	1970
		169*	v Gloucestershire	Chelmsford	1970
		164*	v Glamorgan	Chelmsford	1971
		126	v Warwickshire	Ilford	1971
		106*	v Indians	Colchester (Gar)	1971
		114	v Sussex	Hove	1972
		115	v Kent	Maidstone	1972
		121	v Middlesex	Westcliff	1972
		181*	v Glamorgan	Swansea	1972
		139*	v Yorkshire	Colchester	1972
		113	v Middlesex	Lord's	1973
		114	v Derbyshire	Colchester	1976
		128*	v Surrey	Chelmsford	1976
		111	v Nottinghamshire	Nottingham	1976
		102*	v Nottinghamshire	Nottingham	1976
		103	v Surrey	Chelmsford	1977
		103	v Middlesex	Southend	1977
		106*	v Yorkshire	Middlesbrough	1977
		140*	v Derbyshire	Chesterfield	1979
		122*	v Derbyshire	Colchester	1980
		127	v Worcestershire	Worcester	1981
		123*	v Warwickshire	Birmingham	1981
		165*	v Kent	Chelmsford	1981
		128*	v Surrey	The Oval	1981
		120	v Middlesex	Lord's	1982

Fletcher, K.W.R. (contd)		122	v Surrey	Chelmsford	1982
		124	v Northamptonshire	Northampton	1982
		151*	v Glamorgan	Cardiff	1983
		110	v Surrey	Chelmsford	1983
		131	v Northamptonshire	Chelmsford	1984
		106	v Yorkshire	Leeds	1984
		122	v Worcestershire	Chelmsford	1984
		121	v Middlesex	Lord's	1987
Foster, N.A.	(2)	101*	v Leicestershire	Chelmsford	1990
		107*	v Sussex	Horsham	1991
Francis, B.C.	(7)	121*	v Sussex	Hove	1971
		110	v Hampshire	Westcliff	1971
		115	v Worcestershire	Worcester	1971
		140	v Nottinghamshire	Chelmsford	1971
		121	v Somerset	Chelmsford	1973
		148	v Leicestershire	Leicester	1973
		188*	v Yorkshire	Scarborough	1973
Franklin, H.W.F.	(2)	106	v Middlesex	Leyton	1923
		104	v Somerset	Knowle	1928
Freeman, J.R.	(26)	105*	v Surrey	Leyton	1911
		137*	v Nottinghamshire	Leyton	1911
		100	v Sussex	Leyton	1912
		121*	v Sussex	Leyton	1913
		100	v Derbyshire	Derby	1913
		106	v Lancashire	Leyton	1914
		100*	v Sussex	Hove	1919
		102	v Surrey	Leyton	1921
		286	v Northamptonshire	Northampton	1921
		148	v Hampshire	Bournemouth	1921
		141	v Derbyshire	Leyton	1922
		102	v Worcestershire	Leyton	1922
		135	v Northamptonshire	Northampton	1923
		138	v Worcestershire	Worcester	1923
		123*	v Kent	Gravesend	1924
		113	v Sussex	Eastbourne	1924
		117	v Hampshire	Leyton	1924
		120	v Northamptonshire	Leyton	1924
		125	v Surrey	Leyton	1925
		139	v Oxford University	Chelmsford	1925
		100	v Sussex	Hove	1926
		172*	v Derbyshire	Derby	1926
		113*	v Oxford University	Chelmsford	1926
		118	v Glamorgan	Cardiff	1926
		113	v Leicestershire	Leicester	1926
		133	v Nottinghamshire	Leyton	1926
Garnham, M.A.	(4)	102*	v Cambridge Univ	Cambridge	1991
		117	v Derbyshire	Chelmsford	1991
		123	v Leicestershire	Leicester	1991
		106	v Durham	Chelmsford	1993
Gibb, P.A.	(8)	107	v Yorkshire	Brentwood	1951
		138	v Northamptonshire	Northampton	1951
		141	v Kent	Blackheath	1951
		118	v Nottinghamshire	Clacton	1951
		132	v Northamptonshire	Northampton	1952
		138	v Middlesex	Westcliff	1953
		131	v Worcestershire	Brentwood	1954
		106	v Canadians	Clacton	1954
Gillingham, F.H.	(19)	116	v Leicestershire	Leyton	1903
		103	v Derbyshire	Leyton	1904
		201	v Middlesex	Lord's	1904

Gillingham, F.H. (contd)		102	v Surrey	The Oval	1906
		194	v Gloucestershire	Leyton	1908
		103	v Lancashire	Leyton	1908
		102	v Middlesex	Leyton	1908
		100	v Kent	Leyton	1908
		141	v Cambridge Univ	Leyton	1910
		145	v Kent	Leyton	1910
		128	v Derbyshire	Leyton	1911
		167	v Worcestershire	Stourbridge	1911
		119	v Surrey	Leyton	1913
		105	v Hampshire	Leyton	1913
		121*	v Surrey	The Oval	1914
		125	v Surrey	The Oval	1919
		151	v Sussex	Hove	1920
		128*	v Hampshire	Bournemouth	1920
		100	v Surrey	Leyton	1921
Gladwin, C.		162	v Cambridge Univ	Cambridge	1984
Gooch, G.A.	(79)	114*	v Leicestershire	Chelmsford	1974
		100	v Kent	Colchester	1975
		100*	v Kent	Tunbridge Wells	1976
		136	v Worcestershire	Westcliff	1976
		111	v Lancashire	Manchester	1976
		105*	v Warwickshire	Birmingham	1977
		108	v Kent	Ilford	1978
		129	v Northamptonshire	Ilford	1978
		109	v Derbyshire	Chesterfield	1979
		205	v Cambridge Univ	Cambridge	1980
		108*	v Glamorgan	Swansea	1980
		122	v Kent	Ilford	1980
		108	v Surrey	Chelmsford	1980
		134	v Gloucestershire	Gloucester	1980
		164	v Leicestershire	Leicester	1981
		146	v Northamptonshire	Northampton	1981
		105	v Leicestershire	Colchester	1981
		113	v Glamorgan	Colchester	1981
		122	v Somerset	Taunton	1981
		149	v Kent	Canterbury	1982
		140	v Surrey	The Oval	1982
		127	v Kent	Chelmsford	1982
		174	v Cambridge Univ	Cambridge	1983
		110	v Leicestershire	Chelmsford	1983
		103	v Worcestershire	Colchester	1983
		111	v Yorkshire	Chelmsford	1983
		220	v Hampshire	Southampton	1984
		108	v Nottinghamshire	Chelmsford	1984
		113*	v Leicestershire	Hinckley (LR)	1984
		101	v West Indians	Chelmsford	1984
		227	v Derbyshire	Chesterfield	1984
		131	v Yorkshire	Leeds	1984
		105*	v Middlesex	Lord's	1984
		160*	v Surrey	The Oval	1984
		202	v Nottinghamshire	Nottingham	1985
		125	v Kent	Dartford	1985
		173*	v Somerset	Taunton	1985
		132*	v Surrey	Chelmsford	1985
		145	v Middlesex	Lord's	1985
		142	v Yorkshire	Chelmsford	1985
		151	v Worcestershire	Southend	1986
		171	v Gloucestershire	Bristol	1987
		159	v Northamptonshire	Ilford	1987

Gooch, G.A. (contd)		275	v Kent	Chelmsford	1988
		139	v Surrey	Chelmsford	1988
		113	v Sussex	Ilford	1988
		123	v Surrey	The Oval	1988
		108	v Northamptonshire	Chelmsford	1988
		148	v Derbyshire	Chelmsford	1989
		124*	v Leicestershire	Chelmsford	1989
		158	v Leicestershire	Leicester	1989
		137	v Middlesex	Lord's	1990
		215	v Leicestershire	Chelmsford	1990
		121	v Worcestershire	Worcester	1990
		120	v Middlesex	Ilford	1990
		102*	v New Zealanders	Chelmsford	1990
		177	v Lancashire	Colchester	1990
		174	v Northamptonshire	Northampton	1990
		126	v Northamptonshire	Northampton	1990
		101*	v Cambridge Univ	Cambridge	1991
		106	v Middlesex	Lord's	1991
		173	v Northamptonshire	Colchester	1991
		259	v Middlesex	Chelmsford	1991
		160	v Leicestershire	Chelmsford	1992
		113	v Durham	Hartlepool	1992
		102	v Sussex	Southend	1992
		108*	v Sussex	Southend	1992
		141	v Pakistanis	Chelmsford	1992
		123*	v Derbyshire	Derby	1992
		101	v Gloucestershire	Bristol	1992
		105	v Cambridge Univ	Cambridge	1993
		159*	v Worcestershire	Chelmsford	1993
		109	v Hampshire	Chelmsford	1993
		114	v Hampshire	Chelmsford	1993
		123*	v Hampshire	Southampton	1994
		236	v Kent	Chelmsford	1994
		101	v Worcestershire	Worcester	1994
		205	v Worcestershire	Worcester	1994
		140	v Middlesex	Uxbridge	1994
Greensmith, W.T.		138*	v Kent	Blackheath	1953
Griffiths, C.		105	v Kent	Tunbridge Wells	1952
Hardie, B.R.	(27)	128*	v Middlesex	Ilford	1974
		133	v Warwickshire	Chelmsford	1974
		102*	v Cambridge Univ	Cambridge	1975
		162	v Warwickshire	Birmingham	1975
		118*	v Cambridge Univ	Cambridge	1977
		109	v Surrey	Southend	1978
		100*	v Lancashire	Ilford	1979
		146*	v Hampshire	Bournemouth	1979
		103*	v Northamptonshire	Northampton	1979
		111*	v Warwickshire	Birmingham	1981
		129	v Lancashire	Southend	1981
		114	v Glamorgan	Colchester	1981
		161	v Indians	Chelmsford	1982
		129	v Cambridge Univ	Cambridge	1983
		112*	v Cambridge Univ	Cambridge	1985
		131	v Northamptonshire	Ilford	1985
		113*	v Australians	Chelmsford	1985
		162	v Somerset	Southend	1985
		110	v Yorkshire	Chelmsford	1986
		113*	v Somerset	Taunton	1986
		143	v Cambridge Univ	Cambridge	1987
		111	v Leicestershire	Leicester	1987

Hardie, B.R. (contd)		111	v Sussex	Eastbourne	1987
		142*	v Surrey	The Oval	1989
		101*	v Glamorgan	Swansea	1989
		125	v Hampshire	Southampton	1990
		110*	v Gloucestershire	Ilford	1990
Higgins, G.F.		118	v Warwickshire	Birmingham	1895
Hipkin, A.B.	(2)	102	v Glamorgan	Leyton	1927
		108	v Oxford University	Chelmsford	1927
Hobbs, R.N.S.	(2)	100	v Glamorgan	Ilford	1968
		100	v Australians	Chelmsford	1975
Horsfall, R.	(17)	170	v Hampshire	Bournemouth	1947
		128*	v Surrey	Ilford	1948
		113	v Middlesex	Brentwood	1948
		122	v Worcestershire	Clacton	1948
		110	v Combined Services	Chelmsford	1950
		110	v Glamorgan	Chelmsford	1951
		206	v Kent	Blackheath	1951
		123	v Nottinghamshire	Clacton	1951
		102	v Worcestershire	Romford	1952
		143	v Leicestershire	Brentwood	1952
		135	v Kent	Clacton	1952
		118	v Worcestershire	Worcester	1953
		151*	v Kent	Romford	1953
		103	v Leicestershire	Colchester	1953
		140	v Somerset	Weston-s-Mare	1953
		107	v Warwickshire	Clacton	1953
		117	v Derbyshire	Westcliff	1954
Hussain, N.	(18)	165*	v Leicestershire	Chelmsford	1988
		141	v Warwickshire	Ilford	1989
		127	v Kent	Southend	1989
		105*	v Lancashire	Lytham	1989
		197	v Surrey	The Oval	1990
		128	v Surrey	The Oval	1991
		141	v Northamptonshire	Colchester	1991
		196	v Leicestershire	Leicester	1991
		172*	v Lancashire	Ilford	1992
		118	v England A	Chelmsford	1993
		111	v Cambridge Univ	Cambridge	1993
		152	v Derbyshire	Chelmsford	1993
		107*	v Warwickshire	Ilford	1993
		103	v Leicestershire	Southend	1993
		118	v Sussex	Hove	1993
		102	v Hampshire	Chelmsford	1993
		115*	v Hampshire	Southampton	1994
		101	v Durham	Stockton-on-Tees	1994
Insole, D.J.	(48)	109	v Lancashire	Clacton	1947
		219*	v Yorkshire	Colchester	1949
		147	v Worcestershire	Southend	1949
		107	v Hampshire	Bournemouth	1949
		105	v Worcestershire	Romford	1950
		106	v Warwickshire	Ilford	1950
		100	v Middlesex	Lord's	1950
		122	v Worcestershire	Worcester	1950
		186*	v Worcestershire	Worcester	1951
		158*	v Somerset	Brentwood	1951
		184*	v Sussex	Hove	1951
		124	v Surrey	Ilford	1952
		116	v Indians	Ilford	1952
		130	v Northamptonshire	Colchester	1952
		160*	v Worcestershire	Worcester	1953

Insole, D.J. (contd)		126	v Sussex	Ilford	1953
		137	v Somerset	Chelmsford	1953
		125	v Warwickshire	Birmingham	1954
		156*	v Northamptonshire	Romford	1954
		123*	v Kent	Blackheath	1954
		172*	v Surrey	Colchester	1954
		129	v South Africans	Colchester	1955
		104	v Derbyshire	Chesterfield	1955
		117*	v Gloucestershire	Westcliff	1955
		111	v Kent	Gillingham	1955
		118	v Kent	Gillingham	1955
		142	v Yorkshire	Bradford	1955
		106	v Leicestershire	Leicester	1955
		119	v Yorkshire	Southend	1955
		114*	v Nottinghamshire	Southend	1955
		122	v Kent	Dartford	1956
		159	v Gloucestershire	Romford	1956
		162	v Northamptonshire	Brentwood	1956
		126	v Somerset	Brentwood	1956
		106	v Glamorgan	Ilford	1957
		150*	v Worcestershire	Worcester	1957
		140	v Northamptonshire	Westcliff	1957
		115	v Surrey	Clacton	1957
		108	v Sussex	Hove	1958
		102*	v Glamorgan	Westcliff	1958
		123	v Hampshire	Bournemouth	1959
		180	v Nottinghamshire	Romford	1959
		122	v Glamorgan	Westcliff	1959
		177*	v Gloucestershire	Leyton	1959
		155	v Derbyshire	Chesterfield	1959
		105	v South Africans	Ilford	1960
		105	v Lancashire	Blackpool	1960
		118	v Worcestershire	Worcester	1960
Irani, R.C.	(2)	119	v Worcestershire	Worcester	1994
		102*	v Middlesex	Uxbridge	1994
Irvine, B.L.		109	v Glamorgan	Swansea	1969
Knight, B.R.	(8)	103	v Worcestershire	Leyton	1959
		114	v Surrey	Ilford	1961
		120	v Derbyshire	Burton	1961
		165	v Middlesex	Brentwood	1962
		120	v Warwickshire	Colchester	1962
		124	v Hampshire	Ilford	1963
		101*	v Nottinghamshire	Nottingham	1963
		100	v Surrey	Clacton	1963
Knight, N.V.	(7)	101*	v Lancashire	Manchester	1991
		104*	v Cambridge Univ	Cambridge	1992
		109	v Middlesex	Ilford	1992
		150	v Cambridge Univ	Cambridge	1994
		113	v Warwickshire	Birmingham	1994
		115	v Surrey	Colchester	1994
		157	v Sussex	Chelmsford	1994
Kortright, C.J.	(2)	112	v Leicestershire	Leicester	1898
		131	v Middlesex	Leyton	1900
Lewis, J.J.B.	(4)	116*	v Surrey	The Oval	1990
		133	v Sussex	Hove	1992
		136*	v Nottinghamshire	Nottingham	1993
		109	v Gloucestershire	Chelmsford	1994
Lilley, A.W.	(3)	100*	v Nottinghamshire	Nottingham	1978
		102	v Middlesex	Chelmsford	1987
		113*	v Derbyshire	Chelmsford	1989

Lucas, A.P.	(2)	135	v Somerset	Taunton	1895
		103	v Derbyshire	Leyton	1902
McEwan, K.S.	(52)	119*	v Middlesex	Ilford	1974
		126	v Kent	Dartford	1974
		145	v Glamorgan	Leyton	1975
		106	v Somerset	Taunton	1975
		131	v Cambridge Univ	Cambridge	1976
		112	v Northamptonshire	Northampton	1976
		136	v Kent	Tunbridge Wells	1976
		117	v Surrey	The Oval	1976
		156	v Nottinghamshire	Nottingham	1976
		105	v Somerset	Leyton	1976
		115*	v Derbyshire	Derby	1977
		150	v Cambridge Univ	Cambridge	1977
		100*	v Australians	Chelmsford	1977
		218	v Sussex	Chelmsford	1977
		102	v Warwickshire	Birmingham	1977
		116	v Warwickshire	Birmingham	1977
		106*	v Gloucestershire	Southend	1977
		123	v Worcestershire	Worcester	1977
		109*	v Cambridge Univ	Cambridge	1978
		186	v Northamptonshire	Ilford	1978
		115	v Glamorgan	Cardiff	1978
		149	v Yorkshire	Chelmsford	1978
		128	v Lancashire	Southport	1978
		208*	v Warwickshire	Birmingham	1979
		185	v Derbyshire	Chelmsford	1979
		124	v Yorkshire	Scarborough	1979
		103*	v Sussex	Hove	1980
		140*	v Northamptonshire	Northampton	1980
		106	v Surrey	Chelmsford	1981
		109*	v Leicestershire	Leicester	1981
		102	v Kent	Canterbury	1981
		103	v Hampshire	Southampton	1981
		141	v Leicestershire	Colchester	1981
		102	v Surrey	The Oval	1981
		150*	v Derbyshire	Chesterfield	1982
		116	v Derbyshire	Southend	1982
		128	v Warwickshire	Colchester	1982
		107	v Glamorgan	Cardiff	1983
		151	v Leicestershire	Leicester	1983
		142	v Kent	Tunbridge Wells	1983
		178	v Derbyshire	Derby	1983
		142	v Hampshire	Southend	1983
		104	v Glamorgan	Southend	1983
		181	v Gloucestershire	Colchester	1983
		189*	v Worcestershire	Colchester	1983
		101	v Derbyshire	Ilford	1984
		142*	v Hampshire	Colchester	1984
		104	v Surrey	The Oval	1984
		132	v Lancashire	Manchester	1984
		110	v Cambridge Univ	Cambridge	1985
		121	v Middlesex	Chelmsford	1985
		106	v Gloucestershire	Bristol	1985
McGahey, C.P.	(29)	147	v Somerset	Taunton	1895
		140	v Sussex	Hove	1897
		123	v Leicestershire	Leicester	1897
		115	v Derbyshire	Derby	1898
		145	v Lancashire	Manchester	1898
		130	v Warwickshire	Leyton	1899

McGahey, C.P. (contd)		107	v Sussex	Leyton	1900
		184	v Leicestershire	Leyton	1900
		122	v Derbyshire	Leyton	1900
		142	v Kent	Leyton	1900
		125	v Sussex	Leyton	1901
		114	v Gloucestershire	Leyton	1901
		145*	v Gloucestershire	Leyton	1901
		130*	v Warwickshire	Leyton	1901
		104	v Sussex	Leyton	1902
		126	v Middlesex	Leyton	1902
		110*	v Surrey	Leyton	1903
		144*	v Lancashire	Manchester	1903
		173	v Surrey	The Oval	1904
		225	v Nottinghamshire	Leyton	1904
		277	v Derbyshire	Leyton	1905
		137	v Middlesex	Lord's	1905
		105	v Yorkshire	Leyton	1905
		101	v Kent	Tunbridge Wells	1906
		108	v Kent	Tunbridge Wells	1907
		126	v Gloucestershire	Leyton	1908
		230	v Northamptonshire	Northampton	1908
		150	v Derbyshire	Leyton	1912
		117	v Middlesex	Leyton	1912
McIver, C.D.	(4)	110	v Lancashire	Leyton	1913
		134	v Hampshire	Leyton	1913
		113	v Hampshire	Leyton	1914
		118	v Northamptonshire	Leyton	1914
Mead, W.		119	v Leicestershire	Leyton	1902
Meston, S.P		130	v Lancashire	Leyton	1907
Milner, J.	(3)	135	v Leicestershire	Leicester	1959
		117	v Nottinghamshire	Westcliff	1961
		120	v Hampshire	Cowes	1961
Morris, H.M.	(3)	111	v Middlesex	Lord's	1923
		143	v Somerset	Taunton	1927
		166	v Hampshire	Southampton	1927
Nicholas, F.W.H.		140	v Surrey	Leyton	1926
Nichols, M.S.	(20)	112	v Hampshire	Leyton	1928
		138	v Hampshire	Leyton	1929
		103	v Worcestershire	Leyton	1930
		105	v Yorkshire	Scarborough	1932
		108	v Glamorgan	Swansea	1933
		117	v Worcestershire	Leyton	1933
		135	v Derbyshire	Leyton	1933
		102	v Worcestershire	Chelmsford	1934
		116	v Gloucestershire	Gloucester	1934
		146	v Yorkshire	Huddersfield	1935
		101	v Northamptonshire	Northampton	1936
		110	v Kent	Southend	1936
		205	v Hampshire	Southend	1936
		120	v Hampshire	Portsmouth	1937
		109*	v Northamptonshire	Colchester	1937
		163	v Kent	Gravesend	1938
		133*	v Surrey	Westcliff	1938
		159	v Gloucestershire	Gloucester	1938
		146	v Sussex	Hove	1939
		116*	v Worcestershire	Chelmsford	1939
O'Connor, J.	(71)	102*	v Northamptonshire	Northampton	1922
		111*	v Hampshire	Leyton	1923
		128	v Gloucestershire	Cheltenham	1923
		142	v Leicestershire	Leicester	1925

O'Connor, J. (contd)	111	v Glamorgan	Leyton	1925
	124	v Nottinghamshire	Nottingham	1927
	107	v Kent	Gravesend	1927
	139*	v Leicestershire	Leyton	1927
	101	v Worcestershire	Leyton	1927
	130*	v Yorkshire	Leyton	1928
	123	v Middlesex	Leyton	1928
	157	v Oxford University	Colchester (Gar)	1928
	101	v Somerset	Chelmsford	1928
	124	v Gloucestershire	Chelmsford	1928
	123	v Leicestershire	Leyton	1928
	168*	v Cambridge Univ	Cambridge	1929
	106	v Surrey	The Oval	1929
	109	v Glamorgan	Colchester (Gar)	1929
	151	v Surrey	Leyton	1929
	123	v Warwickshire	Chelmsford	1929
	157	v Hampshire	Leyton	1929
	116	v Kent	Folkestone	1929
	110	v Leicestershire	Southend	1929
	102	v Kent	Leyton	1929
	138	v Gloucestershire	Bristol	1930
	120*	v Gloucestershire	Bristol	1930
	104	v Middlesex	Lord's	1930
	101	v Derbyshire	Derby	1930
	119	v Warwickshire	Leyton	1930
	100	v Kent	Gravesend	1931
	129	v New Zealanders	Leyton	1931
	119	v Kent	Colchester (Gar)	1931
	122	v Lancashire	Clacton	1931
	118*	v Northamptonshire	Northampton	1931
	108	v Leicestershire	Leyton	1931
	112*	v Glamorgan	Cardiff	1932
	115	v Surrey	Leyton	1932
	104	v Surrey	The Oval	1932
	119	v Sussex	Eastbourne	1932
	122*	v Warwickshire	Birmingham	1933
	115	v Hampshire	Leyton	1933
	237	v Somerset	Leyton	1933
	102*	v Lancashire	Leyton	1933
	140	v Gloucestershire	Clacton	1933
	130	v Hampshire	Bournemouth	1933
	112	v Sussex	Hove	1934
	101	v Hampshire	Portsmouth	1934
	105*	v Kent	Brentwood	1934
	248	v Surrey	Brentwood	1934
	143	v Surrey	The Oval	1934
	102*	v Gloucestershire	Westcliff	1934
	106	v Middlesex	Lord's	1934
	174	v Leicestershire	Leicester	1934
	103	v Northamptonshire	Northampton	1934
	139	v Kent	Ilford	1935
	127	v Sussex	Hove	1936
	100	v Kent	Southend	1936
	111	v Nottinghamshire	Clacton	1936
	111	v Cambridge Univ	Brentwood	1937
	107	v Somerset	Ilford	1937
	192	v Northamptonshire	Colchester	1937
	113	v Kent	Gravesend	1938
	129	v Yorkshire	Ilford	1938
	130	v Gloucestershire	Brentwood	1938

O'Connor, J. (contd)		152	v Sussex	Hove	1938
		115*	v Northamptonshire	Rushden	1938
		122	v Middlesex	Lord's	1938
		128	v Middlesex	Lord's	1939
		118*	v Worcestershire	Chelmsford	1939
		194	v Nottinghamshire	Nottingham	1939
		122	v Hampshire	Brentwood	1939
Owen, H.G.P.	(3)	109	v Oxford University	Leyton	1894
		134	v Hampshire	Leyton	1900
		106*	v Derbyshire	Leyton	1901
Pearce, T.N.	(20)	152	v Lancashire	Clacton	1931
		111	v Worcestershire	Chelmsford	1934
		105	v Lancashire	Chelmsford	1935
		132	v Northamptonshire	Northampton	1935
		102	v Sussex	Hove	1936
		110*	v Cambridge Univ	Cambridge	1936
		119*	v Sussex	Colchester	1937
		137*	v Kent	Colchester	1938
		121*	v Sussex	Colchester	1938
		166*	v Somerset	Taunton	1946
		124*	v Derbyshire	Ilford	1946
		116*	v Surrey	The Oval	1946
		156	v Hampshire	Westcliff	1946
		140	v Lancashire	Manchester	1946
		137*	v Worcestershire	Worcester	1947
		127	v Nottinghamshire	Southend	1948
		211*	v Leicestershire	Westcliff	1948
		137	v Lancashire	Blackpool	1948
		111*	v Kent	Ilford	1949
		111	v Derbyshire	Westcliff	1949
Perrin, P.A.	(65)	139	v Warwickshire	Birmingham	1896
		153	v Warwickshire	Leyton	1897
		101	v Hampshire	Leyton	1897
		104	v Derbyshire	Derby	1898
		106*	v Kent	Leyton	1898
		144	v Yorkshire	Sheffield	1899
		104	v Hampshire	Leyton	1899
		168	v Hampshire	Southampton	1899
		196	v Derbyshire	Derby	1899
		109	v Kent	Leyton	1899
		132	v Leicestershire	Leicester	1899
		106	v Gloucestershire	Leyton	1900
		205	v Kent	Leyton	1900
		125	v Warwickshire	Leyton	1900
		134*	v Gloucestershire	Cheltenham	1900
		189	v Kent	Leyton	1901
		101*	v Derbyshire	Leyton	1901
		101	v Sussex	Hove	1901
		104	v Kent	Canterbury	1901
		108*	v Nottinghamshire	Leyton	1901
		121	v Leicestershire	Leicester	1902
		170	v Nottinghamshire	Nottingham	1903
		102*	v Nottinghamshire	Nottingham	1903
		102*	v Derbyshire	Leyton	1903
		110	v Nottinghamshire	Leyton	1903
		100*	v Nottinghamshire	Nottingham	1904
		190	v Sussex	Leyton	1904
		134	v Middlesex	Lord's	1904
		343*	v Derbyshire	Chesterfield	1904
		143	v Lancashire	Leyton	1904

45

Perrin, P.A. (contd)		140	v Middlesex	Lord's	1905
		103*	v Middlesex	Lord's	1905
		173*	v Warwickshire	Leyton	1905
		133	v Surrey	The Oval	1906
		110	v Gloucestershire	Leyton	1906
		106	v West Indians	Leyton	1906
		101	v Kent	Tunbridge Wells	1906
		150	v Sussex	Hastings	1906
		116	v Middlesex	Lord's	1907
		105	v Nottinghamshire	Nottingham	1907
		101*	v Leicestershire	Leyton	1908
		101*	v Lancashire	Leyton	1909
		144	v Cambridge Univ	Cambridge	1910
		114	v Middlesex	Leyton	1911
		101	v Worcestershire	Leyton	1911
		112	v Nottinghamshire	Nottingham	1911
		100*	v Nottinghamshire	Nottingham	1911
		110	v Lancashire	Leyton	1911
		113	v Kent	Leyton	1911
		245	v Derbyshire	Leyton	1912
		107	v Middlesex	Leyton	1912
		104	v Australians	Leyton	1912
		140	v Surrey	Leyton	1913
		103	v Surrey	Leyton	1914
		126	v Kent	Leyton	1914
		105	v Sussex	Leyton	1919
		126	v Kent	Leyton	1919
		101*	v Kent	Leyton	1919
		114	v Northamptonshire	Northampton	1922
		105	v Cambridge Univ	Colchester	1922
		101	v Kent	Southend	1922
		100*	v Derbyshire	Derby	1922
		102*	v Lancashire	Manchester	1923
		122	v Worcestershire	Worcester	1923
		102	v Northamptonshire	Kettering	1925
Phillip, N.		134	v Gloucestershire	Gloucester	1978
Pont, K.R.	(7)	113	v Warwickshire	Birmingham	1973
		110	v Glamorgan	Leyton	1975
		105*	v Somerset	Leyton	1976
		101*	v Surrey	Chelmsford	1977
		101	v Glamorgan	Cardiff	1978
		105	v Kent	Chelmsford	1983
		125*	v Glamorgan	Southend	1983
Pope, D.F.	(7)	123	v Sussex	Hove	1930
		161	v Warwickshire	Leyton	1930
		115	v Somerset	Leyton	1932
		100	v Kent	Brentwood	1934
		108	v Glamorgan	Clacton	1934
		129	v Worcestershire	Worcester	1934
		108	v Gloucestershire	Gloucester	1934
Prichard, P.J.	(23)	100	v Lancashire	Manchester	1984
		147*	v Nottinghamshire	Chelmsford	1986
		128	v Northamptonshire	Colchester	1989
		245	v Leicestershire	Chelmsford	1990
		116	v Cambridge Univ	Cambridge	1990
		116	v Somerset	Bath	1990
		103	v Derbyshire	Derby	1990
		102	v Kent	Chelmsford	1990
		190	v Northamptonshire	Northampton	1991
		129	v Middlesex	Lord's	1991

Prichard, P.J. (contd)		122	v Kent	Southend	1991
		128	v Yorkshire	Colchester	1991
		102	v Leicestershire	Chelmsford	1992
		133	v Kent	Tunbridge Wells	1992
		106	v Leicestershire	Leicester	1992
		136	v Nottinghamshire	Colchester	1992
		123	v Somerset	Chelmsford	1993
		104	v Kent	Maidstone	1993
		106	v Kent	Maidstone	1993
		225*	v Sussex	Hove	1993
		108	v Durham	Stockton-on-Tees	1994
		109	v Kent	Chelmsford	1994
		119	v Gloucestershire	Chelmsford	1994
Pringle, D.R.	(4)	102*	v Hampshire	Southend	1983
		121*	v Surrey	The Oval	1985
		128	v Kent	Chelmsford	1988
		112*	v Sussex	Hove	1992
Reeves, W.	(3)	101	v Surrey	Leyton	1905
		135	v Lancashire	Leyton	1905
		104	v Sussex	Leyton	1906
Russell, C.A.G.	(62)	102	v Hampshire	Leyton	1913
		110	v Lancashire	Manchester	1913
		145	v Leicestershire	Leyton	1914
		116*	v Worcestershire	Worcester	1914
		118	v Yorkshire	Leyton	1919
		122	v Kent	Leyton	1919
		125	v Lancashire	Manchester	1919
		160	v Kent	Canterbury	1919
		117	v Oxford University	Oxford	1920
		197	v Middlesex	Lord's	1920
		168	v Hampshire	Bournemouth	1920
		151	v Worcestershire	Leyton	1921
		108	v Northamptonshire	Northampton	1921
		120	v Middlesex	Leyton	1921
		273	v Northamptonshire	Leyton	1921
		147	v Kent	Leyton	1921
		148	v Lancashire	Leyton	1921
		133	v Somerset	Leyton	1922
		115	v Surrey	The Oval	1922
		118	v Surrey	The Oval	1922
		172	v Northamptonshire	Northampton	1922
		125*	v Sussex	Leyton	1922
		118	v Hampshire	Portsmouth	1922
		110	v Worcestershire	Worcester	1922
		102	v Lancashire	Manchester	1923
		147	v Worcestershire	Worcester	1923
		104	v Gloucestershire	Colchester (Gar)	1924
		108	v South Africans	Colchester (Gar)	1924
		109*	v Nottinghamshire	Worksop	1924
		135*	v Gloucestershire	Leyton	1925
		111	v Somerset	Taunton	1925
		150	v Somerset	Leyton	1925
		104	v Leicestershire	Leicester	1925
		132	v Glamorgan	Swansea	1925
		149	v Hampshire	Southend	1925
		107	v Glamorgan	Leyton	1925
		122*	v Middlesex	Lord's	1926
		180*	v Somerset	Taunton	1926
		171	v Lancashire	Nelson	1926
		103*	v Glamorgan	Leyton	1926

Russell, C.A.G. (contd)		102*	v Derbyshire	Leyton	1926
		156	v Hampshire	Portsmouth	1926
		117	v Somerset	Taunton	1927
		104	v Leicestershire	Leyton	1927
		161	v Hampshire	Southampton	1927
		127	v Hampshire	Chelmsford	1927
		110	v Sussex	Hove	1927
		147	v West Indians	Leyton	1928
		135	v Worcestershire	Leyton	1928
		108*	v Middlesex	Leyton	1928
		113	v Gloucestershire	Chelmsford	1928
		131	v Lancashire	Liverpool	1928
		104	v Lancashire	Liverpool	1928
		153	v Worcestershire	Worcester	1928
		182	v Sussex	Leyton	1928
		111*	v Middlesex	Leyton	1929
		102	v Derbyshire	Derby	1929
		131	v Warwickshire	Coventry (Rover)	1929
		100*	v Warwickshire	Birmingham	1930
		132	v Yorkshire	Dewsbury	1930
		102	v Middlesex	Lord's	1930
		178	v Sussex	Hove	1930
Russell, A.E.		100	v Derbyshire	Chesterfield	1901
Russell, T.M.	(3)	110	v Surrey	Leyton	1896
		122*	v Hampshire	Leyton	1898
		139	v Derbyshire	Derby	1900
Salim Malik	(8)	173	v Kent	Folkestone	1991
		163	v Gloucestershire	Bristol	1991
		215	v Leicestershire	Ilford	1991
		185*	v Surrey	The Oval	1991
		102	v Somerset	Southend	1991
		165	v Derbyshire	Chelmsford	1991
		132	v Derbyshire	Chelmsford	1993
		121	v Nottinghamshire	Nottingham	1993
Savill, L.A.	(4)	100	v Somerset	Brentwood	1956
		115	v Cambridge Univ	Cambridge	1959
		107	v Northamptonshire	Ilford	1959
		115	v Northamptonshire	Northampton	1959
Saville, G.J.	(2)	103	v Cambridge Univ	Harlow	1970
		126*	v Glamorgan	Swansea	1972
Sewell, E.H.D.	(2)	107	v Warwickshire	Birmingham	1904
		106	v Surrey	The Oval	1904
Seymour, A.C.H.		157	v Glamorgan	Cardiff	1991
Shahid, N.	(2)	125	v Lancashire	Colchester	1990
		132	v Kent	Chelmsford	1992
Sheffield, J.R.		108	v Sussex	Hove	1936
Smith, G.J.	(4)	110	v Hampshire	Clacton	1958
		126	v Surrey	Ilford	1961
		148	v Derbyshire	Chelmsford (H)	1961
		103*	v Sussex	Clacton	1961
Smith, N.	(2)	100	v Yorkshire	Middlesbrough	1975
		126	v Somerset	Leyton	1976
Smith, R.	(6)	112	v Derbyshire	Colchester	1948
		147	v South Africans	Ilford	1951
		132	v Warwickshire	Birmingham	1951
		103	v Lancashire	Colchester	1951
		107*	v Northamptonshire	Colchester	1952
		101*	v Northamptonshire	Wellingborough	1955

Name		Score		Opponent	Venue	Year
Smith, T.P.B.	(8)	111	v	Hampshire	Portsmouth	1934
		105	v	Indians	Brentwood	1936
		103	v	Kent	Gravesend	1938
		101	v	Middlesex	Chelmsford	1938
		102	v	Nottinghamshire	Clacton	1939
		106	v	Hampshire	Portsmouth	1946
		163	v	Derbyshire	Chesterfield	1947
		115	v	Northamptonshire	Westcliff	1949
Stephenson, J.P.	(16)	109*	v	Kent	Canterbury	1989
		102	v	Somerset	Chelmsford	1989
		114	v	Surrey	The Oval	1989
		171	v	Lancashire	Lytham	1989
		202*	v	Somerset	Bath	1990
		147	v	New Zealanders	Chelmsford	1990
		131	v	Leicestershire	Leicester	1990
		113	v	Kent	Southend	1991
		116	v	Yorkshire	Colchester	1991
		113	v	Leicestershire	Leicester	1991
		113*	v	Somerset	Taunton	1992
		159*	v	Somerset	Taunton	1992
		123*	v	Sussex	Southend	1992
		113*	v	Nottinghamshire	Nottingham	1993
		122	v	Sussex	Hove	1993
		144	v	Nottinghamshire	Ilford	1994
Taylor, B.	(9)	127	v	Glamorgan	Cardiff	1956
		105	v	Northamptonshire	Wellingborough	1957
		135	v	Middlesex	Lord's	1959
		105*	v	Gloucestershire	Clacton	1962
		104*	v	Worcestershire	Worcester	1965
		117	v	Middlesex	Lord's	1967
		110	v	Surrey	Guildford	1968
		106	v	Cambridge Univ	Harlow	1970
		113*	v	Northamptonshire	Northampton	1970
Taylor, R.M.	(5)	106	v	Yorkshire	Scarborough	1932
		134	v	Derbyshire	Derby	1933
		129	v	Northamptonshire	Colchester	1937
		193	v	Sussex	Colchester	1938
		142	v	Warwickshire	Southend	1946
Tosetti, G.		132*	v	Lancashire	Manchester	1902
Turner, A.J.	(11)	111	v	Yorkshire	Huddersfield	1897
		102*	v	Surrey	Leyton	1898
		109	v	Yorkshire	Sheffield	1899
		124	v	Warwickshire	Birmingham	1899
		111	v	Middlesex	Leyton	1901
		120	v	Nottinghamshire	Leyton	1901
		102	v	Leicestershire	Leicester	1904
		103	v	Derbyshire	Glossop	1905
		117	v	Northamptonshire	Northampton	1908
		117	v	Nottinghamshire	Leyton	1909
		111*	v	Nottinghamshire	Nottingham	1910
Turner, S.	(4)	110*	v	Glamorgan	Ilford	1968
		121	v	Somerset	Taunton	1970
		118*	v	Glamorgan	Swansea	1974
		102	v	Kent	Chelmsford	1979
Turner, W.M.F.	(2)	104*	v	Derbyshire	Leyton	1906
		172	v	Middlesex	Leyton	1919
Vere Hodge, N.	(2)	100*	v	Middlesex	Lord's	1937
		108	v	Nottinghamshire	Nottingham	1937

Vigar, F.H.	(11)	121	v Gloucestershire	Westcliff	1939
		101	v Northamptonshire	Northampton	1946
		111*	v Nottinghamshire	Nottingham	1947
		112	v Warwickshire	Coventry	1947
		125	v Hampshire	Bournemouth	1947
		114*	v Derbyshire	Chesterfield	1947
		103	v Gloucestershire	Ilford	1948
		136	v Kent	Ilford	1949
		119	v Somerset	Bath	1949
		114*	v Leicestershire	Leicester	1949
		144	v Northamptonshire	Northampton	1950
Ward, B.	(4)	115	v Middlesex	Lord's	1967
		128	v Gloucestershire	Bristol	1968
		164*	v Nottinghamshire	Nottingham	1970
		101*	v Worcestershire	Chelmsford	1971
Waterman, A.G.		103	v Somerset	Bath	1938
Waugh, H.P.		128	v Glamorgan	Leyton	1928
Waugh, M.E.	(16)	109	v Hampshire	Ilford	1989
		110	v Middlesex	Uxbridge	1989
		100*	v Australians	Chelmsford	1989
		165	v Leicestershire	Leicester	1989
		166*	v Worcestershire	Worcester	1990
		125	v Hampshire	Southampton	1990
		204	v Gloucestershire	Ilford	1990
		103	v Warwickshire	Birmingham	1990
		126	v Derbyshire	Colchester	1990
		103*	v Sussex	Chelmsford	1990
		207*	v Yorkshire	Middlesbrough	1990
		169	v Kent	Chelmsford	1990
		120	v Kent	Chelmsford	1992
		219*	v Lancashire	Ilford	1992
		125*	v Gloucestershire	Southend	1992
		138*	v Worcestershire	Kidderminster	1992
Wilcox, D.R.	(8)	109	v Yorkshire	Southend	1934
		133	v Hampshire	Southend	1936
		104	v Kent	Westcliff	1937
		129	v Kent	Westcliff	1937
		116	v New Zealanders	Chelmsford	1937
		142	v Worcestershire	Clacton	1937
		102	v Nottinghamshire	Chelmsford	1938
		134	v Warwickshire	Southend	1946
Williams, C.C.P.		119	v Leicestershire	Leicester	1955
Wykes, N.G.		162	v Kent	Leyton	1927

1000 RUNS IN A SEASON

Avery, A.V.	(7)	1939	1335
		1946	1118
		1948	1890
		1950	1380
		1951	1668
		1952	1441
		1953	1128
Bailey, T.E.	(10)	1949	1005
		1952	1274
		1954	1189
		1955	1024
		1957	1202

Bailey, T.E. (contd)		1959	1732
		1960	1597
		1961	1179
		1962	1420
		1963	1420
Barker, G.	(15)	1955	1494
		1956	1159
		1957	1355
		1958	1378
		1959	1391
		1960	1741
		1961	1740
		1962	1475
		1963	1419
		1964	1707
		1965	1289
		1966	1301
		1967	1252
		1969	1060
		1970	1111
Bear, M.J.	(4)	1962	1612
		1963	1170
		1964	1567
		1966	1833
Border, A.R.	(2)	1986	1385
		1988	1393
Carpenter, H.A.	(6)	1898	1011
		1900	1468
		1901	1495
		1904	1121
		1905	1422
		1906	1026
Cray, S.J.	(2)	1947	1233
		1949	1046
Cutmore, J.A.	(11)	1925	1069
		1926	1556
		1927	1162
		1928	1170
		1929	1399
		1930	1588
		1931	1175
		1932	1485
		1933	1813
		1934	1876
		1935	1218
Denness, M.H.	(2)	1977	1343
		1979	1032
Dodds, T.C.	(13)	1946	1050
		1947	1858
		1948	1780
		1949	1696
		1950	1584
		1951	1345
		1952	1797
		1953	1050
		1954	1275
		1955	1364
		1956	1228
		1957	1151
		1958	1069

Douglas, J.W.H.T.	(8)	1908	1010
		1911	1047
		1912	1049
		1914	1151
		1920	1200
		1921	1211
		1923	1043
		1927	1046
Eastman, L.C.	(5)	1929	1298
		1933	1338
		1937	1057
		1938	1033
		1939	1027
Edmeades, B.E.A.	(5)	1967	1152
		1969	1249
		1970	1620
		1972	1257
		1975	1084
Fane, F.L.		1902	1028
Fletcher, K.W.R.	(19)	1963	1282
		1964	1445
		1965	1437
		1966	1374
		1967	1754
		1968	1523
		1969	1035
		1970	1218
		1971	1325
		1972	1755
		1976	1588
		1977	1331
		1978	1127
		1979	1006
		1980	1349
		1981	1180
		1982	1238
		1983	1077
		1984	1056
Francis, B.C.	(2)	1971	1578
		1973	1384
Freeman, J.R.	(7)	1919	1000
		1921	1557
		1922	1094
		1923	1186
		1924	1327
		1925	1273
		1926	1958
Gibb, P.A.	(4)	1951	1330
		1952	1474
		1953	1241
		1955	1219
Gladwin, C.		1984	1396
Gooch, G.A	(15)	1976	1273
		1980	1019
		1981	1184
		1982	1632
		1983	1481
		1984	2559
		1985	1706
		1987	1174

Gooch, G.A. (contd)		1988	1754
		1989	1073
		1990	1688
		1991	1219
		1992	1466
		1993	1350
		1994	1385
Hardie, B.R.	(11)	1974	1168
		1975	1522
		1978	1044
		1979	1170
		1980	1084
		1981	1339
		1982	1432
		1983	1042
		1984	1077
		1985	1374
		1987	1370
Horsfall, R.	(4)	1948	1302
		1951	1655
		1952	1560
		1953	1731
Hussain, N.	(2)	1991	1307
		1993	1420
Insole, D.J.	(11)	1950	1669
		1951	1664
		1952	1658
		1953	1329
		1954	1763
		1955	2142
		1956	1877
		1957	1540
		1958	1161
		1959	1874
		1960	1225
Irvine, B.L.	(2)	1968	1439
		1969	1235
Knight, B.R.	(5)	1961	1106
		1962	1493
		1963	1412
		1964	1046
		1965	1001
McEwan, K.S.	(12)	1974	1040
		1975	1174
		1976	1821
		1977	1702
		1978	1682
		1979	1387
		1980	1217
		1981	1420
		1982	1421
		1983	2176
		1984	1755
		1985	1293
McGahey, C.P.	(9)	1898	1024
		1900	1106
		1901	1627
		1902	1030
		1903	1061
		1904	1189

McGahey, C.P. (contd)		1905	1645
		1906	1217
		1907	1165
Milner, J.		1961	1308
Nichols, M.S.	(9)	1929	1281
		1932	1381
		1933	1311
		1934	1219
		1935	1171
		1936	1224
		1937	1159
		1938	1310
		1939	1363
O'Connor, J.	(16)	1923	1218
		1925	1054
		1926	1402
		1927	1334
		1928	2256
		1929	2224
		1930	1504
		1931	1634
		1932	1299
		1933	2077
		1934	2308
		1935	1603
		1936	1343
		1937	1475
		1938	1839
		1939	1716
Pearce, T.N.	(4)	1935	1018
		1946	1321
		1947	1392
		1948	1567
Perrin, P.A.	(17)	1898	1073
		1899	1491
		1900	1138
		1901	1426
		1902	1062
		1903	1428
		1904	1421
		1905	1119
		1906	1883
		1907	1077
		1908	1077
		1911	1281
		1914	1261
		1921	1123
		1922	1301
		1923	1135
		1925	1023
Pope, D.F.	(4)	1930	1280
		1932	1172
		1933	1132
		1934	1750
Prichard, P.J.	(5)	1986	1342
		1988	1202
		1990	1407
		1992	1485
		1993	1319
Reeves, W.		1905	1172

Russell, C.A.G.	(13)	1913	1072
		1914	1429
		1919	1387
		1920	2042
		1921	1935
		1922	2243
		1923	1249
		1924	1286
		1925	1942
		1926	1906
		1927	1759
		1928	2062
		1930	1355
Salim Malik		1991	1972
Savill, L.A.		1959	1197
Saville, G.J.		1970	1133
Smith, G.J.	(3)	1960	1367
		1961	1754
		1962	1115
Smith, R.	(3)	1947	1201
		1950	1109
		1951	1254
Smith, T.P.B.		1947	1065
Stephenson, J.P.	(5)	1989	1318
		1990	1730
		1991	1421
		1992	1401
		1993	1011
Taylor, B.	(8)	1956	1219
		1957	1163
		1959	1630
		1960	1358
		1964	1225
		1966	1264
		1967	1282
		1970	1176
Taylor, R.M.	(2)	1933	1181
		1938	1099
Vigar, F.H.	(3)	1947	1537
		1949	1449
		1950	1020
Waugh, M.E.	(3)	1989	1537
		1990	2072
		1992	1314
Wilcox, D.R.	(2)	1937	1253
		1938	1025

MOST HUNDREDS IN A SEASON

9	J.O'Connor	1929		7	C.A.G.Russell	1922
	J.O'Connor	1934			C.A.G.Russell	1925
	D.J.Insole	1955			G.A.Gooch	1992
8	C.A.G.Russell	1928			N.Hussain	1993
	K.S.McEwan	1977				
	K.S.McEwan	1983				
	G.A.Gooch	1984				
	G.A.Gooch	1990				
	M.E.Waugh	1990				

MOST RUNS IN A SEASON

G.A.Gooch	2559 in 1984	D.J.Insole	2142 in 1955
J.O'Connor	2308 in 1934	J.O'Connor	2077 in 1933
J.O'Connor	2256 in 1928	M.E.Waugh	2072 in 1990
C.A.G.Russell	2243 in 1922	C.A.G.Russell	2062 in 1928
J.O'Connor	2224 in 1929	C.A.G.Russell	2042 in 1920
K.S.McEwan	2176 in 1983		

10,000 RUNS FOR ESSEX

	Career	M	I	NO	Runs	HS	Avge	100
K.W.R.Fletcher	1962-1988	574	920	122	29434	228*	36.88	45
P.A.Perrin	1896-1928	525	894	88	29172	343*	36.19	65
J.O'Connor	1921-1939	516	866	76	27819	248	35.21	71
G.A.Gooch	1973-1994	346	569	54	26719	275	51.88	79
C.A.G.Russell	1908-1930	379	628	51	23610	273	40.91	62
G.Barker	1954-1971	444	797	46	21895	181*	29.15	30
T.E.Bailey	1946-1967	482	774	152	21460	205	34.50	22
D.J.Insole	1947-1963	345	574	54	20113	219*	38.67	48
C.P.McGahey	1894-1921	400	685	61	19079	277	30.57	29
T.C.Dodds	1946-1959	380	663	17	18565	157	28.73	17
B.Taylor	1949-1973	539	901	69	18240	135	21.92	9
K.S.McEwan	1974-1985	282	458	41	18088	218	43.37	52
B.R.Hardie	1973-1990	374	601	78	17945	162	34.31	27
J.W.H.T.Douglas	1901-1928	459	746	108	17915	210*	28.07	18
J.A.Cutmore	1924-1936	342	593	36	15937	238*	28.61	15
M.S.Nichols	1924-1939	418	664	66	15736	205	26.31	20
J.R.Freeman	1905-1928	336	577	56	14507	286	27.84	26
A.V.Avery	1935-1954	268	453	33	14045	234	33.60	25
H.A.Carpenter	1894-1920	262	466	24	13043	199	29.50	22
L.C.Eastman	1920-1939	442	679	49	12965	161	20.57	7
B.E.A.Edmeades	1961-1976	335	555	69	12593	163	25.91	14
F.L.Fane	1895-1922	292	512	30	12599	217	26.13	18
M.J.Bear	1954-1968	322	562	44	12564	137	24.25	9
P.J.Prichard	1984-1994	224	359	43	11498	245	36.38	23
T.N.Pearce	1929-1950	231	376	48	11139	211*	33.96	20
R.Smith	1934-1956	419	646	81	11125	147	19.69	6

LEADING CAREER AVERAGES

	Career	M	I	NO	Runs	HS	Avge	100
M.E.Waugh	1988-1992	65	100	17	5101	219*	61.45	16
Salim Malik	1991-1993	39	63	11	2889	215	55.55	8
A.R.Border	1986-1988	40	64	12	2778	169*	53.42	10
G.A.Gooch	1973-1994	346	569	54	26719	275	51.88	79
N.Hussain	1987-1994	120	178	23	6738	147	43.47	18
K.S.McEwan	1974-1985	282	458	41	18088	218	43.37	52
C.A.G.Russell	1908-1930	379	628	51	23610	273	40.91	62
D.J.Insole	1947-1963	345	574	54	20113	219*	38.67	48
B.C.Francis	1971-1973	47	84	7	2962	188*	38.46	7
J.J.B.Lewis	1990-1994	45	76	12	2422	136*	37.84	4
N.V.Knight	1991-1994	46	74	9	2454	157	37.75	7
K.W.R.Fletcher	1962-1988	574	920	122	29434	228*	36.88	45
P.J.Prichard	1984-1994	224	359	43	11498	245	36.38	23
P.A.Perrin	1896-1928	525	894	88	29172	343*	36.19	65
A.J.Turner	1897-1910	68	116	12	3730	124	35.86	11

J.P.Stephenson	1985-1994	171	293	28	9383	202*	35.40	16
J.O'Connor	1921-1939	516	866	76	27819	248	35.21	71
B.L.Irvine	1968-1969	54	89	12	2674	109	34.71	1
T.E.Bailey	1946-1967	482	774	152	21460	205	34.50	22
B.R.Hardie	1973-1990	374	601	78	17945	162	34.31	27
T.N.Pearce	1929-1950	231	376	48	11139	211*	33.96	21
L.G.Crawley	1926-1936	56	91	4	2949	222	33.89	6
A.V.Avery	1935-1954	268	453	33	14045	234	33.60	25
H.P.Crabtree	1931-1947	24	41	1	1281	146	32.02	4
F.H.Gillingham	1903-1928	181	307	21	9160	201	32.02	19
M.H.Denness	1977-1980	83	137	9	4050	195	31.64	6
N.Shahid	1989-1994	65	97	16	2523	132	31.14	2
D.R.Wilcox	1928-1947	118	186	8	5482	142	30.79	8
C.P.McGahey	1894-1921	400	685	61	19079	277	30.57	29

MOST HUNDREDS IN A CAREER

79	G.A.Gooch	27	B.R.Hardie
71	J.O'Connor	26	J.R.Freeman
65	P.A.Perrin	25	A.V.Avery
62	C.A.G.Russell	23	P.J.Prichard
52	K.S.McEwan	22	T.E.Bailey
48	D.J.Insole	22	H.A.Carpenter
45	K.W.R.Fletcher	20	M.S.Nichols
30	G.Barker	20	T.N.Pearce
29	C.P.McGahey		

MOST FIFTIES IN A CAREER

	100s	50s	Total
K.W.R.Fletcher	45	176	221
P.A.Perrin	65	145	210
G.A.Gooch	79	129	208
J.O'Connor	71	125	196
C.A.G.Russell	62	117	179
D.J.Insole	48	97	145
G.Barker	30	112	142
T.E.Bailey	22	119	141
K.S.McEwan	52	82	134
C.P.McGahey	29	97	126
T.C.Dodds	17	107	124
B.R.Hardie	27	89	116
J.A.Cutmore	15	87	102

SECTION 3 - PARTNERSHIP RECORDS

HIGHEST PARTNERSHIP FOR EACH WICKET

For Essex

1st	316	G.A.Gooch & P.J.Prichard	v Kent	Chelmsford	1994
2nd	403	G.A.Gooch & P.J.Prichard	v Leicestershire	Chelmsford	1990
3rd	347*	M.E.Waugh & N.Hussain	v Lancashire	Ilford	1992
4th	314	Salim Malik & N.Hussain	v Surrey	The Oval	1991
5th	316	N.Hussain & M.A.Garnham	v Leicestershire	Leicester	1991
6th	206	J.W.H.T.Douglas & J.O'Connor	v Gloucestershire	Cheltenham	1923
	206	B.R.Knight & R.A.G.Luckin	v Middlesex	Brentwood	1962
7th	261	J.W.H.T.Douglas & J.R.Freeman	v Lancashire	Leyton	1914
8th	263	D.R.Wilcox & R.M.Taylor	v Warwickshire	Southend	1946
9th	251	J.W.H.T.Douglas & S.N.Hare	v Derbyshire	Leyton	1921
10th	218	F.H.Vigar & T.P.B.Smith	v Derbyshire	Chesterfield	1947

(Essex is the only team in the World, apart from New South Wales, to have double century stands for all ten wickets)

Against Essex

1st	555	P.Holmes & H.Sutcliffe	for Yorkshire	Leyton	1932
2nd	429*	J.G.Dewes & G.H.G.Doggart	for Cambridge Univ	Cambridge	1949
3rd	362	W.Bardsley & C.G.Macartney	for Australians	Leyton	1912
4th	361	A.O.Jones & J.Gunn	for Nottinghamshire	Leyton	1905
5th	347	D.Brookes & D.W.Barrick	for Northamptonshire	Northampton	1952
6th	256*	C.J.Tavare & A.P.E.Knott	for Kent	Chelmsford	1982
7th	344	K.S.Ranjitsinhji & W.Newham	for Sussex	Leyton	1902
8th	191*	W.Rhodes & G.G.Macaulay	for Yorkshire	Harrogate	1922
9th	160*	E.H.Hendren & F.J.Durston	for Middlesex	Leyton	1927
10th	173	A.Ducat & A.Sandham	for Surrey	Leyton	1921

LEADING PARTNERSHIPS FOR EACH WICKET FOR ESSEX

First Wicket
(Qualification 200)

316	G.A.Gooch & P.J.Prichard	v Kent	Chelmsford	1994
270	A.V.Avery & T.C.Dodds	v Surrey	The Oval	1946
263	G.A.Gooch & B.R.Hardie	v Cambridge Univ	Cambridge	1983
254	G.A.Gooch & J.P.Stephenson	v Derbyshire	Chelmsford	1989
238	G.A.Gooch & J.P.Stephenson	v Leicestershire	Chelmsford	1992
233	T.C.Dodds & A.V.Avery	v Somerset	Westcliff	1952
227	G.A.Gooch & J.P.Stephenson	v Northamptonshire	Northampton	1990
220	G.A.Gooch & J.P.Stephenson	v Northamptonshire	Northampton	1990
214	G.A.Gooch & J.P.Stephenson	v Worcestershire	Southend	1986
212	C.D.McIver & C.A.G.Russell	v Leicestershire	Leyton	1914
210	C.D.McIver & C.A.G.Russell	v Hampshire	Leyton	1913
209	F.L.Fane & J.W.H.T.Douglas	v Middlesex	Leyton	1906
208	T.C.Dodds & A.V.Avery	v Derbyshire	Derby	1948
207	F.L.Fane & J.W.H.T.Douglas	v Kent	Leyton	1908
206	A.C.H.Seymour & J.P.Stephenson	v Glamorgan	Cardiff	1991
200	T.C.Dodds & S.J.Cray	v Kent	Maidstone	1947

Second Wicket
(Qualification 200)

403	G.A.Gooch & P.J.Prichard	v Leicestershire	Chelmsford	1990
321	G.A.Gooch & K.S.McEwan	v Northamptonshire	Ilford	1978
294	A.V.Avery & P.A.Gibb	v Northamptonshire	Northampton	1952
288*	G.J.Saville & K.W.R.Fletcher	v Glamorgan	Swansea	1972
246	J.P.Stephenson & P.J.Prichard	v Yorkshire	Colchester	1991
242*	J.P.Stephenson & J.J.B.Lewis	v Nottinghamshire	Nottingham	1993
237*	H.A.Carpenter & C.A.G.Russell	v Worcestershire	Worcester	1914
236	F.L.Fane & P.A.Perrin	v Leicestershire	Leicester	1899
235*	F.L.Fane & P.A.Perrin	v Nottinghamshire	Leyton	1901
232	H.A.Carpenter & P.A.Perrin	v Kent	Leyton	1901
225	J.P.Stephenson & P.J.Prichard	v Somerset	Bath	1990
221	J.W.H.T.Douglas & P.A.Perrin	v Nottinghamshire	Nottingham	1911
221	D.R.Wilcox & M.S.Nichols	v Hampshire	Southend	1936
219	J.A.Cutmore & J.O'Connor	v Derbyshire	Derby	1930
216	J.P.Stephenson & P.J.Prichard	v Kent	Southend	1991
215	F.L.Fane & P.A.Perrin	v Lancashire	Leyton	1911
215	J.P.Stephenson & N.Hussain	v Sussex	Hove	1993
211	D.F.Pope & J.O'Connor	v Warwickshire	Leyton	1930
209	J.W.H.T.Douglas & J.R.Freeman	v Worcestershire	Worcester	1920
208*	H.A.Carpenter & P.A.Perrin	v Sussex	Leyton	1905
207	B.R.Hardie & K.S.McEwan	v Cambridge Univ	Cambridge	1977
206	J.A.Cutmore & J.O'Connor	v Surrey	The Oval	1929
205	C.Bray & J.O'Connor	v Middlesex	Leyton	1928
201	C.A.G.Russell & J.R.Freeman	v Hampshire	Bournemouth	1921

Third Wicket
(Qualification 200)

347*	M.E.Waugh & N.Hussain	v Lancashire	Ilford	1992
343	P.A.Gibb & R.Horsfall	v Kent	Blackheath	1951
333	R.M.Taylor & J.O'Connor	v Northamptonshire	Colchester	1937
328	H.A.Carpenter & C.P.McGahey	v Surrey	The Oval	1904
323	C.P.McGahey & P.A.Perrin	v Kent	Leyton	1900
312	P.A.Perrin & C.P.McGahey	v Derbyshire	Leyton	1912
291	P.A.Perrin & F.H.Gillingham	v Cambridge Univ	Cambridge	1910
272	G.A.Gooch & M.E.Waugh	v Leicestershire	Leicester	1989
263	D.F.Pope & C.A.G.Russell	v Sussex	Hove	1930
252	G.Barker & J.Milner	v Leicestershire	Leicester	1959
250	J.O'Connor & C.A.G.Russell	v Leicestershire	Leyton	1927
242	M.E.Waugh & B.R.Hardie	v Gloucestershire	Ilford	1990
240	F.H.Gillingham & P.A.Perrin	v Surrey	Leyton	1913
239	M.E.Waugh & P.J.Prichard	v Kent	Chelmsford	1990
235	H.A.Carpenter & C.P.McGahey	v Sussex	Leyton	1900
235	C.A.G.Russell & P.A.Perrin	v Kent	Leyton	1919
233	P.A.Perrin & C.P.McGahey	v Middlesex	Lord's	1905
233	J.O'Connor & C.A.G.Russell	v Gloucestershire	Chelmsford	1928
232	J.O'Connor & C.A.G.Russell	v Worcestershire	Worcester	1928
228	L.G.Crawley & C.A.G.Russell	v Glamorgan	Swansea	1928
225	A.V.Avery & J.O'Connor	v Middlesex	Lord's	1939
225	F.H.Vigar & R.Horsfall	v Hampshire	Bournemouth	1947
223	L.C.Eastman & C.A.G.Russell	v Derbyshire	Derby	1929
216	J.O'Connor & J.A.Cutmore	v Surrey	Leyton	1932
209	M.S.Nichols & J.O'Connor	v Kent	Southend	1936
208*	B.Ward & K.W.R.Fletcher	v Nottinghamshire	Nottingham	1970
208	G.A.Gooch & K.S.McEwan	v Surrey	The Oval	1984
207	C.A.G.Russell & P.A.Perrin	v Northamptonshire	Northampton	1922
206	H.A.Carpenter & C.P.McGahey	v Middlesex	Lord's	1906
206	K.S.McEwan & K.W.R.Fletcher	v Yorkshire	Chelmsford	1977

203	J.A.Cutmore & J.O'Connor	v Hampshire	Bournemouth	1933
203	B.R.Hardie & M.E.Waugh	v Hampshire	Ilford	1989
202*	K.S.McEwan & K.W.R.Fletcher	v Northamptonshire	Northampton	1980

Fourth Wicket
(Qualification 200)

314	Salim Malik & N.Hussain	v Surrey	The Oval	1991
298	A.V.Avery & R.Horsfall	v Worcestershire	Clacton	1948
290	Salim Malik & N.Hussain	v Derbyshire	Chelmsford	1993
287	G.A.Gooch & N.Hussain	v Northamptonshire	Colchester	1991
271	J.O'Connor & T.N.Pearce	v Lancashire	Clacton	1931
268	H.Carpenter & T.M.Russell	v Derbyshire	Derby	1900
259	G.A.Gooch & D.R.Pringle	v Kent	Chelmsford	1988
258	K.S.McEwan & K.W.R.Fletcher	v Sussex	Chelmsford	1977
256	C.A.G.Russell & P.A.Perrin	v Worcestershire	Worcester	1923
245	G.A.Gooch & R.C.Irani	v Worcestershire	Worcester	1994
239*	D.J.Insole & T.E.Bailey	v Nottinghamshire	Southend	1955
236	C.P.McGahey & A.J.Turner	v Northamptonshire	Northampton	1908
236	L.A.Savill & T.E.Bailey	v Cambridge Univ	Cambridge	1959
233	C.A.C.Russell & H.M.Morris	v Hampshire	Southampton	1927
229	C.A.G.Russell & P.A.Perrin	v Somerset	Leyton	1925
227	P.A.Perrin & F.H.Gillingham	v Middlesex	Lord's	1904
227	R.Horsfall & D.J.Insole	v Worcestershire	Worcester	1953
219	K.S.McEwan & K.W.R.Fletcher	v Warwickshire	Birmingham	1979
216*	B.R.Hardie & K.W.R.Fletcher	v Surrey	The Oval	1981
215	A.V.Avery & D.J.Insole	v Sussex	Hove	1951
214	B.R.Hardie & K.W.R.Fletcher	v Sussex	Eastbourne	1987
210	J.O'Connor & M.S.Nichols	v Hampshire	Leyton	1929
210	T.N.Pearce & M.S.Nichols	v Worcestershire	Chelmsford	1934
208	G.J.Saville & B.Taylor	v Cambridge Univ	Harlow	1970
206	G.F.Higgins & J.Burns	v Warwickshire	Birmingham	1895
205	G.Barker & B.Taylor	v Northamptonshire	Northampton	1970
203	J.A.Cutmore & M.S.Nichols	v Worcestershire	Leyton	1930
202	C.A.G.Russell & J.W.H.T.Douglas	v Northamptonshire	Leyton	1921
200	C.C.P.Williams & D.J.Insole	v Leicestershire	Leicester	1955
200	K.S.McEwan & K.R.Pont	v Glamorgan	Leyton	1975

In addition to the above there was a partnership of 207 for the fourth wicket against Nottinghamshire at Nottingham in 1939. This consisted of two stands, 41 between J.O'Connor and M.S.Nichols and 166 between O'Connor and R.M.Taylor after Nichols had retired hurt.

Fifth Wicket
(Qualification 175)

316	N.Hussain & M.A.Garnham	v Leicestershire	Leicester	1991
287	J.O'Connor & C.T.Ashton	v Surrey	Brentwood	1934
216	D.J.Insole & T.E.Bailey	v Hampshire	Bournemouth	1959
202	D.J.Insole & T.E.Bailey	v Somerset	Chelmsford	1953
200	J.R.Freeman & P.A.Perrin	v Oxford University	Chelmsford	1925
190*	K.W.R.Fletcher & B.R.Hardie	v Derbyshire	Colchester	1980
187	T.C.Dodds & T.N.Pearce	v Leicestershire	Leicester	1947
185	F.H.Gillingham & C.P.McGahey	v Derbyshire	Leyton	1911
184	D.J.Insole & T.E.Bailey	v South Africans	Colchester	1955
183	K.W.R.Fletcher & K.R.Pont	v Surrey	Chelmsford	1977
179	B.R.Knight & B.Taylor	v Kent	Ilford	1964
178	K.S.McEwan & K.R.Pont	v Gloucestershire	Colchester	1983
178	A.R.Border & J.P.Stephenson	v Derbyshire	Derby	1988
177	M.S.Nichols & T.N.Pearce	v Gloucestershire	Gloucester	1938
176	C.A.G.Russell & J.W.H.T.Douglas	v West Indians	Leyton	1928

Sixth Wicket
(Qualification 175)

206	J.W.H.T.Douglas & J.O'Connor	v Gloucestershire	Cheltenham	1923
206	B.R.Knight & R.A.G.Luckin	v Middlesex	Brentwood	1962
205	P.A.Perrin & C.P.McGahey	v Kent	Tunbridge Wells	1906
194	N.Hussain & J.J.B.Lewis	v Surrey	The Oval	1990
186	C.P.Buckenham & S.P.Meston	v Lancashire	Leyton	1907
178	T.E.Bailey & R.Smith	v Lancashire	Colchester	1951

Seventh Wicket
(Qualification 150)

261	J.W.H.T.Douglas & J.R.Freeman	v Lancashire	Leyton	1914
174*	M.A.Garnham & D.R.Pringle	v Sussex	Horsham	1989
171	T.E.Bailey & B.R.Knight	v Worcestershire	Leyton	1959
169	J.W.H.T.Douglas & A.E.Russell	v Derbyshire	Chesterfield	1901
169	M.A.Garnham & D.R.Pringle	v Derbyshire	Chelmsford	1991
163	J.O'Connor & D.F.Pope	v Somerset	Leyton	1933
152	N.Shahid & D.R.Pringle	v Kent	Chelmsford	1992
151	A.J.Turner & R.P.Keigwin	v Lancashire	Leyton	1904
150	M.S.Nichols & L.C.Eastman	v Worcestershire	Leyton	1933

Eighth Wicket
(Qualification 150)

263	D.R.Wilcox & R.M.Taylor	v Warwickshire	Southend	1946
214	J.A.Cutmore & T.P.B.Smith	v Indians	Brentwood	1936
206	K.R.Pont & N.Smith	v Somerset	Leyton	1976
192	S.Turner & R.N.S.Hobbs	v Glamorgan	Ilford	1968
186	K.W.R.Fletcher & D.E.East	v Gloucestershire	Southend	1985
184	A.P.Lucas & T.M.Russell	v Somerset	Taunton	1895
184	M.S.Nichols & T.P.B.Smith	v Kent	Gravesend	1938
183	D.J.Insole & R.Smith	v Worcestershire	Worcester	1951
183	T.E.Bailey & C.Griffiths	v Kent	Tunbridge Wells	1952
163	W.Reeves & C.P.Buckenham	v Sussex	Leyton	1906
156	W.T.Greensmith & F.H.Rist	v Kent	Blackheath	1953
152	F.H.Vigar & R.Smith	v Derbyshire	Colchester	1948

Ninth Wicket
(Qualification 150)

251	J.W.H.T.Douglas & S.N.Hare	v Derbyshire	Leyton	1921
184	C.A.G.Russell & L.C.Eastman	v Middlesex	Lord's	1920
179	C.P.McGahey & C.P.Buckenham	v Nottinghamshire	Leyton	1904
160	J.W.H.T.Douglas & H.W.F.Franklin	v Middlesex	Leyton	1923
160	D.R.Wilcox & R.Smith	v Yorkshire	Southend	1947

Tenth Wicket
(Qualification 100)

218	F.H.Vigar & T.P.B.Smith	v Derbyshire	Chesterfield	1947
157	C.A.G.Russell & A.B.Hipkin	v Somerset	Taunton	1926
149	K.Farnes & T.H.Wade	v Somerset	Taunton	1936
122	W.Reeves & G.M.Louden	v Surrey	Leyton	1919
122	S.Turner & D.L.Acfield	v Glamorgan	Swansea	1974
110	J.R.Sheffield & T.H.Wade	v Warwickshire	Chelmsford	1929
106	F.W.Gilligan & M.S.Nichols	v Kent	Canterbury	1926
101*	J.W.H.T.Douglas & B.Tremlin	v Derbyshire	Leyton	1914

LEADING PARTNERSHIPS FOR EACH WICKET
AGAINST ESSSEX

First Wicket
(Qualification 200)

555	P.Holmes & H.Sutcliffe	Yorkshire	Leyton	1932
322	H.Storer & J.Bowden	Derbyshire	Derby	1929
306	D.L.Haynes & M.A.Roseberry	Middlesex	Ilford	1990
305	John Langridge & H.W.Grenwood	Sussex	Hove	1935
293	R.M.Prideaux & C.Milburn	Northamptonshire	Clacton	1966
283	A.E.Fagg & P.R.Sunnucks	Kent	Colchester	1938
279	C.F.Walters & H.H.I.H.Gibbons	Worcestershire	Chelmsford	1934
268	P.Holmes & H.Sutcliffe	Yorkshire	Leyton	1928
243	N.F.M.Popplewell & P.M.Roebuck	Somerset	Southend	1985
240	G.Boycott & P.J.Sharpe	Yorkshire	Colchester (Gar)	1971
238*	S.Smith & A.C.Shirreff	Combined Services	Chelmsford	1950
238	A.O.Jones & J.Iremonger	Nottinghamshire	Leyton	1901
237	C.Washbrook & W.Place	Lancashire	Colchester	1946
235	R.Anson & F.A.Tarrant	Middlesex	Leyton	1914
234	J.W.Lee & F.S.Lee	Somerset	Leyton	1932
228	N.J.Lenham & C.W.J.Athey	Sussex	Hove	1993
216	J.B.Hobbs & A.Sandham	Surrey	Leyton	1925
216	G.Cook & W.Larkins	Northamptonshire	Northampton	1980
212	P.E.Richardson & D.Kenyon	Worcestershire	Worcester	1953
208	M.R.Benson & N.R.Taylor	Kent	Chelmsford	1988
207	D.Kenyon & R.G.A.Headley	Worcestershire	Romford	1960
205	D.G.W.Fletcher & E.A.Bedser	Surrey	Ilford	1952
201*	W.W.Keeton & C.B.Harris	Nottinghamshire	Nottingham	1936

Second Wicket
(Qualification 200)

429*	J.G.Dewes & G.H.G.Doggart	Cambridge Univ	Cambridge	1949
352	W.H.Ashdown & F.E.Woolley	Kent	Brentwood	1934
316*	M.J.Stewart & K.F.Barrington	Surrey	The Oval	1962
314	H.Sutcliffe & E.Oldroyd	Yorkshire	Southend	1924
289*	J.C.Balderstone & D.I.Gower	Leicestershire	Leicester	1981
273	L.J.Todd & L.E.G.Ames	Kent	Maidstone	1947
270	W.M.Woodfull & C.G.Macartney	Australians	Leyton	1926
264*	T.S.Curtis & T.M.Moody	Worcestershire	Ilford	1991
250	H.T.W.Hardinge & James Seymour	Kent	Leyton	1923
241	M.R.Barton & P.B.H.May	Surrey	Southend	1951
237	E.H.Bowley & K.S.Duleepsinhji	Sussex	Hove	1931
237	T.C.Middleton & C.L.Smith	Hampshire	Southampton	1990
236	F.A.Lowson & J.V.Wilson	Yorkshire	Sheffield	1950
232*	J.B.Hobbs & R.J.Gregory	Surrey	The Oval	1932
231	F.C.Gardner & A.V.Wolton	Warwickshire	Westcliff	1954
229*	F.A.Tarrant & J.W.Hearne	Middlesex	Leyton	1914
220	G.T.S.Stevens & J.W.Hearne	Middlesex	Leyton	1925
220	G.M.Turner & J.M.Parker	Worcestershire	Leyton	1972
219	W.A.Brown & D.G.Bradman	Australians	Southend	1948
217	R.H.Spooner & J.T.Tyldesley	Lancashire	Leyton	1909
216	J.B.Hobbs & E.G.Hayes	Surrey	Leyton	1905
216	R.T.Robinson & M.Newell	Nottinghamshire	Chelmsford	1987
212	C.N.Woolley & R.Haywood	Northamptonshire	Northampton	1921
210	G.D.Barlow & C.T.Radley	Middlesex	Chelmsford	1983
210	C.L.Smith & M.C.J.Nicholas	Hampshire	Portsmouth	1988

207	S.Coe & H.Whitehead	Leicestershire	Leyton	1914
203	D.R.Turner & R.M.C.Gilliat	Hampshire	Portsmouth	1973

(after C.G.Greenidge retired hurt when the partnership had reached 8)

202	M.J.Stewart & K.F.Barrington	for Surrey	The Oval	1963
201	E.H.Bowley & K.S.Duleepsinhji	for Sussex	Hove	1930

Third Wicket
(Qualification 200)

362	W.Bardsley & C.G.Macartney	Australians	Leyton	1912
355	W.Bardsley & V.S.Ransford	Australians	Leyton	1909
319*	D.L.Haynes & M.W.Gatting	Middlesex	Uxbridge	1989
317	A.Ducat & T.F.Shepherd	Surrey	Leyton	1928
313	D.E.Davies & W.E.Jones	Glamorgan	Brentwood	1948
296	R.H.Spooner & J.Hallows	Lancashire	Leyton	1904
284	E.T.Killick & G.C.Grant	Cambridge Univ	Cambridge	1929
273	W.Place & G.A.Edrich	Lancashire	Clacton	1947
268	M.R.Benson & G.R.Cowdrey	Kent	Maidstone	1990
266	J.D.Inchmore & J.M Parker	Worcestershire	Worcester	1974

(after G.M.Turner retired hurt when the partnership had reached 6)

259	C.L.Townsend & W Troup	Gloucestershire	Clifton	1899
245	W.H.Ashdown & L.E.G.Ames	Kent	Brentwood	1934
245	B.J.Booth & C.C.Inman	Leicestershire	Romford	1967
239	K.S.Duleepsinhji & H.W.Parks	Sussex	Chelmsford	1931
239	R.I.Alikhan & D.M.Ward	Surrey	The Oval	1990
236*	G.D.Barlow & C.T.Radley	Middlesex	Chelmsford	1976
236	W.W.Keeton & J.Hardstaff, jun	Nottinghamshire	Nottingham	1947
234	G.Gunn & A.O.Jones	Nottinghamshire	Leyton	1904
230	D.Brookes & F.Jakeman	Northamptonshire	Chelmsford	1951
223	J.Iddon & N.Oldfield	Lancashire	Ilford	1938
220*	A.E.Dipper & W.R.Hammond	Gloucestershire	Bristol	1927
220*	M.A.Atherton & N.H.Fairbrother	Lancashire	Colchester	1990
215	D.Smith & G.M.Lee	Derbyshire	Leyton	1931
210*	E.Tyldesley & J.Sharp	Lancashire	Leyton	1921
210*	F.T.Prentice & M.Tompkin	Leicestershire	Leicester	1947
210	G.P.Howarth & M.D.Crowe	New Zealanders	Chelmsford	1983
208	B.O.Allen & W.R.Hammond	Gloucestershire	Brentwood	1937
204	H.S.Squires & B.Constable	Surrey	Southend	1949
203	D.M.Green & Javed Burki	Oxford University	Brentwood	1960

Fourth Wicket
(Qualification 200)

361	A.O.Jones & J.Gunn	Nottinghamshire	Leyton	1905
275	R.D.K.Winlaw & J.H.Human	Cambridge Univ	Cambridge	1934
273	Mushtaq Mohammad & W.Larkins	Northamptonshire	Chelmsford	1975
271	T.W.Graveney & B.L.D'Oliveira	Worcestershire	Worcester	1966
256	R.Abel & F.C.Holland	Surrey	The Oval	1895
256	E.H.Hendren & F.T.Mann	Middlesex	Leyton	1923
247	M.Leyland & L.Hutton	Yorkshire	Hull	1936
242	M.C.Cowdrey & J.F.Pretlove	Kent	Blackheath	1959
229*	S.J.Cook & R.J.Harden	Somerset	Chelmsford	1989
228	K.Ibadulla & J.A.Jameson	Warwickshire	Ilford	1964
220	James Seymour & D.W.Jennings	Kent	Tunbridge Wells	1914
212	G.Boycott & J.H.Hampshire	Yorkshire	Colchester (Gar)	1970
209	A.W.Carr & W.R.D.Payton	Nottinghamshire	Worksop	1924
209	C.E.B.Rice & J.D.Birch	Nottinghamshire	Chelmsford	1981
209	W.Larkins & R.J.Bailey	Northamptonshire	Northampton	1990
206*	P.A.Cottey & I.V.A.Richards	Glamorgan	Southend	1990

63

Fifth Wicket
(Qualification 175)

347	D.Brookes & D.W.Barrick	Northamptonshire	Northampton	1952
268	W.G.Quaife & W.Quaife	Warwickshire	Leyton	1900
268	M.W.Gatting & J.E.Emburey	Middlesex	Chelmsford	1983
251	D.M.Smith & P.Moores	Sussex	Southend	1992
236	W.W.Keeton & A.W.Carr	Nottinghamshire	Nottingham	1932
219	M.J.Procter & J.C.Foat	Gloucestershire	Gloucester	1978
211	S.E.Leary & P.H.Jones	Kent	Gravesend	1960
211	W.Larkins & A.J.Lamb	Northamptonshire	Northampton	1990
208	J.Douglas & C.M.Wells	Middlesex	Leyton	1902
208	B.L.Reynolds & G.E.Tribe	Northamptonshire	Brentwood	1956
204	J.J.Whitaker & P.N.Hepworth	Leicestershire	Leicester	1991
203	M.J.Horton & G.Dews	Worcestershire	Leyton	1959
202	L.E.G.Ames & B.H.Valentine	Kent	Gravesend	1938
192	T.S.Fishwick & A.F.A.Lilley	Warwickshire	Leyton	1901
190	W.H.Ashdown & C.S.Hurst	Kent	Tonbridge	1922
182*	D.W.Barrick & B.S.Crump	Northamptonshire	Leyton	1960
180	C.J.B.Wood & S.Coe	Leicestershire	Leicester	1914

Sixth Wicket
(Qualification 175)

256*	C.J.Tavare & A.P.E.Knott	Kent	Chelmsford	1982
212	G.M.Lee & T.S.Worthington	Derbyshire	Chesterfield	1932
207	J.Hallows & J.J.Broughton	Lancashire	Leyton	1901
202	J.R.Gray & G.Hill	Hampshire	Southampton	1952
210	J.E.Timms & A.D.G.Matthews	Northamptonshire	Clacton	1934
200	D.Denton & G.H.Hirst	Yorkshire	Bradford	1902
191	R.E.Hitchcock & A.Townsend	Warwickshire	Birmingham	1955
189	A.P.Day & S.H.Day	Kent	Leyton	1909
186*	L.P.Hedges & G.T.S.Stevens	Oxford University	Oxford	1920
179	Javed Miandad & P.W.G.Parker	Sussex	Hove	1976

Seventh Wicket
(Qualification 150)

344	K.S.Ranjitsinhji & W.Newham	Sussex	Leyton	1902
325	G.Brown & C.H.Abercrombie	Hampshire	Leyton	1913
222	G.R.Cowdrey & S.A.Marsh	Kent	Chelmsford	1988
194	H.Whitehead & W.W.Odell	Leicestershire	Leicester	1905
179	M.C.Cowdrey & S.E.Leary	Kent	Romford	1968
177	J.Sharp & A.H.Hornby	Lancashire	Manchester	1904
166	A.Ducat & H.Strudwick	Surrey	Leyton	1921
159	D.C.S.Compton & W.F.F.Price	Middlesex	Lord's	1938
156	D.Brookes & A.W.Childs-Clarke	Northamptonshire	Northampton	1947
152	V.W.C.Jupp & A.H.Bakewell	Northamptonshire	Leyton	1928
152	P.A.Nixon & G.J.Parsons	Leicestershire	Leicester	1994
150	C.Hallows & R.K.Tyldesley	Lancashire	Southend	1923

Eight Wicket
(Qualification 150)

191*	W.Rhodes & G.G.Macaulay	Yorkshire	Harrogate	1922
177	W.G.Quaife & A.E.M.Whittle	Warwickshire	Birmingham	1904
174	W.E.Jones & G.Lavis	Glamorgan	Cardiff	1947
164	M.R.Hallam & C.T.Spencer	Leicestershire	Leicester	1964
157	A.L.Hilder & C.Wright	Kent	Gravesend	1924
155	A.Morton & J.Horsley	Derbyshire	Leyton	1924

Ninth Wicket
(Qualification 150)

160*	E.H.Hendren & F.J.Durston	Middlesex	Leyton	1927
152	E.Martin & H.R.Murrell	Middlesex	Leyton	1919

Tenth Wicket
(Qualification 100)

173	A.Ducat & A.Sandham	Surrey	Leyton	1921
143	A.H.D.Gibbs & J.J.Bridges	Somerset	Weston-s-Mare	1919
130	G.R.Cox & G.Stannard	Sussex	Hove	1919
118	R.J.L.Hammond & J.H.G.Deighton	Combined Services	Chelmsford	1950
103	A.Dolphin & Ernest Smith	Yorkshire	Leyton	1919
102	James Seymour & A.Fielder	Kent	Leyton	1911

CENTURY PARTNERSHIPS FOR FIRST WICKET IN EACH INNINGS

For Essex

191 & 104	C.A.G.Russell & F.A.Loveday	v Lancashire	Leyton	1921
122 & 140	F.H.Gillingham & C.A.G.Russell	v Surrey	The Oval	1922
135 & 100*	G.A.Gooch & J.P.Stephenson	v Nottinghamshire	Southend	1990
227 & 220	G.A.Gooch & J.P.Stephenson	v Northamptonshire	Northampton	1990

Against Essex

121 & 176	J.D.B.Robertson & S.M.Brown	Middlesex	Colchester	1947
103 & 185	A.Turner & B.M.Laird	Australians	Chelmsford	1975
145 & 170	T.J.Boon & N.E.Briers	Leicestershire	Chelmsford	1990

SECTION 4 - INDIVIDUAL RECORDS - BOWLING

BEST BOWLING PERFORMANCES IN AN INNINGS

For Essex

10-32	H.Pickett	v Leicestershire	Leyton	1895
10-90	T.E.Bailey	v Lancashire	Clacton	1949
9-32	M.S.Nichols	v Nottinghamshire	Nottingham	1936
9-37	M.S.Nichols	v Gloucestershire	Gloucester	1938
9-40	W.Mead	v Hampshire	Southampton	1900
9-47	J.W.H.T.Douglas	v Derbyshire	Leyton	1921
9-52	W.Mead	v Hampshire	Southampton	1895
9-59	M.S.Nichols	v Hampshire	Chelmsford	1927
9-61	K.D.Boyce	v Cambridge Univ	Brentwood	1966
9-75	W.Mead	v Leicestershire	Leyton	1896
9-77	T.P.B.Smith	v Middlesex	Colchester	1947
9-93	F.G.Bull	v Surrey	The Oval	1897
9-108	T.P.B.Smith	v Kent	Maidstone	1948
9-116	M.S.Nichols	v Middlesex	Leyton	1930
9-117	T.P.B.Smith	v Nottinghamshire	Southend	1948
9-126	B.Tremlin	v Derbyshire	Leyton	1905

Against Essex

10-40	E.G.Dennett	for Gloucestershire	Bristol	1906
10-45	T.Richardson	for Surrey	The Oval	1894
10-53	A.P.Freeman	for Kent	Southend	1930
9-26	A.E.G.Baring	for Hampshire	Colchester (Garrison)	1931
9-28	W.Rhodes	for Yorkshire	Leyton	1899
9-37	D.L.Underwood	for Kent	Westcliff	1966
9-39	W.Rhodes	for Yorkshire	Leyton	1929
9-40	C.F.Root	for Worcestershire	Worcester	1924
9-44	C.W.L.Parker	for Gloucestershire	Gloucester	1925
9-44	H.Verity	for Yorkshire	Leyton	1933
9-48	H.Verity	for Yorkshire	Westcliff	1936
9-55	H.J.Pallett	for Warwickshire	Leyton	1894
9-59	W.H.Lockwood	for Surrey	Leyton	1902
9-59	J.C.Clay	for Glamorgan	Westcliff	1937
9-62	B.L.Muncer	for Glamorgan	Brentwood	1948
9-67	C.Blythe	for Kent	Canterbury	1903
9-94	W.H.Lockwood	for Surrey	The Oval	1900
9-121	W.E.Bowes	for Yorkshire	Scarborough	1933
9-131	J.A.Newman	for Hampshire	Chelmsford	1927

SEVEN OR MORE WICKETS IN AN INNINGS FOR ESSEX

Acfield, D.L.	(4)	7-36	v Sussex	Ilford	1973
		7-57	v Surrey	The Oval	1976
		8-55	v Kent	Canterbury	1981
		7-100	v Lancashire	Manchester	1983
Andrew, S.J.W.	(2)	7-47	v Lancashire	Manchester	1993
		7-69	v Glamorgan	Cardiff	1993
Ashton, C.T.		7-51	v Gloucestershire	Cheltenham	1923
Bailey, J.A.		7-32	v Nottinghamshire	Southend	1953
Bailey, T.E.	(10)	10-90	v Lancashire	Clacton	1949
		7-45	v Somerset	Brentwood	1951
		7-61	v Derbyshire	Burton-on-Trent	1957

Bailey, T.E. (contd)		8-49	v Hampshire	Romford	1957
		8-29	v Derbyshire	Westcliff	1958
		7-19	v Surrey	Leyton	1958
		7-81	v South Africans	Ilford	1960
		7-40	v Yorkshire	Leeds	1960
		7-40	v Hampshire	Leyton	1961
		7-55	v Yorkshire	Southend	1961
Benham, C.E.		7-60	v Sussex	Horsham	1908
Boyce, K.D.	(3)	9-61	v Cambridge University	Brentwood	1966
		7-80	v Northamptonshire	Northampton	1969
		7-36	v Northamptonshire	Northampton	1972
Buckenham, C.P.	(10)	8-53	v Surrey	Leyton	1903
		8-33	v Sussex	Leyton	1904
		7-153	v Surrey	Leyton	1906
		7-99	v Sussex	Leyton	1907
		8-64	v Lancashire	Liverpool	1909
		7-39	v Surrey	Leyton	1909
		8-59	v Gloucestershire	Leyton	1909
		8-40	v Worcestershire	Leyton	1910
		7-115	v Surrey	Leyton	1911
		7-37	v Somerset	Weston-s-Mare	1914
Bull, F.G.	(6)	8-44	v Yorkshire	Bradford	1896
		7-73	v Yorkshire	Leyton	1896
		9-93	v Surrey	The Oval	1897
		7-93	v Derbyshire	Leyton	1897
		7-63	v Lancashire	Leyton	1897
		7-113	v Lancashire	Leyton	1897
Childs, J.H.	(6)	7-51	v Glamorgan	Swansea	1986
		8-61	v Northamptonshire	Colchester	1986
		8-58	v Gloucestershire	Colchester	1986
		7-58	v Kent	Folkestone	1986
		7-35	v Cambridge University	Cambridge	1989
		7-38	v Hampshire	Ilford	1989
Clarke, C.B.		7-130	v Northamptonshire	Northampton	1959
Dixon, J.G.		7-61	v Dublin University	Brentwood	1922
Douglas, J.W.H.T.	(25)	7-73	v Lancashire	Leyton	1906
		8-33	v Leicestershire	Southend	1906
		7-86	v Kent	Leyton	1907
		7-100	v Surrey	The Oval	1909
		7-103	v Northamptonshire	Leyton	1912
		7-106	v Sussex	Hove	1919
		7-50	v Aust Imperial Forces	Southend	1919
		7-87	v Gloucestershire	Clifton	1919
		7-69	v Northamptonshire	Leyton	1920
		8-39	v Derbyshire	Derby	1920
		7-47	v Middlesex	Leyton	1920
		7-61	v Lancashire	Leyton	1920
		7-91	v Worcestershire	Leyton	1921
		7-65	v Worcestershire	Leyton	1921
		9-47	v Derbyshire	Leyton	1921
		7-17	v Hampshire	Bournemouth	1921
		7-74	v Hampshire	Bournemouth	1921
		7-62	v Northamptonshire	Southend	1922
		8-45	v Gloucestershire	Cheltenham	1922
		7-110	v Sussex	Leyton	1923
		7-119	v Surrey	Leyton	1923
		8-90	v Somerset	Colchester	1923
		7-89	v Worcestershire	Worcester	1923
		7-72	v Hampshire	Leyton	1923
		7-66	v Nottinghamshire	Worksop	1924

East, R.E.	(12)	8-70	v Warwickshire	Westcliff	1967
		7-52	v Warwickshire	Leyton	1968
		8-63	v Warwickshire	Leyton	1968
		7-37	v Leicestershire	Leyton	1968
		7-48	v Northamptonshire	Leyton	1969
		7-40	v Somerset	Leyton	1971
		8-30	v Nottinghamshire	Ilford	1977
		8-57	v Derbyshire	Leyton	1977
		8-90	v Glamorgan	Leyton	1977
		8-41	v Northamptonshire	Northampton	1978
		7-49	v Kent	Canterbury	1981
		7-55	v Kent	Chelmsford	1981
Eastman, L.C.	(2)	7-28	v Somerset	Taunton	1922
		7-51	v Lancashire	Manchester	1934
Edmeades, B.E.A.	(2)	7-43	v Derbyshire	Derby	1965
		7-37	v Glamorgan	Leyton	1966
Farnes, K.	(6)	7-72	v Somerset	Taunton	1933
		7-21	v Surrey	Southend	1933
		7-59	v Yorkshire	Southend	1934
		7-84	v Middlesex	Colchester	1936
		7-41	v Derbyshire	Ilkeston	1937
		8-38	v Glamorgan	Clacton	1938
Foster, N.A.	(3)	7-33	v Warwickshire	Chelmsford	1987
		7-105	v Northamptonshire	Northampton	1989
		8-99	v Lancashire	Manchester	1991
Gooch, G.A.		7-14	v Worcestershire	Ilford	1982
Greensmith, W.T.	(4)	8-59	v Gloucestershire	Bristol	1956
		7-69	v Cambridge University	Cambridge	1959
		7-46	v Lancashire	Blackpool	1961
		8-116	v Middlesex	Brentwood	1962
Hipkin, A.B.	(2)	8-71	v Gloucestershire	Bristol	1924
		7-34	v Glamorgan	Swansea	1927
Hobbs, R.N.S.	(4)	8-63	v Glamorgan	Swansea	1966
		7-73	v Worcestershire	Chelmsford	1968
		7-59	v Derbyshire	Leyton	1970
		7-118	v Glamorgan	Swansea	1972
Ilott, M.C.		7-85	v Surrey	The Oval	1993
Kasprowicz, M.S.		7-87	v Somerset	Weston-s-Mare	1994
Knight, B.R.	(6)	7-68	v Glamorgan	Westcliff	1959
		7-55	v Glamorgan	Westcliff	1960
		7-42	v Glamorgan	Clacton	1962
		8-70	v Gloucestershire	Bristol	1963
		7-68	v Middlesex	Southend	1963
		8-69	v Nottinghamshire	Nottingham	1963
Kortright, C.J.	(8)	8-94	v Warwickshire	Birmingham	1895
		8-63	v Leicestershire	Leyton	1895
		7-57	v Somerset	Taunton	1895
		7-50	v Derbyshire	Leyton	1895
		7-72	v Surrey	Leyton	1895
		7-60	v Warwickshire	Leyton	1898
		7-57	v Gloucestershire	Leyton	1898
		8-57	v Yorkshire	Leyton	1900
Laker, J.C.	(2)	7-73	v Kent	Dover	1962
		7-89	v Leicestershire	Leicester	1963
Lever, J.K.	(13)	7-90	v Somerset	Leyton	1971
		8-128	v Gloucestershire	Cheltenham	1976
		7-32	v Sussex	Hove	1978
		7-27	v Lancashire	Ilford	1979
		7-41	v Leicestershire	Chelmsford	1979
		8-49	v Warwickshire	Birmingham	1979

Lever, J.K. (contd)		7-40	v Hampshire	Bournemouth	1979
		8-49	v Yorkshire	Leeds	1981
		7-63	v Cambridge University	Cambridge	1983
		7-55	v Sussex	Hove	1983
		7-78	v Yorkshire	Chelmsford	1983
		8-37	v Gloucestershire	Bristol	1984
		7-48	v Surrey	Chelmsford	1989
Louden, G.M.	(8)	7-42	v Lancashire	Leyton	1919
		8-122	v Sussex	Leyton	1919
		8-36	v Derbyshire	Southend	1920
		7-144	v Australians	Southend	1921
		7-84	v Surrey	The Oval	1922
		7-22	v Worcestershire	Leyton	1922
		7-105	v Surrey	Leyton	1922
		8-48	v Sussex	Hove	1922
McGahey, C.P.		7-27	v Nottinghamshire	Leyton	1906
Mead, W.	(27)	7-87	v Yorkshire	Leyton	1894
		7-66	v Oxford University	Leyton	1894
		7-88	v Middlesex	Leyton	1895
		8-67	v Hampshire	Southampton	1895
		9-52	v Hampshire	Southampton	1895
		7-73	v Leicestershire	Leicester	1895
		7-56	v Yorkshire	Harrogate	1895
		9-75	v Leicestershire	Leyton	1896
		7-60	v Oxford University	Oxford	1898
		7-100	v Hampshire	Leyton	1898
		7-34	v Sussex	Leyton	1899
		7-37	v Yorkshire	Leyton	1899
		7-90	v Yorkshire	Leyton	1899
		7-53	v Hampshire	Leyton	1899
		7-62	v Surrey	The Oval	1900
		7-36	v Sussex	Eastbourne	1900
		9-40	v Hampshire	Southampton	1900
		8-103	v Leicestershire	Leicester	1900
		7-70	v Gloucestershire	Cheltenham	1900
		7-20	v Sussex	Hove	1902
		7-34	v Surrey	The Oval	1903
		7-27	v Sussex	Leyton	1903
		7-50	v Leicestershire	Leyton	1903
		8-65	v Leicestershire	Leyton	1903
		7-13	v Derbyshire	Leyton	1906
		8-39	v Nottinghamshire	Leyton	1907
		8-35	v Worcestershire	Leyton	1911
Miller, G.		7-59	v Lancashire	Manchester	1987
Morris, P.E.	(3)	8-106	v Somerset	Leyton	1922
		7-43	v Worcestershire	Leyton	1922
		7-72	v Gloucestershire	Leyton	1923
Nichols, M.S.	(20)	7-90	v Gloucestershire	Leyton	1926
		7-89	v Derbyshire	Ilkeston	1927
		7-112	v Hampshire	Southampton	1927
		9-59	v Hampshire	Chelmsford	1927
		7-72	v Yorkshire	Leeds	1927
		8-46	v Derbyshire	Southend	1927
		7-77	v Nottinghamshire	Westcliff	1935
		7-37	v Yorkshire	Huddersfield	1935
		8-58	v Derbyshire	Chesterfield	1935
		7-15	v Glamorgan	Neath	1935
		9-32	v Nottinghamshire	Nottingham	1936
		7-50	v Gloucestershire	Clacton	1936
		7-61	v Gloucestershire	Bristol	1937

Name		Figures	Opponent	Venue	Year
Nichols, M.S. (contd)		9-116	v Middlesex	Leyton	1930
		7-55	v Somerset	Taunton	1931
		7-68	v Warwickshire	Chelmsford	1932
		7-52	v Gloucestershire	Cheltenham	1933
		7-52	v Kent	Chelmsford	1933
		7-52	v Gloucestershire	Clacton	1933
		7-84	v Lancashire	Southend	1934
O'Connor, J.	(2)	7-55	v Leicestershire	Leicester	1926
		7-52	v Leicestershire	Leicester	1928
Phelan, P.J.	(3)	7-63	v Oxford University	Oxford	1962
		8-109	v Kent	Blackheath	1964
		7-80	v Worcestershire	Brentwood	1965
Pickett, H.		10-32	v Leicestershire	Leyton	1895
Preston, K.C.		7-55	v Northamptonshire	Peterborough	1956
Price, E.J.		8-125	v Worcestershire	Worcester	1949
Pringle, D.R.	(5)	7-32	v Middlesex	Chelmsford	1983
		7-53	v Kent	Canterbury	1984
		7-46	v Yorkshire	Chelmsford	1986
		7-44	v Warwickshire	Ilford	1989
		7-18	v Glamorgan	Swansea	1989
Ralph, L.H.R.	(2)	7-77	v Worcestershire	Romford	1956
		7-42	v Gloucestershire	Romford	1956
Read, A.H.		7-75	v Northamptonshire	Northampton	1908
Read, H.D.	(2)	7-35	v Surrey	Brentwood	1934
		7-114	v Northamptonshire	Clacton	1934
Reeves, W.	(4)	7-75	v Middlesex	Lord's	1904
		7-88	v Lancashire	Manchester	1907
		7-79	v Yorkshire	Leyton	1909
		7-33	v Northamptonshire	Northampton	1920
Smith, R.	(7)	7-51	v Worcestershire	Chelmsford	1946
		7-56	v Nottinghamshire	Clacton	1946
		7-91	v Warwickshire	Brentwood	1947
		7-97	v Surrey	The Oval	1948
		8-87	v Leicestershire	Leicester	1950
		7-80	v Gloucestershire	Westcliff	1955
		8-65	v Glamorgan	Pontypridd	1955
Smith, T.P.B.	(20)	7-64	v Northamptonshire	Northampton	1931
		8-155	v Worcestershire	Chelmsford	1936
		7-56	v Northamptonshire	Colchester	1937
		7-140	v Glamorgan	Llanelli	1937
		7-47	v Surrey	Colchester	1939
		7-85	v Worcestershire	Worcester	1939
		7-75	v Lancashire	Manchester	1946
		7-92	v Cambridge University	Cambridge	1947
		9-77	v Middlesex	Colchester	1947
		7-138	v Middlesex	Colchester	1947
		7-129	v Hampshire	Colchester	1947
		8-98	v Leicestershire	Clacton	1947
		9-117	v Nottinghamshire	Southend	1948
		9-108	v Kent	Maidstone	1948
		8-123	v Worcestershire	Worcester	1948
		7-54	v Surrey	The Oval	1950
		7-44	v Kent	Clacton	1950
		7-75	v Leicestershire	Leicester	1950
		7-139	v Surrey	Chelmsford	1950
		7-88	v Surrey	The Oval	1951
Stephenson, J.W.A.	(2)	7-66	v South Africans	Southend	1935
		8-46	v Cambridge University	Brentwood	1937
Such, P.M.		7-66	v Hampshire	Southampton	1994
Taylor, R.M.		7-99	v Somerset	Taunton	1946

Topley, T.D.		7-75	v Derbyshire	Chesterfield	1988
Tremlin, B.	(3)	9-126	v Derbyshire	Leyton	1905
		7-72	v Australians	Leyton	1905
		7-171	v Aust Imperial Forces	Leyton	1919
Vigar, F.H.	(3)	8-128	v Leicestershire	Clacton	1946
		8-169	v Leicestershire	Leicester	1946
		7-102	v Somerset	Clacton	1949
Young, H.I.	(5)	7-32	v Australians	Leyton	1899
		7-49	v Kent	Gravesend	1899
		7-100	v Warwickshire	Birmingham	1899
		8-54	v Warwickshire	Birmingham	1899
		7-48	v Derbyshire	Chesterfield	1901

MOST WICKETS IN A MATCH

For Essex

17-119	W.Mead	v Hampshire	Southampton	1895
16-215	T.P.B.Smith	v Middlesex	Colchester	1947
15-113	K.Farnes	v Glamorgan	Clacton	1938
15-115	W.Mead	v Leicestershire	Leyton	1903
15-115	R.E.East	v Warwickshire	Leyton	1968
15-154	H.I.Young	v Warwickshire	Birmingham	1899
15-165	M.S.Nichols	v Gloucestershire	Gloucester	1938
14-81	T.E.Bailey	v Hampshire	Romford	1957
14-91	J.W.H.T.Douglas	v Hampshire	Bournemouth	1921
14-119	K.Farnes	v Worcestershire	Leyton	1938
14-127	W.Mead	v Yorkshire	Leyton	1899
14-132	W.Mead	v Leicestershire	Leyton	1896
14-156	J.W.H.T.Douglas	v Worcestershire	Leyton	1921
14-176	F.G.Bull	v Lancashire	Leyton	1897

(In addition W.Mead took 17 wickets for 205 against the Australians at Leyton in 1893 before Essex became first-class)

Against Essex

17-56	C.W.L.Parker	for Gloucestershire	Gloucester	1925
17-91	H.Verity	for Yorkshire	Leyton	1933
16-83	B.Dooland	for Nottinghamshire	Nottingham	1954
16-94	A.P.Freeman	for Kent	Southend	1930
16-103	T.G.Wass	for Nottinghamshire	Nottingham	1908
15-56	W.Rhodes	for Yorkshire	Leyton	1899
15-88	E.G.Dennett	for Gloucestershire	Bristol	1906
15-95	T.Richardson	for Surrey	The Oval	1894
15-100	H.Verity	for Yorkshire	Westcliff	1936
15-106	R.T.D.Perks	for Worcestershire	Worcester	1937
15-106	F.D.Stephenson	for Nottinghamshire	Nottingham	1989
15-116	G.A.Davidson	for Derbyshire	Leyton	1898
15-141	C.L.Townsend	for Gloucestershire	Clifton	1898
15-142	A.P.Freeman	for Kent	Gravesend	1931
15-161	B.L.Muncer	for Glamorgan	Brentwood	1948
14-68	W.Rhodes	for Yorkshire	Harrogate	1900
14-70	S.F.Barnes	for Lancashire	Leyton	1903
14-77	E.Wainwright	for Yorkshire	Bradford	1896
14-89	A.D.Pougher	for Leicestershire	Leyton	1894
14-94	C.T.Spencer	for Leicestershire	Colchester	1959
14-100	H.J.Pallett	for Warwickshire	Leyton	1894
14-111	W.Brearley	for Lancashire	Manchester	1908
14-115	A.P.Freeman	for Kent	Gravesend	1935
14-127	W.H.Lockwood	for Surrey	The Oval	1900

14-132	A.D.Pougher	for Leicestershire	Leyton	1896
14-146	J.W.Hearne	for Middlesex	Leyton	1914
14-146	J.C.Clay	for Glamorgan	Westcliff	1937
14-160	W.Brearley	for Lancashire	Manchester	1904
14-160	M.W.Booth	for Yorkshire	Leyton	1914
14-165	F.P.Ryan	for Glamorgan	Swansea	1925
14-167	T.W.J.Goddard	for Gloucestershire	Bristol	1946
14-174	J.Gunn	for Nottinghamshire	Leyton	1903
14-181	A.P.Freeman	for Kent	Canterbury	1928
14-185	T.Richardson	for Surrey	Leyton	1900
14-213	T.Forrester	for Derbyshire	Leyton	1914

OUTSTANDING INNINGS ANALYSES

For Essex

O	M	R	W				
7.3	4	4	6	N.Phillip	v Surrey	Chelmsford	1983
7.2	5	3	5	T.E.Bailey	v Cambridge University	Cambridge	1965
4.4	1	4	5	J.W.A.Stephenson	v Somerset	Wells	1939
2.1	2	0	4	L.C.Eastman	v Somerset	Weston-super-Mare	1934

Against Essex

O	M	R	W				
17	10	12	8	C.W.L.Parker	for Gloucestershire	Gloucester	1925
5.1	3	2	5	N.Gifford	for Warwickshire	Nuneaton	1983
3.3	2	1	4	A.G.Slater	for Derbyshire	Leyton	1913

OUTSTANDING MATCH ANALYSES

For Essex

14-81	(6-32 & 8-49)	T.E.Bailey	v Hampshire	Romford	1957
14-91	(7-17 & 7-74)	J.W.H.T.Douglas	v Hampshire	Bournemouth	1921
13-69	(7-36 & 6-33)	W.Mead	v Sussex	Eastbourne	1900
13-70	(7-20 & 6-50)	W.Mead	v Sussex	Hove	1902
12-59	(7-33 & 5-26)	W.Reeves	v Northamptonshire	Northampton	1920

Against Essex

17-56	(9-44 & 8-12)	C.W.L.Parker	for Gloucestershire	Gloucester	1925
17-91	(8-47 & 9-44)	H.Verity	for Yorkshire	Leyton	1933
16-83	(8-39 & 8-44)	B.Dooland	for Nottinghamshire	Nottingham	1954
15-56	(9-28 & 6-28)	W.Rhodes	for Yorkshire	Leyton	1899
12-29	(7-12 & 5-17)	G.H.Hirst	for Yorkshire	Leyton	1901

HAT-TRICKS

For Essex

J.W.H.T.Douglas	v Yorkshire	Leyton	1905
H.I.Young	v Leicestershire	Leyton	1907
B.Tremlin	v Derbyshire	Derby	1914
P.C.E.Toone	v Kent	Leyton	1920

G.M.Louden	v Somerset	Southend	1921
J.W.H.T.Douglas	v Sussex	Leyton	1923
A.B.Hipkin	v Lancashire	Blackpool	1924
J.O'Connor	v Worcestershire	Worcester	1925
M.S.Nichols	v Yorkshire	Leeds	1931
H.D.Read	v Gloucestershire	Bristol	1935
K.Farnes	v Nottinghamshire	Clacton	1939
P.Cousens	v Combined Services	Chelmsford	1950
T.E.Bailey	v Glamorgan	Newport	1950
S.Turner	v Surrey	The Oval	1971
K.D.Boyce	v Warwickshire	Chelmsford	1974
N.Phillip	v Northamptonshire	Wellingborough	1983

Against Essex

W.M.Bradley	for Kent	Leyton	1899
J.T.Hearne *(4 in 5)*	for Middlesex	Lord's	1902
W.E.Benskin	for Leicestershire	Southend	1906
T.G.Wass	for Nottinghamshire	Nottingham	1908
J.W.Hearne	for Middlesex	Lord's	1911
A.Drake	for Yorkshire	Huddersfield	1912
M.W.Booth	for Yorkshire	Leyton	1912
V.W.C.Jupp	for Sussex	Leyton	1919
C.N.Woolley	for Northamptonshire	Northampton	1920
R.H.B.Bettington	for Oxford University	Oxford	1920
V.W.C.Jupp	for Sussex	Colchester	1921

(he scored a century in the same match)

J.W.Hearne	for Middlesex	Leyton	1922
C.W.L.Parker	for Gloucestershire	Chelmsford	1930
A.E.G.Rhodes	for Derbyshire	Colchester	1948
R.G.Marlar	for Cambridge Univ	Cambridge	1952
A.V.Bedser	for Surrey	The Oval	1953
F.W.Moore	for Lancashire	Chelmsford	1956
K.Higgs	for Lancashire	Blackpool	1960
L.J.Coldwell	for Worcestershire	Brentwood	1965
A.C.Smith	for Warwickshire	Clacton	1965

(he started the match as the wicket-keeper, then took off his pads and bowled)

G.A.Cope	for Yorkshire	Colchester	1970
M.J.Procter	for Gloucestershire	Westcliff	1972

(all lbw, he also scored a century in the same match)

M.J.Procter	for Gloucestershire	Southend	1977
G.R.Dilley	for Kent	Chelmsford	1986
S.T.Clarke *(4 in 5)*	for Surrey	Colchester	1987

FOUR WICKETS WITH FIVE CONSECUTIVE BALLS

For Essex

The feat has not been performed for Essex

Against Essex

J.T.Hearne	for Middlesex	Lord's	1902
S.T.Clarke	for Surrey	Colchester	1987

OUTSTANDING SPELLS OF WICKET-TAKING

For Essex

Wkts	Balls				
7	29	T.E.Bailey	v Glamorgan	Brentwood	1950
5	8	J.W.H.T.Douglas	v Yorkshire	Leyton	1905

Against Essex

Wkts	Balls				
7	25	J.W.Hearne	for Middlesex	Lord's	1910
7	28	W.Rhodes	for Yorkshire	Leyton	1929
5	8	G.A.Cope	for Yorkshire	Colchester	1970

BOWLERS UNCHANGED IN BOTH INNINGS

For Essex

W.Mead (12-73) & W.Reeves (8-98)	v Nottinghamshire	Leyton	1907
J.W.H.T.Douglas (11-98) & B.Tremlin (9-115)	v Surrey	The Oval	1914
J.W.H.T.Douglas (9-62) & B.Tremlin (10-52)	v Derbyshire	Derby	1914

Against Essex

G.H.Hirst (12-29) & W.Rhodes (6-37)	for Yorkshire	Leyton	1901
E.G.Dennett (15-88) & F.G.Roberts (5-111)	for Gloucestershire	Bristol	1906
T.G.Wass (16-103) & A.W.Hallam (4-44)	for Nottinghamshire	Nottingham	1908
W.Huddleston (8-101) & H.Dean (11-102)	for Lancashire	Liverpool	1909
G.J.Thompson (9-55) & S.G.Smith (10-72)	for Northants	Northampton	1912

WICKET WITH FIRST BALL IN FIRST-CLASS CRICKET

For Essex

M.Berkley	v Yorkshire	Halifax	1894
R.H.Sharp	v Gloucestershire	Leyton	1925

Against Essex

H.G.Curgenven	for Derbyshire	Leyton	1896
L.W.Cook	for Lancashire	Manchester	1907
G.D.Hough	for Kent	Leyton	1919

NO-BALLED FOR THROWING

For Essex

D.J.Insole	v Northamptonshire	Northampton	1952

(As a protest against the opposing captain's refusal to declare)

Against Essex

D.B.Pearson	for Worcestershire	Worcester	1959

MOST WICKETS IN A SEASON

T.P.B.Smith	172 in 1947	W.Mead	128 in 1907
M.S.Nichols	160 in 1938	B.R.Knight	125 in 1963
T.P.B.Smith	152 in 1937	J.W.H.T.Douglas	124 in 1920
K.C.Preston	140 in 1957	T.P.B.Smith	124 in 1950
J.W.H.T.Douglas	139 in 1923	W.Mead	122 in 1900
M.S.Nichols	138 in 1935	C.P.Buckenham	122 in 1906
M.S.Nichols	136 in 1937	B.R.Knight	121 in 1965
R.Smith	133 in 1952	M.S.Nichols	120 in 1927
T.P.B.Smith	132 in 1938	M.S.Nichols	120 in 1933
W.Mead	128 in 1895	T.E.Bailey	120 in 1961

100 WICKETS IN A SEASON

Bailey, T.E.	(4)	1958	106
		1960	113
		1961	120
		1962	111
Buckenham, C.P.		1906	122
Bull, F.G.	(2)	1897	109
		1898	101
Douglas, J.W.H.T.	(5)	1914	118
		1920	124
		1921	110
		1922	102
		1923	139
Edmeades, B.E.A.		1966	106
Foster, N.A.	(2)	1986	100
		1991	102
Hipkin, A.B.		1924	112
Knight, B.R.	(3)	1959	101
		1963	125
		1965	121
Lever, J.K	(4)	1978	102
		1979	104
		1983	116
		1984	116
Mead, W.	(5)	1895	128
		1899	118
		1900	122
		1903	114
		1907	128
Nichols, M.S.	(11)	1926	114
		1927	120
		1929	100
		1930	111
		1932	106
		1933	120
		1935	138
		1936	108
		1937	136
		1938	160
		1939	119
Preston, K.C.		1957	140
Ralph, L.H.R.		1957	102
Reeves, W.		1904	106

Smith, R.	(7)	1946	116
		1947	118
		1948	101
		1949	104
		1950	101
		1952	133
		1953	119
Smith, T.P.B.	(6)	1933	116
		1937	152
		1938	132
		1946	113
		1947	172
		1950	124
Tremlin, B.		1914	101
Young, H.I.		1899	100

500 WICKETS FOR ESSEX

	Career	Runs	Wkts	Avge	BB	5wi	10wm
T.P.B.Smith	1929-1951	42314	1610	26.28	9-77	117	27
M.S.Nichols	1924-1939	34201	1608	21.26	9-32	108	22
T.E.Bailey	1946-1967	35042	1593	21.99	10-90	91	10
J.K.Lever	1967-1989	34669	1473	23.54	8-37	77	11
W.Mead	1894-1913	28423	1472	19.30	9-40	117	30
J.W.H.T.Douglas	1901-1928	33653	1443	23.32	9-47	93	21
R.Smith	1934-1956	39817	1317	30.23	8-63	73	10
K.C.Preston	1948-1964	30288	1155	26.22	7-55	37	2
R.E.East	1965-1984	25804	1010	25.54	8-30	49	10
L.C.Eastman	1920-1939	26102	975	26.77	7-28	29	3
C.P.Buckenham	1899-1914	24629	934	26.36	8-33	72	16
D.L.Acfield	1966-1986	23509	855	27.49	8-55	30	4
S.Turner	1965-1986	20987	810	25.90	6-26	27	1
R.N.S.Hobbs	1961-1975	19844	763	26.00	8-63	32	5
B.R.Knight	1955-1966	17162	761	22.55	8-69	39	8
N.A.Foster	1980-1993	17626	747	23.60	8-99	42	7
W.T.Greensmith	1947-1963	20711	720	28.76	8-59	21	2
K.D.Boyce	1966-1977	15704	662	23.72	9-61	30	6
W.Reeves	1897-1921	16137	581	27.77	7-33	37	5
D.R.Pringle	1978-1993	14365	566	25.38	7-18	20	2
J.O'Connor	1921-1939	17523	537	32.63	7-52	17	2
A.B.Hipkin	1923-1931	13377	518	25.82	8-71	18	3
J.H.Childs	1985-1994	14427	517	27.90	8-58	29	6

LEADING CAREER AVERAGES

	Career	Runs	Wkts	Avge	BB	5wi	10wm
K.Farnes	1930-1939	7086	367	19.307	8-38	28	5
W.Mead	1894-1913	28423	1472	19.309	9-40	117	30
C.J.Kortright	1894-1897	9036	440	20.53	8-57	35	8
H.D.Read	1933-1935	2765	131	21.10	7-35	7	1
M.S.Nichols	1924-1939	34201	1608	21.26	9-32	108	22
J.C.Laker	1962-1964	2367	111	21.32	7-73	7	2
F.G.Bull	1895-1900	7923	365	21.70	5-93	29	5
G.M.Louden	1912-1927	9066	415	21.84	8-36	33	5
T.E.Bailey	1946-1967	35042	1593	21.99	10-90	91	10

B.R.Knight	1955-1966	17162	761	22.55	8-69	39	8
J.A.Bailey	1953-1958	4553	198	22.99	7-32	11	-
J.W.H.T.Douglas	1901-1928	33653	1443	23.32	9-47	93	21
J.K.Lever	1967-1989	34669	1473	23.53	8-37	77	11
N.A.Foster	1980-1993	17626	747	23.59	8-99	42	7
K.D.Boyce	1966-1977	15704	662	23.72	9-61	30	6
J.W.A.Stephenson	1934-1939	4156	174	23.88	8-46	10	1
L.H.R.Ralph	1953-1961	11053	460	24.02	7-42	19	3
H.Pickett	1894-1897	2780	114	24.38	10-32	4	1
H.J.Palmer	1924-1932	3477	142	24.48	6-68	6	-
H.I.Young	1898-1912	9092	368	24.70	8-54	18	3
N.Phillip	1978-1985	10638	423	25.14	6-4	18	1
D.R.Pringle	1978-1993	14365	566	25.37	7-18	20	2
R.E.East	1965-1984	25804	1010	25.54	8-30	49	10
A.B.Hipkin	1923-1931	13377	518	25.82	8-71	18	3
B.E.A.Edmeades	1961-1976	9688	374	25.903	7-37	10	1
S.Turner	1965-1986	20987	810	25.909	6-26	27	1
B.Tremlin	1900-1919	11734	452	25.96	9-126	23	4
R.N.S.Hobbs	1961-1975	19844	763	26.00	8-63	32	5
K.C.Preston	1948-1964	30288	1155	26.22	7-55	37	2
T.P.B.Smith	1929-1951	42314	1610	26.28	9-77	117	27
C.P.Buckenham	1899-1914	24629	934	26.36	8-33	72	16
L.C.Eastman	1920-1939	26102	975	26.77	7-28	29	3
C.A.G.Russell	1908-1930	7480	276	27.10	5-25	5	-
D.L.Acfield	1966-1986	23509	855	27.49	8-55	30	4
W.Reeves	1897-1921	16137	581	27.77	7-33	37	5
J.H.Childs	1985-1994	14427	517	27.90	8-58	29	6
P.M.Such	1990-1994	5742	205	28.00	7-66	14	3
T.D.Topley	1985-1994	9431	336	28.06	7-75	12	1
P.J.Phelan	1958-1965	8510	300	28.36	8-109	17	2
W.T.Greensmith	1947-1963	20711	720	28.76	8-59	21	2
V.J.Evans	1932-1937	3843	129	29.79	6-47	5	1
A.M.Jorden	1966-1970	3501	117	29.92	4-29	-	-

SECTION 5 - INDIVIDUAL RECORDS - ALL-ROUND CRICKET

THE MATCH DOUBLE - 100 RUNS and 10 WICKETS

For Essex

C.P.McGahey	66 & 91	6-86 & 6-71	v Gloucestershire	Clifton	1901
C.P.McGahey	89 & 14	7-27 & 3-37	v Nottinghamshire	Leyton	1906
J.W.H.T.Douglas	8 & 123*	7-91 & 7-65	v Worcestershire	Leyton	1921
J.W.H.T.Douglas	210*	9-47 & 2-0	v Derbyshire	Leyton	1921
M.S.Nichols	73 & 33	5-67 & 5-37	v Sussex	Horsham	1933
M.S.Nichols	146	4-17 & 7-37	v Yorkshire	Huddersfield	1935
T.P.B.Smith	1 & 101	2-69 & 8-99	v Middlesex	Chelmsford	1938
M.S.Nichols	159	9-37 & 6-126	v Gloucestershire	Gloucester	1938
T.E.Bailey	59 & 71*	6-32 & 8-49	v Hampshire	Romford	1957
T.E.Bailey	60* & 46	7-40 & 5-61	v Yorkshire	Leeds	1960
K.D.Boyce	113	6-25 & 6-48	v Leicestershire	Chelmsford	1975

Against Essex

A.D.Pougher	5 & 109*	6-29 & 8-60	for Leicestershire	Leyton	1894
A.E.Trott	112	8-54 & 3-84	for Middlesex	Lord's	1901
J.W.Hearne	106*	7-54 & 7-92	for Middlesex	Leyton	1914
J.W.Hearne	88 & 37*	5-78 & 5-91	for Middlesex	Lord's	1914
V.W.C.Jupp	102 & 33*	6-61 & 6-78	for Sussex	Colchester	1921
V.W.C.Jupp	56 & 70	5-34 & 7-71	for Northamptonshire	Colchester	1925
P.G.H.Fender	104	3-48 & 7-76	for Surrey	Leyton	1926
V.W.C.Jupp	113	7-42 & 5-79	for Northamptonshire	Leyton	1928

HUNDRED and A HAT-TRICK AGAINST ESSEX

V.W.C.Jupp	102	for Sussex	Colchester	1921
M.J.Procter	102	for Gloucestershire	Westcliff	1972

(The feat has not been performed for Essex)

THE SEASON DOUBLE - 1000 RUNS and 100 WICKETS

	Season	Runs	Avge	Wkts	Avge
J.W.H.T.Douglas	1914	1151	39.68	118	18.88
J.W.H.T.Douglas	1920	1200	35.29	124	20.98
J.W.H.T.Douglas	1921	1211	46.57	110	18.10
J.W.H.T.Douglas	1923	1043	30.67	139	22.01
M.S.Nichols	1929	1281	29.11	100	25.56
M.S.Nichols	1932	1381	32.11	106	25.52
M.S.Nichols	1933	1311	29.13	120	21.55
M.S.Nichols	1935	1171	24.39	138	15.70
M.S.Nichols	1936	1224	29.85	108	18.47
M.S.Nichols	1937	1159	25.19	136	18.56
M.S.Nichols	1938	1310	35.40	160	18.31
M.S.Nichols	1939	1363	35.86	119	17.84
R.Smith	1947	1201	27.93	118	36.74
T.P.B.Smith	1947	1065	23.66	172	27.13
R.Smith	1950	1109	23.59	101	34.57
T.E.Bailey	1960	1597	40.94	113	20.26
T.E.Bailey	1961	1179	29.47	120	20.25
T.E.Bailey	1962	1420	36.41	111	21.00
B.R.Knight	1963	1412	30.04	125	21.94
B.R.Knight	1965	1001	21.76	121	18.52

THE SEASON DOUBLE - 500 RUNS and 50 WICKETS SINCE THE REDUCTION OF COUNTY CHAMPIONSHIP MATCHES IN 1969

	Season	Runs	Avge	Wkts	Avge
K.D.Boyce	1969	892	27.03	72	23.55
R.N.S.Hobbs	1970	568	20.28	90	21.18
S.Turner	1970	545	16.02	70	23.51
K.D.Boyce	1970	728	16.17	87	26.47
K.D.Boyce	1971	690	18.64	62	28.37
K.D.Boyce	1972	994	31.06	81	19.85
R.E.East	1973	537	16.27	64	23.90
S.Turner	1974	951	33.96	69	18.33
K.D.Boyce	1975	555	27.75	72	18.18
S.Turner	1976	541	20.03	81	23.07
S.Turner	1977	504	21.91	77	23.16
N.Phillip	1978	645	26.87	71	22.40
S.Turner	1979	561	21.57	61	21.06
N.Phillip	1981	720	21.81	51	33.82
N.Phillip	1982	783	27.00	82	22.46
D.R.Pringle	1984	577	25.08	59	25.88
D.R.Pringle	1985	654	24.22	53	29.35
D.R.Pringle	1987	705	29.37	55	21.87
N.A.Foster	1990	530	26.50	94	26.62
N.A.Foster	1991	513	28.50	102	20.96

10,000 RUNS and 1,000 WICKETS / 500 CATCHES OR DISMISSALS

	Career	Runs	Wickets
T.E.Bailey	1946-1967	21460	1593
J.W.H.T.Douglas	1901-1928	17915	1443
M.S.Nichols	1924-1939	15736	1608
R.Smith	1934-1956	11125	1317
B.Taylor	1949-1973	18240	1231 dismissals
K.W.R.Fletcher	1962-1988	29434	519 catches

SECTION 6 - INDIVIDUAL RECORDS - WICKET-KEEPING

MOST DISMISSALS IN AN INNINGS

For Essex

8 (All ct)	D.E.East	v Somerset	Taunton	1985

(The first eight wickets to fall, Somerset declared with nine wickets down)

6 (3c,3s)	T.M.Russell	v Lancashire	Manchester	1898
6 (2c,4s)	T.M.Russell	v Kent	Canterbury	1901
6 (5c,1s)	K.L.Gibson	v Derbyshire	Leyton	1911
6 (2c,4s)	F.W.Gilligan	v Gloucestershire	Cheltenham	1928
6 (4c,2s)	T.H.Wade	v Lancashire	Clacton	1947
6 (All ct)	D.E.East	v Sussex	Hove	1983
6 (All ct)	M.A.Garnham	v Warwickshire	Chelmsford	1991

Against Essex

7 (All ct)	K.J.Piper	for Warwickshire	Birmingham	1994
6 (4c,2s)	L.H.Compton	for Middlesex	Lord's	1953
6 (All ct)	M.G.Griffith	for Sussex	Clacton	1964
6 (All ct)	G.R.Cass	for Worcestershire	Worcester	1973
6 (All ct)	D.J.S.Taylor	for Somerset	Taunton	1981
6 (All ct)	B.N.French	for Nottinghamshire	Nottingham	1982
6 (All ct)	E.W.Jones	for Glamorgan	Cardiff	1982
6 (All ct)	R.J.Parks	for Hampshire	Colchester	1984

MOST DISMISSALS IN A MATCH

For Essex

9 (7c,2s)	K.L.Gibson	v Derbyshire	Leyton	1911
9 (All ct)	D.E.East	v Sussex	Hove	1983
8 (All ct)	T.M.Russell	v Kent	Leyton	1899
8 (7c,1s)	P.A.Gibb	v Kent	Tunbridge Wells	1952
8 (5c,3s)	B.Taylor	v Leicestershire	Leicester	1970
8 (All ct)	D.E.East	v Derbyshire	Southend	1982
8 (All ct)	D.E.East	v Lancashire	Ilford	1985
8 (All ct)	D.E.East	v Somerset	Taunton	1985
8 (3c,5s)	D.E.East	v Kent	Folkestone	1986

Against Essex

9 (All ct)	P.A.Nixon	for Leicestershire	Leicester	1992
9 (8c,1s)	K.J.Piper	for Warwickshire	Birmingham	1994

MOST DISMISSALS IN A SEASON

	Season	Total	Ct	St
B.Taylor	1962	89	79	10
P.A.Gibb	1952	83	66	17
D.E.East	1986	83	64	19
P.A.Gibb	1953	79	64	15
B.Taylor	1961	79	70	9
T.H.Wade	1938	78	62	16
D.E.East	1984	77	76	1
T.H.Wade	1947	76	38	38
B.Taylor	1963	76	71	5
B.Taylor	1964	76	66	10
D.E.East	1985	76	72	4
D.E.East	1982	74	65	9
B.Taylor	1957	73	59	14
B.Taylor	1956	70	58	12
B.Taylor	1959	70	58	12
B.Taylor	1970	70	51	19

(These figures exclude catches made when not keeping wicket)

MOST DISMISSALS IN A CAREER
(These figures include some catches taken in the field)

	Career	Total	Ct	St
B.Taylor	1949-1973	1231	1040	191
T.H.Wade	1929-1950	590	413	177
D.E.East	1981-1989	533	480	53
N.Smith	1973-1981	428	381	47
P.A.Gibb	1951-1956	336	273	63
T.M.Russell	1894-1905	334	246	88
M.A.Garnham	1989-1994	284	266	18
J.R.Freeman	1905-1928	276	230	46
J.R.Sheffield	1929-1936	248	194	54
A.E.Russell	1898-1910	207	163	44

SECTION 7 - INDIVIDUAL RECORDS - FIELDING

MOST CATCHES IN AN INNINGS

For Essex

5	F.H.Gillingham	v Surrey	The Oval	1919
5	M.S.Nichols	v Sussex	Hove	1926
5	F.H.Vigar	v Middlesex	Westcliff	1946
5	F.H.Vigar	v Northamptonshire	Brentwood	1946
5	F.H.Vigar	v Surrey	The Oval	1951
5	D.J.Insole	v Lancashire	Blackpool	1958
5	G.A.Gooch	v Gloucestershire	Cheltenham	1982
5	N.V.Knight	v Warwickshire	Birmingham	1994

Against Essex

6	F.A.Tarrant	for Middlesex	Leyton	1926
5	A.H.Bakewell	for Northamptonshire	Leyton	1928
5	A.B.Sellers	for Yorkshire	Leyton	1933
5	G.Hughes	for Glamorgan	Swansea	1964

MOST CATCHES IN A MATCH

For Essex

6	W.M.F.Turner	v Leicestershire	Leicester	1914
6	M.S.Nichols	v Sussex	Hove	1926
6	F.H.Vigar	v Nottinghamshire	Ilford	1950
6	K.D.Boyce	v Hampshire	Bournemouth	1967
6	K.W.R.Fletcher	v Glamorgan	Brentwood	1967
6	R.E.East	v Northamptonshire	Westcliff	1973
6	K.W.R.Fletcher	v Worcestershire	Worcester	1977
6	K.W.R.Fletcher	v Derbyshire	Southend	1978
6	G.A.Gooch	v Gloucestershire	Cheltenham	1982
6	G.A.Gooch	v Middlesex	Lord's	1985

Against Essex

8	A.H.Bakewell	for Northamptonshire	Leyton	1928
7	A.B.Sellers	for Yorkshire	Leyton	1933
7	T.A.Dean	for Hampshire	Colchester	1947
7	G.Hughes	for Glamorgan	Swansea	1964

MOST CATCHES IN A SEASON

40	K.W.R.Fletcher	1966
39	K.W.R.Fletcher	1965
38	K.C.Preston	1958
37	N.Hussain	1991
36	T.P.B.Smith	1933
35	K.C.Preston	1957
35	G.A.Gooch	1983
34	A.B.Hipkin	1927
34	A.B.Hipkin	1929
34	R.M.Taylor	1938
34	N.Hussain	1994
33	K.D.Boyce	1967
32	L.C.Eastman	1933
32	T.E.Bailey	1959
32	K.C.Preston	1962
31	M.E.Waugh	1989
30	H.A.Carpenter	1906
30	W.M.F.Turner	1906
30	A.B.Hipkin	1926
30	R.N.S.Hobbs	1966
30	K.W.R.Fletcher	1967
30	G.J.Saville	1971
30	B.R.Hardie	1979
30	B.R.Hardie	1983

MOST CATCHES IN A CAREER

	Career	Catches	
K.W.R.Fletcher	1962-1988	519	
K.C.Preston	1948-1964	344	
G.A.Gooch	1973-1994	343	
T.P.B.Smith	1929-1951	330	
T.E.Bailey	1946-1967	320	
B.R.Hardie	1973-1990	289	
P.A.Perrin	1896-1928	284	
C.A.G.Russell	1908-1930	280	
M.S.Nichols	1924-1939	279	
D.J.Insole	1947-1963	279	*(he also took 1 stumping)*
J.W.H.T.Douglas	1901-1928	265	
L.C.Eastman	1920-1939	254	
R.E.East	1965-1984	251	

SECTION 8 - MISCELLANEOUS

BEST PERFORMANCES EACH SEASON

Year	Most runs		Most wickets	
1895	976	H.A.Carpenter	128	W.Mead
1896	719	P.A.Perrin	70	F.G.Bull
1897	964	P.A.Perrin	109	F.G.Bull
1898	1073	P.A.Perrin	101	F.G.Bull
1899	1491	P.A.Perrin	118	W.Mead
1900	1468	H.A.Carpenter	122	W.Mead
1901	1627	C.P.McGahey	79	W.Mead
1902	1062	P.A.Perrin	86	W.Mead
1903	1428	P.A.Perrin	114	W.Mead
1904	1421	P.A.Perrin	106	W.Reeves
1905	1645	C.P.McGahey	99	B.Tremlin
1906	1883	P.A.Perrin	122	C.P.Buckenham
1907	1165	C.P.McGahey	128	W.Mead
1908	1077	P.A.Perrin	68	J.W.H.T.Douglas
1909	728	P.A.Perrin	97	C.P.Buckenham
1910	792	J.W.H.T.Douglas	85	C.P.Buckenham
1911	1281	P.A.Perrin	97	C.P.Buckenham
1912	1049	J.W.H.T.Douglas	63	W.Mead
1913	1072	C.A.G.Russell	57	C.P.Buckenham
1914	1429	C.A.G.Russell	118	J.W.H.T.Douglas
1919	1387	C.A.G.Russell	98	J.W.H.T.Douglas
1920	2042	C.A.G.Russell	124	J.W.H.T.Douglas
1921	1935	C.A.G.Russell	110	J.W.H.T.Douglas
1922	2243	C.A.G.Russell	102	J.W.H.T.Douglas
1923	1249	C.A.G.Russell	139	J.W.H.T.Douglas
1924	1337	J.R.Freeman	112	A.B.Hipkin
1925	1942	C.A.G.Russell	81	A.B.Hipkin
1926	1958	J.R.Freeman	114	M.S.Nichols
1927	1759	C.A.G.Russell	120	M.S.Nichols
1928	2256	J.O'Connor	68	J.O'Connor
1929	2224	J.O'Connor	100	M.S.Nichols
1930	1588	J.A.Cutmore	111	M.S.Nichols
1931	1634	J.O'Connor	97	M.S.Nichols
1932	1485	J.A.Cutmore	106	M.S.Nichols
1933	2100	J.O'Connor	120	M.S.Nichols
1934	2308	J.O'Connor	85	L.C.Eastman
1935	1603	J.O'Connor	138	M.S.Nichols
1936	1343	J.O'Connor	108	M.S.Nichols
1937	1475	J.O'Connor	152	T.P.B.Smith
1938	1839	J.O'Connor	160	M.S.Nichols
1939	1716	J.O'Connor	119	M.S.Nichols
1946	1321	T.N.Pearce	116	R.Smith
1947	1858	T.C.Dodds	172	T.P.B.Smith
1948	1890	A.V.Avery	101	R.Smith
1949	1696	T.C.Dodds	104	R.Smith
1950	1669	D.J.Insole	124	T.P.B.Smith
1951	1668	A.V.Avery	95	R.Smith
1952	1797	T.C.Dodds	133	R.Smith
1953	1731	R.Horsfall	119	R.Smith
1954	1763	D.J.Insole	88	T.E.Bailey
1955	2142	D.J.Insole	94	K.C.Preston
1956	1877	D.J.Insole	96	K.C.Preston
1957	1540	D.J.Insole	140	K.C.Preston
1958	1378	G.Barker	106	T.E.Bailey

BEST PERFORMANCES EACH SEASON (Contd)

Year	Most runs		Most wickets	
1959	1874	D.J.Insole	101	B.R.Knight
1960	1741	G.Barker	113	T.E.Bailey
1961	1754	G.J.Smith	120	T.E.Bailey
1962	1612	M.J.Bear	111	T.E .Bailey
1963	1420	T.E.Bailey	125	B.R.Knight
1964	1707	G.Barker	89	B.R.Knight
1965	1437	K.W.R.Fletcher	121	B.R.Knight
1966	1833	M.J.Bear	106	B.E.A.Edmeades
1967	1754	K.W.R.Fletcher	81	K.D.Boyce
1968	1523	K.W.R.Fletcher	88	K.D.Boyce
1969	1249	B.E.A.Edmeades	73	R.E.East
1970	1620	B.E.A.Edmeades	90	R.N.S.Hobbs
1971	1578	B.C.Francis	67	R.E.East
1972	1755	K.W.R.Fletcher	81	K.D.Boyce
1973	1384	B.C.Francis	64	R.E.East
1974	1168	B.R.Hardie	69	S.Turner
1975	1522	B.R.Hardie	85	J.K.Lever
1976	1821	K.S.McEwan	81	S.Turner
1977	1702	K.S.McEwan	77	S.Turner
1978	1682	K.S.McEwan	102	J.K.Lever
1979	1387	K.S.McEwan	104	J.K.Lever
1980	1349	K.W.R.Fletcher	61	R.E.East
1981	1420	K.S.McEwan	80	J.K.Lever
1982	1632	G.A.Gooch	82	N.Phillip
1983	2176	K.S.McEwan	116	J.K.Lever
1984	2559	G.A.Gooch	116	J.K.Lever
1985	1706	G.A.Gooch	77	J.K.Lever
1986	1385	A.R.Border	100	N.A.Foster
1987	1370	B.R.Hardie	71	N.A.Foster
1988	1754	G.A.Gooch	66	N.A.Foster
1989	1537	M.E.Waugh	89	D.R.Pringle
1990	2072	M.E.Waugh	94	N.A.Foster
1991	1972	Salim Malik	102	N.A.Foster
1992	1485	P.J.Prichard	67	J.H.Childs
1993	1420	N.Hussain	62	J.H.Childs
1994	1385	G.A.Gooch	60	M.S.Kasprowicz

CAPTAINS OF ESSEX

1894	A.P.Lucas
1895-1902	H.G.P.Owen
1903	C.J.Kortright
1904-1906	F.L.Fane
1907-1910	C.P.McGahey
1911-1928	J.W.H.T.Douglas (P.A.Perrin acted as captain in 1926 when Douglas was absent)
1929-1932	H.M.Morris
1933-1938	T.N.Pearce & D.R.Wilcox
1939	D.R.Wilcox, F.St.G.Unwin & J.W.A.Stephenson
1946-1949	T.N.Pearce
1950	T.N.Pearce & D.J.Insole
1951-1960	D.J.Insole
1961-1966	T.E.Bailey
1967-1973	B.Taylor
1974-1985	K.W.R.Fletcher
1986-1987	G.A.Gooch
1988	K.W.R.Fletcher
1989-1994	G.A.Gooch

MOST APPEARANCES FOR ESSEX

	Career	Matches
K.W.R.Fletcher	1962-1988	574
B.Taylor	1949-1973	539
P.A.Perrin	1896-1928	525
J.O'Connor	1921-1939	516
T.E.Bailey	1946-1967	482
J.W.H.T.Douglas	1901-1928	459
G.Barker	1954-1971	444
J.K.Lever	1967-1989	443
L.C.Eastman	1920-1939	442
T.P.B.Smith	1929-1951	434
R.Smith	1934-1956	419
M.S.Nichols	1924-1939	418
R.E.East	1965-1984	405
C.P.McGahey	1894-1921	400

COUNTY CAPS AWARDED SINCE 1946

1946	H.P.Crabtree, T.C.Dodds, R.F.T.Paterson, F.H.Vigar
1947	T.E.Bailey, L.S.Clark, S.J.Cray
1948	R.Horsfall, F.Rist
1949	D.J.Insole, G.R.Pullinger
1951	P.A.Gibb, K.C.Preston
1952	W.T.Greensmith
1954	J.A.Bailey
1955	G.Barker
1956	B.Taylor
1957	L.H.R.Ralph
1958	M.J.Bear
1959	B.R.Knight, L.A.Savill
1960	G.J.Smith
1961	J.Milner
1962	J.C.Laker
1963	K.W.R.Fletcher
1964	R.N.S.Hobbs, P.J.Phelan
1965	B.E.A.Edmeades
1967	K.D.Boyce, R.E.East
1968	B.L.Irvine
1970	D.L.Acfield, J.K.Lever, G.J.Saville, S.Turner, B.Ward
1971	B.C.Francis
1974	B.R.Hardie, K.S.McEwan
1975	G.A.Gooch, N.Smith
1976	K.R.Pont
1977	M.H.Denness
1978	N.Philip
1982	D.E.East, D.R.Pringle
1983	N.A.Foster
1984	C.Gladwin
1986	A.R.Border, J.H.Childs, A.W.Lilley, P.J.Prichard
1988	G.Miller, T.D.Topley
1989	N.Hussain, J.P.Stephenson, M.E.Waugh
1990	M.A.Garnham
1991	Salim Malik, P.M.Such
1993	M.C.Ilott
1994	R.C.Irani, M.S.Kasprowicz, N.V.Knight, J.J.B.Lewis

YOUNGEST PLAYERS ON DEBUT

16y 322d	B.Taylor	v Cambridge University	Cambridge	1949
17y 3d	S.J.Cray	v Worcestershire	Southend	1938
17y 15d	W.T.Greensmith	v Gloucestershire	Bristol	1947
17y 101d	B.R.Knight	v Worcestershire	Worcester	1955
17y 154d	R.D.Clark	v Lancashire	Leyton	1912
17y 216d	K.R.Pont	v Jamaica	Leyton	1970
17y 265d	M.C.Ilott	v Cambridge University	Cambridge	1988
17y 338d	A.L.Gibson	v Surrey	Leyton	1895
17y 338d	L.A.Savill	v Glamorgan	Llanelli	1953
17y 361d	R.E.East	v Oxford University	Romford	1965
18y 1d	N.A.Foster	v Kent	Ilford	1980
18y 1d	B.J.Hyam	v Glamorgan	Cardiff	1983
18y 7d	R.C.Harvey	v T.N.Pearce's XI	Chelmsford	1952
18y 31d	P.Cousens	v Lancashire	Manchester	1950
18y 58d	D.R.Wilcox	v Hampshire	Portsmouth	1928
18y 64d	J.K.Lever	v Cambridge University	Cambridge	1967
18y 66d	K.W.R.Fletcher	v Glamorgan	Ebbw Vale	1962
18y 76d	W.M.F.Turner	v Warwickshire	Birmingham	1899
18y 76d	O.C.Bristowe	v Middlesex	Leyton	1913
18y 124d	K.A.Butler	v Cambridge University	Cambridge	1989
18y 184d	R.J.Rollins	v Pakistanis	Chelmsford	1992
18y 215d	M.K.Fosh	v Cambridge University	Cambridge	1976
18y 235d	G.R.R.Brown	v Lancashire	Leyton	1924
18y 271d	R.Herbert	v Warwickshire	Leyton	1976
18y 295d	G.Tosetti	v Oxford University	Oxford	1898
18y 314d	P.A.Hector	v Cambridge University	Cambridge	1977
18y 325d	L.D.Womersley	v Derbyshire	Derby	1910
18y 345d	J.G.Dixon	v Northamptonshire	Northampton	1914
18y 346d	J.W.H.T.Douglas	v Yorkshire	Leyton	1901
18y 352d	H.R.H.Williams	v Surrey	The Oval	1919
18y 354d	D.L.Acfield	v Kent	Westcliff	1966
18y 355d	K.Farnes	v Gloucestershire	Chelmsford	1930

OLDEST PLAYERS ON DEBUT

46y 136d	E.S.Missen	v Hampshire	Colchester	1921
44y 6d	P.W.Turrell	v Oxford University	Chelmsford	1927
43y 37d	H.Hailey	v Leicestershire	Leyton	1894
42y 210d	B.K.Castor	v Cambridge University	Cambridge	1932
41y 57d	C.B.Clarke	v Oxford University	Oxford	1959
40y 288d	F.Appleyard	v Yorkshire	Harrogate	1946
40y 92d	J.C.Laker	v Derbyshire	Ilford	1962
39y 55d	G.M.Locks	v Lancashire	Liverpool	1928
38y 272d	M.A.Green	v Somerset	Colchester (G)	1930
37y 305d	P.A.Gibb	v Worcestershire	Worcester	1951
37y 83d	A.P.Lucas	v Leicestershire	Leyton	1894
36y 255d	C.E.L.Orman	v M.C.C.	Lord's	1896
36y 184d	L.F.Parslow	v Somerset	Taunton	1946
36y 154d	M.H.Denness	v Derbyshire	Derby	1977
36y 139d	F.C.Hawker	v Lancashire	Manchester	1937
36y 76d	R.J.Richards	v Jamaica	Leyton	1970
36y 52d	M.Mackinnon	v Surrey	Leyton	1927
35y 288d	C.J.Round	v Hampshire	Colchester	1921
35y 193d	O.Martyn	v Northamptonshire	Southend	1922
35y 115d	L.C.S.Jerman	v Combined Services	Chelmsford	1950

*(In addition A.W.Lapham, born in 1879, made his debut in 1921 either aged 41 or 42, but
no date of birth has been traced)*

OLDEST PLAYERS TO APPEAR FOR ESSEX
(age on last day of last match)

52y 287d	F.H.Gillingham	v Surrey	Leyton	1928
52y 127d	P.A.Perrin	v Sussex	Leyton	1928
51y 49d	H.A.Carpenter	v Somerset	Weston-s-Mare	1920
50y 178d	A.P.Lucas	v South Africans	Leyton	1907
47y 71d	F.L.Fane	v Dublin University	Brentwood	1922
46y 267d	P.E.Morris	v Hampshire	Bournemouth	1924
46y 136d	E.S.Missen	v Middlesex	Colchester	1921
45y 360d	W.Reeves	v Middlesex	Leyton	1921
45y 360d	J.W.H.T.Douglas	v Leicestershire	Leyton	1928
45y 123d	W.Mead	v Kent	Leyton	1913
45y 51d	W.M.F.Turner	v Worcestershire	Leyton	1926

LONG CAREERS

The following players careers lasted for 20 years and more from their first season to their last. Some players did not appear in every season, mainly because of the two World Wars.

33 seasons	P.A.Perrin	1896-1928
28 seasons	C.P.McGahey	1894-1921
28 seasons	F.L.Fane	1895-1922
28 seasons	W.M.F.Turner	1899-1926
28 seasons	J.W.H.T.Douglas	1901-1928
26 seasons	F.H.Gillingham	1903-1928
25 seasons	W.Reeves	1897-1921
25 seasons	B.Taylor	1949-1973
25 seasons	K.W.R.Fletcher	1962-1986
24 seasons	J.R.Freeman	1905-1928
23 seasons	C.A.G.Russell	1908-1930
23 seasons	T.P.B.Smith	1929-1951
23 seasons	R.Smith	1934-1956
23 seasons	J.K.Lever	1967-1989
22 seasons	T.N.Pearce	1929-1950
22 seasons	T.H.Wade	1929-1950
22 seasons	T.E.Bailey	1946-1967
22 seasons	S.Turner	1965-1986
22 seasons	G.A.Gooch	1973-1994
21 seasons	C.D.McIver	1902-1922
21 seasons	D.L.Acfield	1966-1986
20 seasons	W.Mead	1894-1913
20 seasons	B.Tremlin	1900-1919
20 seasons	L.C.Eastman	1920-1939
20 seasons	D.R.Wilcox	1928-1947
20 seasons	F.Rist	1934-1953
20 seasons	A.V.Avery	1935-1954

OLDEST LIVED PLAYERS

		Career	Born	Died
95y 310d	P.S.Whitcombe	1922	3 Oct 1893	9 Aug 1989
95y 159d	C.Bray	1927-1937	6 Apr 1898	12 Sep 1993
92y 83d	J.Burns	1894-1896	20 Jun 1865	11 Sep 1957
91y 166d	L.D.Sears	1925	12 Jan 1901	27 Jun 1992
90y 216d	F.C.Hawker	1937	21 Jul 1900	22 Feb 1991
89y 346d	B.K.Castor	1932	21 Oct 1889	2 Oct 1979
89y 232d	R.P.Keigwin	1903-1919	8 Apr 1883	26 Nov 1972
89y 175d	C.V.Jenkinson	1922-1923	15 May 1891	6 Nov 1980
88y 310d	H.I.Young	1898-1912	5 Feb 1876	12 Dec 1964
88y 158d	T.N.Pearce	1929-1950	3 Nov 1905	10 Apr 1994

(Some dates of birth have not been traced so there could be others not listed above)

BENEFITS AND TESTIMONIALS

1897	H.Pickett
1900	W.Mead
1901	H.A.Carpenter
1921	W.Reeves
1925	H.I.Young
1926	J.R.Freeman
1928	C.A.G.Russell
1933	J.O'Connor
1936	M.S.Nichols
1939	L.C.Eastman
1947	T.P.B.Smith
1948	T.H.Wade
1950	A.V.Avery
1951	R.Smith
1953	F.H.Vigar
1954	F.Rist (Testimonial)
1955	R.Smith (Testimonial)
1957	T.C.Dodds
1959	K.C.Preston
1961	L.H.R.Ralph and H.Dalton (Testimonial)
1963	W.T.Greensmith
1965	G.Barker
1966	B.Taylor
1967	T.E.Bailey (Testimonial)
1968	M.J.Bear
1971	G.Barker (Testimonial)
1973	K.W.R.Fletcher
1974	R.N.S.Hobbs
1975	B.E.A.Edmeades
1977	K.D.Boyce
1978	R.E.East
1979	S.Turner
1980	J.K.Lever
1981	D.L.Acfield
1982	K.W.R.Fletcher (Testimonial)
1983	B.R.Hardie
1984	K.S.McEwan

1985	G.A.Gooch
1986	K.R.Pont
1989	J.K.Lever (Testimonial)
1991	D.E.East
1992	D.R.Pringle
1993	N.A.Foster
1994	J.H.Childs

FAMILY LINKS

FATHERS AND SONS
Freeman, E.C. (1894-1896)   E.J. (1904-1912)
Leiper, J.M. (1950)   R.J. (1981-1982)
Mead, W. (1894-1913)   H. (1913-1914)
Read, A.H. (1904-1910)   H.D. (1933-1935)
Russell, A.E. (1898-1910)   C.A.G. (1908-1930)
Wilcox, D.R. (1928-1947)   J.W.T. (1964-1967)

BROTHERS
Ashton, C.T. (1921-1938)   H. (1921-1939)   P. (1924)
Burrell, H.J.E. (1895)   R.J. (1894-1895)
Crawley, C.L. (1929)   L.G. (1926-1936)
Daer, A.G. (1925-1935)   H.B. (1938-1939)
Douglas, C.H. (1912-1919)   J.W.H.T. (1901-1928)
Eastman, G.F. (1926-1929)   L.C. (1920-1939)
Franklin, H.W.F. (1921-1931) R.C. (1924)
Keigwin, H.D. (1906-1907)   R.P. (1903-1919)
Meston, A.H. (1926-1927)   S.P. (1907-1908)
Pont, I.L. (1985-1988)   K.R. (1970-1986)
Russell, A.E. (1898-1910)   T.M. (1894-1905)
Turner, A.J. (1897-1910)   W.M.F. (1899-1926)
Unwin, E.J. (1932-1939)   F.St.G. (1932-1950)

UNCLE AND NEPHEW
Gosling, R.C. (1894-1896)   C.H. (1930)
Carpenter, H.A. (1894-1920)   O'Connor, J. (1921-1939)

COUSINS
Smith, R. (1934-1956)   T.P.B. (1929-1951)

SECOND COUSINS
Saville, G.J. (1963-1974)   Gooch, G.A. (1973-1994)

UNIVERSITY BLUES

CAMBRIDGE

H.W.de Zoete	Eton	1897, 1898
R.P.Keigwin	Clifton	1903, 1904, 1905, 1906
G.B.Davies	Rossall	1913, 1914
H.Ashton	Winchester	1920, 1921, 1922
C.T.Ashton	Winchester	1921, 1922, 1923
N.G.Wykes	Oundle	1928
K.Farnes	Royal Liberty	1931, 1932, 1933
D.R.Wilcox	Dulwich	1931, 1933, 1934
A.G.Powell	Charterhouse	1934
J.H.Pawle	Harrow	1936, 1937
T.E.Bailey	Dulwich	1947, 1948
D.J.Insole	Sir George Monoux, Walthamstow	1947, 1948, 1949
C.J.M.Kenny	Ampleforth	1952
A.Hurd	Chigwell	1958, 1959, 1960
G.C.Pritchard	King's Canterbury	1964
D.L.Acfield	Brentwood	1967, 1968
A.M.Jorden	Monmouth	1968, 1969, 1970
R.K.Baker	Brentwood	1973, 1974
M.K.Fosh	Harrow	1977, 1978
D.R.Pringle	Felsted	1979, 1980, 1981

*(Pringle was appointed captain of Cambridge in 1982 but missed his Blue
as he played for England during the University Match)*

A.K.Golding	Colchester Royal Grammar	1986

The following should also be noted.
A.P.Lucas (Uppingham) played for Cambridge in 1875, 1876, 1877 and 1878 while with Surrey.
R.C.Gosling (Eton) played for Cambridge in 1888, 1889 and 1890 before Essex was first-class.
L.G.Crawley (Harrow) played for Cambridge in 1923, 1924 and 1925 while with Worcestershire.
P.A.Gibb (St Edward's, Oxford) played for Cambridge in 1935, 1936, 1937 and 1938 while with Yorkshire.
R.M.Pearson (Batley GS) played for Cambridge in 1991, 1992 and 1993 while with Northamptonshire.

OXFORD

H.A.Arkwright	Eton	1895
F.L.Fane	Charterhouse	1896, 1898
C.D.McIver	Forest	1903, 1904
O.C.Bristowe	Eton	1914
F.W.Gilligan	Dulwich	1919, 1920
H.W.F.Franklin	Christ's Hospital	1924
J.V.Richardson	Uppingham	1925
B.H.Belle	Forest	1936
C.C.P.Williams	Westminster	1953, 1954, 1955
J.A.Bailey	Christ's Hospital	1956, 1957, 1958

SECTION 9 - RECORDS AGAINST EACH OPPONENT

COUNTIES

ESSEX v DERBYSHIRE

Home		P	W	L	D	A
Leyton	1895-1977	33	15	6	12	-
Southend	1920-1988	10	4	2	4	-
Brentwood	1935	1	-	1	-	-
Chelmsford	1936-1993	9	6	2	1	-
Clacton	1938-1959	2	2	-	-	-
Ilford	1946-1984	5	2	1	2	-
Colchester (Castle Park)	1948-1990	8	4	-	4	-
Westcliff	1949-1974	4	-	3	1	-
Romford	1951-1963	2	1	-	1	-
Chelmsford (Hoffman's)	1961	1	-	-	1	-
Colchester (Garrison)	1966	1	-	-	1	-
HOME TOTAL		76	34	15	27	-
GRAND TOTAL		152	62	28	62	1

Away		P	W	L	D	A
Derby	1895-1994	40	17	3	20	-
Chesterfield	1901-1988	22	4	7	11	-
Glossop	1903-1905	2	2	-	-	-
Ilkeston	1927-1975	5	2	1	2	-
Burton-on-Trent	1949-1972	6	3	2	1	-
Buxton	1958	1	-	-	1	1
AWAY TOTAL		76	28	13	35	1

Highest innings total	609-4d	Leyton	1912
Highest innings total against	552	Chesterfield	1928
Lowest innings total	58	Burton-on-T	1949
Lowest innings total against	31	Derby	1914
Highest match aggregate	1391-31	Chesterfield	1904
Lowest match aggregate	329-30	Southend	1939
Highest individual innings	343* P.A.Perrin	Chesterfield	1904
Highest individual innings against	232 H.Storer	Derby	1933
Best bowling in an innings	9-47 J.W.H.T.Douglas	Leyton	1921
Best bowling in an innings against	8-50 C.Gladwin	Chesterfield	1954
Best bowling in a match	13-103 C.J.Kortright	Leyton	1895
Best bowling in a match against	15-116 G.A.Davidson	Leyton	1898

ESSEX v DURHAM

Home		P	W	L	D
Chelmsford	1993	1	-	1	-
GRAND TOTAL		3	2	1	-

Away		P	W	L	D
Hartlepool	1992	1	1	-	-
Stockton-on-Tees	1994	1	1	-	-
AWAY TOTAL		2	2	-	-

Highest innings total	423	Stockton-on-T	1994
Highest innings total against	483	Chelmsford	1993
Lowest innings total	154	Chelmsford	1993
Lowest innings total against	175	Stockton-on-T	1994
Highest match aggregate	1218-38	Chelmsford	1993
Lowest match aggregate	915-30	Stockton-on-T	1994

Highest individual innings			113	G.A.Gooch	Hartlepool	1992					
Highest individual innings against			150*	P.Bainbridge	Chelmsford	1993					

Best bowling in an innings	6-61	M.S.Kasprowicz	Stockton-on-T	1994
Best bowling in an innings against	6-110	J.Wood	Stockton-on-T	1994

Best bowling in a match	9-154	J.H.Childs	Chelmsford	1993
Best bowling in a match against	8-134	A.C.Cummins	Chelmsford	1993

ESSEX v GLAMORGAN

Home		P	W	L	D	A	Away		P	W	L	D	A
Leyton	1925-1977	8	3	-	5	-	Swansea	1925-1989	17	5	2	10	-
Colchester	1929-1930	2	2	-	-	-	Cardiff	1926-1961	10	3	3	4	-
(Garrison)							(Arms Park)						
Chelmsford	1931-1992	9	3	1	5	-	Cowbridge	1931	1	-	-	1	-
Clacton	1932-1964	7	4	-	3	-	Neath	1934-1935	2	1	-	1	-
Westcliff	1936-1960	8	5	1	2	-	Pontypridd	1936-1955	2	1	-	1	1
Ilford	1939-1979	8	2	2	4	-	Llanelli	1937-1965	4	1	2	1	-
Brentwood	1948-1967	3	1	1	1	-	Newport	1946-1960	4	1	1	2	-
Colchester	1954-1988	5	1	1	3	-	Ebbw Vale	1949-1962	4	-	2	2	-
(Castle Park)							Cardiff	1967-1993	7	1	2	4	-
Southend	1983-1994	4	2	-	2	-	(Sophia Gardens)						
HOME TOTAL		54	23	6	25	-	AWAY TOTAL		51	13	12	26	1
GRAND TOTAL		105	36	18	51	1							

Highest innings total	499-8d	Swansea	1928
Highest innings total against	586-5d	Brentwood	1948

Lowest innings total	74	Leyton	1966
Lowest innings total against	43	Neath	1935

Highest match aggregate	1307-26	Southend	1990
Lowest match aggregate	240-16	Ilford	1939

Highest individual innings	222	L.G.Crawley	Swansea	1928
Highest individual innings against	215	D.E.Davies	Brentwood	1948

Best bowling in an innings	8-38	K.Farnes	Clacton	1938
Best bowling in an innings against	9-59	J.C.Clay	Westcliff	1937

Best bowling in a match	15-113	K.Farnes	Clacton	1938
Best bowling in a match against	15-161	B.L.Muncer	Brentwood	1948

ESSEX v GLOUCESTERSHIRE

Home		P	W	L	D	T	A	Away	Years	P	W	L	D	T	A
Leyton	1898-1963	18	8	3	6	1	-	Clifton	1898-1919	4	-	2	2	-	-
Colchester	1920-1986	6	2	2	2	-	-	Cheltenham	1900-1982	10	2	5	3	-	-
(Castle Park)								Bristol	1906-1993	30	9	12	9	-	-
Colchester	1924	1	-	1	-	-	-	(County Ground)							
(Garrison)								Gloucester	1921-1980	12	2	5	5	-	-
Chelmsford	1928-1994	4	-	2	2	-	1	Bristol	1927	1	-	-	1	-	-
Southend	1932-1992	6	3	1	2	-	-	(Packer Ground)							
Clacton	1933-1962	5	3	2	-	-	-	Stroud	1957-1961	2	1	1	-	-	-
Westcliff	1934-1975	6	2	4	-	-	-	AWAY TOTAL		59	14	25	20	-	-
Brentwood	1937-1946	3	1	2	-	-	-								
Ilford	1948-1990	5	1	1	3	-	-								
Romford	1956-1967	3	3	-	-	-	-								
HOME TOTAL		57	23	18	15	1	1								
GRAND TOTAL		116	37	43	35	1	1								

Highest innings total	578-6d		Bristol (PG))	1927
Highest innings total against	523		Chelmsford	1928
Lowest innings total	63		Gloucester	1925
Lowest innings total against	67		Leyton	1908
Highest match aggregate	1344-28		Leyton	1901
Lowest match aggregate	380-34		Cheltenham	1922
Highest individual innings	238*	J.A.Cutmore	Bristol (PG)	1927
Highest individual innings against	244	W.R.Hammond	Chelmsford	1928
Best bowling in an innings	9-37	M.S.Nichols	Gloucester	1938
Best bowling in an innings against	10-40	E.G.Dennett	Bristol	1906
Best bowling in a match	15-165	M.S.Nichols	Gloucester	1938
Best bowling in a match against	17-56	C.W.L.Parker	Gloucester	1925

ESSEX v HAMPSHIRE

Home		P	W	L	D	A
Leyton	1895-1961	17	7	1	9	1
Colchester	1920-1984	6	1	3	2	-
(Castle Park)						
Southend	1925-1987	7	2	3	2	-
Chelmsford	1927-1993	13	6	2	5	-
Colchester	1931	1	1	-	-	-
(Garrison)						
Brentwood	1938-1953	3	2	-	1	-
Westcliff	1946-1971	5	2	1	2	-
Romford	1950-1965	5	1	1	3	-
Clacton	1954-1958	2	-	1	1	-
Ilford	1963-1989	5	3	2	-	-
HOME TOTAL		64	25	14	25	1
GRAND TOTAL		126	41	32	53	1

Away		P	W	L	D	A
Southampton	1895-1994	24	9	8	7	-
Portsmouth	1913-1988	18	2	5	11	-
Bournemouth	1914-1992	19	5	4	10	-
Cowes	1961	1	-	1	-	-
AWAY TOTAL		62	16	18	28	-

Highest innings total	584-9d		Southampton	1927
Highest innings total against	534-7d		Leyton	1913
Lowest innings total	69		Colchester (G)	1931
Lowest innings total against	54		Southampton	1931
Highest match aggregate	1333-29		Leyton	1913
Lowest match aggregate	352-30		Southampton	1931
Highest individual innings	220	G.A.Gooch	Southampton	1989
Highest individual innings against	230	G.Brown	Bournemouth	1920
Best bowling in an innings	9-40	W.Mead	Southampton	1900
Best bowling in an innings against	9-26	A.E.G.Baring	Colchester (G)	1931
Best bowling in a match	17-119	W.Mead	Southampton	1895
Best bowling in a match against	13-78	H.Baldwin	Southampton	1895

ESSEX v KENT

Home		P	W	L	D	A
Leyton	1898-1973	30	5	10	15	1
Southend	1922-1991	6	2	2	2	-
Colchester (Garrison)	1926-1931	2	1	-	1	-
Chelmsford	1933-1994	14	6	2	6	-
Brentwood	1934-1969	2	-	2	-	-
Ilford	1935-1987	9	4	1	4	-
Westcliff	1937-1966	3	1	2	-	-
Colchester (Castle Park)	1938-1984	5	2	1	2	1
Clacton	1950-1958	6	4	1	1	-
Romford	1953-1968	3	2	-	1	-
Harlow	1970	1	-	1	-	-
HOME TOTAL		81	27	22	32	1
GRAND TOTAL		163	43	54	66	1

Away		P	W	L	D	A
Tonbridge	1898-1922	5	1	4	-	-
Gravesend	1899-1960	14	6	6	2	-
Maidstone	1900-1993	11	1	2	8	-
Canterbury	1901-1989	14	1	5	8	-
Tunbridge Wells	1906-1992	14	3	7	4	-
Catford	1909	1	-	-	1	-
Dover	1920-1969	5	-	3	2	-
Folkestone	1929-1991	7	2	2	3	-
Gillingham	1939-1955	2	-	2	-	-
Blackheath	1951-1964	5	-	1	4	-
Dartford	1956-1985	4	2	-	2	-
AWAY TOTAL		82	16	32	34	-

Highest innings total	616	Chelmsford	1988
Highest innings total against	803-4d	Brentwood	1934
Lowest innings total	34	Brentwood	1969
Lowest innings total against	43	Southend	1925
Highest match aggregate	1570-29	Chelmsford	1988
Lowest match aggregate	292-32	Westcliff	1966
Highest individual innings	275	G.A.Gooch	Chelmsford	1988
Highest individual innings against	332	W.H.Ashdown	Brentwood	1934
Best bowling in an innings	9-108	T.P.B.Smith	Maidstone	1948
Best bowling in an innings against	10-53	A.P.Freeman	Southend	1930
Best bowling in a match	13-155	J.W.H.T.Douglas	Leyton	1907
Best bowling in a match against	16-94	A.P.Freeman	Southend	1930

ESSEX v LANCASHIRE

Home		P	W	L	D	T	A
Leyton	1897-1973	30	6	7	17	-	-
Colchester (Castle Park)	1922-1990	7	1	2	4	-	-
Southend	1923-1988	6	2	2	2	-	-
Colchester (Garrison)	1928	1	-	1	-	-	-
Clacton	1931-1955	5	2	2	1	-	-
Chelmsford (County Ground)	1935-1994	5	1	4	-	-	-
Ilford	1938-1992	7	2	1	4	-	-
Brentwood	1952-1964	5	1	0	3	1	-
Chelmsford (Hoffman's)	1959	1	-	1	-	-	-
HOME TOTAL		67	15	20	31	1	-
GRAND TOTAL		135	28	43	63	-	1

Away		P	W	L	D	T	A
Manchester	1897-1993	43	8	15	20	-	1
Liverpool	1899-1982	12	1	6	5	-	-
Blackpool	1924-1980	9	2	2	5	-	-
Nelson	1926	1	-	-	1	-	-
Southport	1972-1978	2	1	-	1	-	-
Lytham	1989	1	1	-	-	-	-
AWAY TOTAL		68	13	23	32	-	1

Highest innings total	559-9	Leyton	1904
Highest innings total against	510	Clacton	1947
Lowest innings total	77	Leyton	1968
Lowest innings total against	70	Southport	1978

| Highest match aggregate | 1298-24 | Colchester | 1990 |
| Lowest match aggregate | 385-31 | Leyton | 1903 |

| Highest individual innings | 219* | M.E.Waugh | Ilford | 1992 |
| Highest individual innings against | 266 | E.Paynter | Manchester | 1937 |

| Best bowling in an innings | 10-90 | T.E.Bailey | Clacton | 1949 |
| Best bowling in an innings against | 8-37 | S.F.Barnes | Leyton | 1903 |

| Best bowling in a match | 14-176 | F.G.Bull | Leyton | 1897 |
| Best bowling in a match against | 14-70 | S.F.Barnes | Leyton | 1903 |

ESSEX v LEICESTERSHIRE

Home		P	W	L	D	A	Away		P	W	L	D	A
Leyton †	1894	1	-	1	-	-	Leicester †	1894	1	-	-	1	-
Leyton	1895-1972	22	6	5	11	2	(Aylestone Road)						
Southend	1906-1993	4	1	2	1	-	Leicester	1895-1934	25	8	5	12	-
Colchester	1926-1969	2	1	1	-	-	(Aylestone Road)						
(Garrison)							Leicester	1946-1994	38	8	10	20	-
Chelmsford	1932-1992	16	6	2	8	-	(Grace Road)						
Clacton	1946-1966	3	-	1	2	-	Loughborough	1948	1	-	-	1	-
Westcliff	1948-1950	2	-	-	2	-	Ashby-de-la-Zouch						
Colchester	1949-1982	8	3	2	3	-		1951-1954	2	-	-	2	-
(Castle Park)							Hinckley	1952-1962	3	3	-	-	-
Romford	1951-1967	2	-	1	1	-	(Coventry Road)						
Brentwood	1952-1957	3	2	1	-	-	Coalville	1958	1	-	1	-	-
Ilford	1956-1991	5	1	1	3	-	Hinckley	1984	1	-	-	1	-
HOME TOTAL		68	20	17	31	2	(Leicester Road)						
							AWAY TOTAL		72	19	16	37	-

GRAND TOTAL 140 39 33 68 2
† Friendly matches

| Highest innings total | 761-6d | Chelmsford | 1990 |
| Highest innings total against | 673 | Leicester | 1899 |

| Lowest innings total | 53 | Leicester | 1977 |
| Lowest innings total against | 45 | Brentwood | 1957 |

| Highest match aggregate | 1530-19 | Chelmsford | 1990 |
| Lowest match aggregate | 286-14 | Leyton | 1968 |

| Highest individual innings | 245 | P.J.Prichard | Chelmsford | 1990 |
| Highest individual innings against | 189* | C.C.Lewis | Chelmsford | 1990 |

| Best bowling in an innings | 10-32 | H.Pickett | Leyton | 1895 |
| Best bowling in an innings against | 8-41 | C.T.Spencer | Colchester | 1959 |

| Best bowling in a match | 15-115 | W.Mead | Leyton | 1903 |
| Best bowling in a match against | 14-89 | A.D.Pougher | Leyton | 1894 |

ESSEX v MIDDLESEX

Home		P	W	L	D	A		Away		P	W	L	D	A
Leyton	1895-1965	31	6	10	15	1		Lord's	1895-1991	73	13	30	30	1
Clacton	1934	1	-	-	1	-		Uxbridge	1989-1994	2	-	-	2	-
Ilford	1935-1992	5	2	1	2	-		AWAY TOTAL		75	13	30	32	1
Colchester	1936-1993	7	1	2	4	-								
(Castle Park)														
Chelmsford	1937-1991	13	6	3	4	-								
Southend	1939-1982	7	1	2	4	-								
Westcliff	1946-1972	8	-	3	5	-								
Brentwood	1948-1962	3	2	-	1	-								
HOME TOTAL		75	18	21	36	1								
GRAND TOTAL		150	31	51	68	2								

Highest innings total	566-6d	Chelmsford	1991
Highest innings total against	634-7d	Chelmsford	1983
Lowest innings total	64	Lord's	1902
Lowest innings total against	51	Chelmsford	1991
Highest match aggregate	1531-23	Uxbridge	1994
Lowest match aggregate	312-33	Lord's	1925
Highest individual innings	259	G.A.Gooch	Chelmsford	1991
Highest individual innings against	285*	J.W.Hearne	Leyton	1929
Best bowling in an innings	9-77	T.P.B.Smith	Colchester	1947
Best bowling in an innings against	8-40	F.J.Durston	Leyton	1928
Best bowling in a match	16-215	T.P.B.Smith	Colchester	1947
Best bowling in a match against	14-146	J.W.Hearne	Leyton	1914

ESSEX v NORTHAMPTONSHIRE

Home		P	W	L	D	T		Away		P	W	L	D	T
Leyton	1906-1974	19	8	5	6	-		Northampton	1906-1993	55	10	11	34	-
Southend	1907-1981	6	4	1	1	-		Kettering	1925-1953	4	1	2	1	-
Colchester	1925-1927	2	1	1	-	-		Peterborough	1937-1966	4	2	2	0	-
(Garrison)								Rushden	1938-1954	2	1	-	1	-
Clacton	1934-1966	5	1	2	2	-		Wellingborough	1955-1983	6	2	2	2	-
Colchester	1935-1991	8	4	1	3	-		AWAY TOTAL		71	16	17	38	-
(Castle Park)														
Ilford	1936-1987	8	3	1	3	1								
Westcliff	1938-1976	5	2	-	3	-								
Brentwood	1946-1956	3	1	1	1	-								
Chelmsford	1951-1994	14	4	4	6	-								
Romford	1954-1963	3	1	2	-	-								
HOME TOTAL		73	29	18	25	1								
GRAND TOTAL		144	45	35	63	1								

Highest innings total	604-7d	Northampton	1921
Highest innings total against	636-6d	Chelmsford	1990
Lowest innings total	44	Colchester	1986
Lowest innings total against	45	Southend	1923
Highest match aggregate	1388-36	Chelmsford	1990
Lowest match aggregate	419-30	Northampton	1912

Highest individual innings	286	J.R.Freeman	Northampton	1921
Highest individual innings against	258*	F.Jakeman	Northampton	1951

Best bowling in an innings	8-41	R.E.East	Northampton	1978
Best bowling in an innings against	7-34	B.S.Bedi	Chelmsford	1972
	7-34	N.G.B.Cook	Chelmsford	1992

Best bowling in a match	13-118	T.P.B.Smith	Colchester	1937
Best bowling in a match against	12-94	S.G.Smith	Northampton	1913

ESSEX v NOTTINGHAMSHIRE

Home		P	W	L	D
Leyton	1901-1967	18	2	6	10
Southend	1927-1990	10	3	3	4
Colchester †	1929	1	-	1	-
(Garrison)					
Westcliff	1934-1965	4	1	1	2
Clacton	1936-1951	4	2	-	2
Chelmsford	1938-1987	8	3	1	4
Brentwood	1949-1964	3	1	-	2
Ilford	1950-1994	5	2	1	2
Colchester	1958	1	-	-	1
(Garrison)					
Romford	1959-1966	2	2	-	-
Colchester	1988-1992	2	1	1	-
(Castle Park)					
HOME TOTAL		58	17	14	27
GRAND TOTAL		115	28	27	60
† Friendly matches					

Away		P	W	L	D
Nottingham	1901-1993	53	10	12	31
Worksop	1924-1938	2	1	-	1
Nottingham †	1929	1	-	1	-
Newark	1972	1	-	-	1
AWAY TOTAL		57	11	13	33

Highest innings total	593-7		Clacton	1951
Highest innings total against	662-8d		Nottingham	1947

Lowest innings total	44		Nottingham	1910
Lowest innings total against	58		Southend	1931

Highest match aggregate	1332-30		Leyton	1901
Lowest match aggregate	345-40		Leyton	1907

Highest individual innings	225	C.P.McGahey	Leyton	1904
Highest individual innings against	274	A.O.Jones	Leyton	1905

Best bowling in an innings	9-32	M.S.Nichols	Nottingham	1936
Best bowling in an innings against	8-25	T.G.Wass	Nottingham	1902

Best bowling in a match	12-73	W.Mead	Leyton	1907
Best bowling in a match against	16-83	B.Dooland	Nottingham	1954

ESSEX v SOMERSET

Home		P	W	L	D	T	A	Away		P	W	L	D	T	A
Leyton	1895-1976	13	3	4	6	-	-	Taunton	1895-1992	32	13	4	15	-	-
Colchester	1923-1978	5	5	-	-	-	-	Weston-super-Mare							
(Castle Park)									1914-1994	13	5	3	5	-	-
Southend	1921-1991	5	4	1	-	-	-	Bath	1921-1990	11	3	4	4	1	1
Ilford	1924-1980	6	2	2	2	-	-	Knowle	1928	1	1	-	-	-	-
Chelmsford	1926-1993	14	6	3	4	1	-	Frome	1935	1	-	1	-	-	-
Colchester	1927-1972	3	2	-	1	-	-	Wells	1939	1	1	-	-	-	-
(Garrison)								Yeovil	1960-1967	2	-	-	2	-	-
Clacton	1935-1949	2	-	2	-	-	-	AWAY TOTAL		61	23	12	26	-	1
Westcliff	1939-1974	8	2	3	3	-	-								
Brentwood	1951-1963	5	2	1	2	-	-								
Romford	1955	1	1	-	-	-	-								
HOME TOTAL		62	27	16	18	1	-								
GRAND TOTAL		123	50	28	44	1	1								

Highest innings total	692		Taunton	1895
Highest innings total against	488		Clacton	1949
Lowest innings total	69		Ilford	1924
Lowest innings total against	48		Bath	1951
	48		Westcliff	1961
Highest match aggregate	1193-29		Leyton	1976
Lowest match aggregate	343-30		Weston-s-Mare	1934
Highest individual innings	237	J.O'Connor	Leyton	1933
Highest individual innings against	193*	S.J.Cook	Southend	1991
Best bowling in an innings	8-90	J.W.H.T.Douglas	Colchester	1923
Best bowling in an innings against	8-67	B.A.Langford	Ilford	1958
Best bowling in a match	13-98	K.Farnes	Taunton	1933
Best bowling in a match against	13-61	J.C.White	Ilford	1924

ESSEX v SURREY

Home		P	W	L	D	A	Away		P	W	L	D	A
Leyton †	1894	1	-	1	-	-	The Oval †	1894-1947	3	-	2	1	-
Leyton	1895-1969	36	5	22	9	-	The Oval	1895-1993	80	15	31	34	3
Southend	1907-1978	7	2	3	2	-	Guildford	1968	1	-	-	1	-
Brentwood	1934-1960	4	1	1	2	-	AWAY TOTAL		84	15	33	36	3
Clacton	1935-1963	4	2	1	1	-							
Chelmsford	1937-1991	18	7	2	9	-							
Westcliff	1938	1	1	-	-	-							
Colchester	1939-1994	5	2	1	2	-							
(Castle Park)													
Ilford	1948-1974	7	1	2	4	-							
Romford	1959-1968	2	-	1	1	-							
Colchester	1970	1	-	-	1	-							
(Garrison)													
HOME TOTAL		86	21	34	31	-							
GRAND TOTAL		170	36	67	67	3							
† Friendly matches													

Highest innings total	616-5d		The Oval	1904
Highest innings total against	613-6d		The Oval	1990
Lowest innings total	37		Leyton	1899
Lowest innings total against	14		Chelmsford	1983

Highest match aggregate	1292-26		The Oval	1990
Lowest match aggregate	339-30		Leyton	1958

Highest individual innings	248	J.O'Connor	Brentwood	1934
Highest individual innings against	290*	A.Ducat	Leyton	1921

Best bowling in an innings	9-93	F.G.Bull	The Oval	1897
Best bowling in an innings against	10-45	T.Richardson	The Oval	1894

Best bowling in a match	13-113	T.P.B.Smith	The Oval	1950
Best bowling in a match against	15-95	T.Richardson	The Oval	1894

ESSEX v SUSSEX

Home		P	W	L	D	T	Away		P	W	L	D	T
Leyton	1897-1933	25	9	5	11	-	Hove	1897-1993	48	17	13	17	1
Southend	1914-1992	7	6	-	1	-	Eastbourne	1900-1987	13	2	1	10	-
Colchester	1921-1985	7	2	1	4	-	Hastings	1906-1968	3	1	1	1	-
(Castle Park)							Horsham	1908-1991	6	1	1	4	-
Ilford	1924-1988	11	4	2	5	-	Worthing	1955-1962	3	1	2	-	-
Colchester	1925-1969	2	-	1	1	-	AWAY TOTAL		73	22	18	32	1
(Garrison)													
Chelmsford	1931-1994	6	1	2	3	-							
Clacton	1932-1964	4	1	2	1	-							
Brentwood	1935-1967	7	1	3	3	-							
Westcliff	1971-1975	2	1	1	-	-							
HOME TOTAL		71	25	17	29	-							
GRAND TOTAL		144	47	35	61	1							

Highest innings total	560-9d		Leyton	1933
Highest innings total against	611		Leyton	1905

Lowest innings total	71		Hove	1902
Lowest innings total against	47		Southend	1914

Highest match aggregate	1808-20		Hove	1993
Lowest match aggregate	408-30		Southend	1914

Highest individual innings	228*	K.W.R.Fletcher	Hastings	1968
Highest individual innings against	230	K.S.Ranjitsinhji	Leyton	1902

Best bowling in an innings	8-33	C.P.Buckenham	Leyton	1904
Best bowling in an innings against	8-22	A.E.Relf	Hove	1909

Best bowling in a match	13-69	W.Mead	Eastbourne	1900
Best bowling in a match against	12-57	M.W.Tate	Hove	1923

ESSEX v WARWICKSHIRE

Home		P	W	L	D	Away		P	W	L	D
Leyton †	1894	1	-	-	1	Birmingham †	1894	1	-	1	-
Leyton	1895-1976	16	5	5	6	Birmingham	1895-1994	46	7	15	24
Chelmsford	1929-1991	7	5	-	2	Coventry	1929	1	1	-	-
Southend	1946-1980	5	1	-	4	(Rover)					
Brentwood	1947-1949	2	1	1	-	Coventry	1947-1965	3	1	1	1
Ilford	1950-1993	6	4	-	2	(Courtaulds)					
Clacton	1951-1965	5	3	-	2	Nuneaton	1983	1	-	1	-
Westcliff	1954-1967	4	2	2	-	AWAY TOTAL		52	9	18	25
Colchester	1956-1982	6	2	1	3						
(Castle Park)											
HOME TOTAL		52	23	9	20						
GRAND TOTAL		104	32	27	45						

† Friendly matches

Highest innings total	522-8d		Leyton	1930
Highest innings total against	614-8d		Birmingham	1904
Lowest innings total	47		Leyton	1968
Lowest innings total against	53		Birmingham	1957
Highest match aggregate	1350-27		Birmingham	1977
Lowest match aggregate	267-31		Birmingham	1894
Highest individual innings	208*	K.S.McEwan	Birmingham	1979
Highest individual innings against	223*	W.G.Quaife	Leyton	1900
Best bowling in an innings	8-49	J.K.Lever	Birmingham	1979
Best bowling in an innings against	9-55	H.J.Pallett	Leyton	1894
Best bowling in a match	15-115	R.E.East	Leyton	1968
Best bowling in a match against	14-100	H.J.Pallett	Leyton	1894

ESSEX v WORCESTERSHIRE

Home		P	W	L	D
Leyton	1910-1972	22	11	5	6
Colchester	1914-1989	5	2	1	2
(Castle Park)					
Chelmsford	1934-1993	17	5	6	6
Clacton	1937-1948	2	2	-	-
Southend	1938-1986	4	1	1	2
Romford	1950-1966	7	1	2	4
Brentwood	1954-1969	3	1	-	2
Ilford	1967-1991	3	-	-	3
Westcliff	1976	1	-	-	1
HOME TOTAL		64	23	15	26
GRAND TOTAL		127	38	27	62

Away		P	W	L	D
Bournville	1910	1	-	-	1
Stourbridge	1911	1	1	-	-
Worcester	1914-1994	59	14	12	33
Dudley	1964	1	-	-	1
Kidderminster	1992	1	-	-	1
AWAY TOTAL		63	15	12	36

Highest innings total	560-5d		Leyton	1921
Highest innings total against	515		Chelmsford	1934
Lowest innings total	65		Chelmsford	1947
	65		Chelmsford	1973
Lowest innings total against	49		Leyton	1922
Highest match aggregate	1333-29		Worcester	1994
Lowest match aggregate	489-31		Chelmsford	1953
Highest individual innings	214*	A.V.Avery	Clacton	1948
Highest individual innings against	231*	Nawab of Pataudi		
			Worcester	1933
Best bowling in an innings	8-35	W.Mead	Leyton	1911
Best bowling in an innings against	9-40	C.F.Root	Worcester	1924
Best bowling in a match	14-119	K.Farnes	Worcester	1938
Best bowling in a match against	15-106	R.T.D.Perks	Worcester	1937

ESSEX v YORKSHIRE

Home		P	W	L	D	A	Away		P	W	L	D	A
Leyton †	1894	1	-	1	-	-	Halifax †	1894	1	-	1	-	-
Leyton	1895-1974	36	5	20	11	-	Harrogate	1895-1961	7	1	4	2	-
Southend	1920-1989	8	3	4	1	-	Bradford	1896-1966	11	-	10	1	-
Colchester	1935-1991	6	-	3	3	-	Huddersfield	1897-1937	5	2	2	1	-
(Castle Park)							Sheffield	1899-1969	11	2	5	4	-
Westcliff	1936-1968	4	1	2	1	-	(Bramall Lane)						
Ilford	1937-1982	5	1	3	1	-	Leeds	1901-1994	14	2	6	6	-
Brentwood	1951	1	-	-	1	-	Dewsbury	1907-1933	5	-	4	1	-
Clacton	1952-1963	2	-	1	1	-	Hull	1908-1971	8	-	3	5	-
Romford	1954-1958	2	-	1	1	-	Scarborough	1932-1979	6	1	4	1	-
Colchester	1970-1971	2	-	1	1	-	Middlesbrough	1958-1990	4	1	2	1	-
(Garrison)							Sheffield	1988	1	1	-	-	1
Chelmsford	1972-1993	7	3	1	3	-	(Abbeydale Park)						
HOME TOTAL		74	13	37	24	-	AWAY TOTAL		73	10	41	22	1
GRAND TOTAL		147	23	78	46	1							

† Friendly matches

Highest innings total	524-7d	Leeds	1984
Highest innings total against	555-1d	Leyton	1932
Lowest innings total	30	Leyton	1901
Lowest innings total against	31	Huddersfield	1935
Highest match aggregate	1244-31	Southend	1947
Lowest match aggregate	175-29	Leyton	1901
Highest individual innings	219* D.J.Insole	Colchester	1949
Highest individual innings against	313 H.Sutcliffe	Leyton	1932
Best bowling in an innings	8-44 F.G.Bull	Bradford	1896
Best bowling in an innings against	9-28 W.Rhodes	Leyton	1899
Best bowling in a match	14-127 W.Mead	Leyton	1899
Best bowling in a match against	17-91 H.Verity	Leyton	1933

UNIVERSITIES

ESSEX v CAMBRIDGE UNIVERSITY

Home		P	W	L	D	Away		P	W	L	D
Colchester	1922-1923	2	1	-	1	Cambridge	1910-1994	46	16	1	29
(Castle Park)						(Fenner's)					
Chelmsford	1933-1956	2	-	1	1						
Westcliff	1935	1	-	1	-						
Brentwood	1937-1956	4	3	-	1						
Harlow	1970	1	1	-	-						
HOME TOTAL		10	5	2	3						
GRAND TOTAL		56	21	3	32						

Highest innings total	463-4d	Cambridge	1984
Highest innings total against	464-8d	Cambridge	1929
Lowest innings total	120	Cambridge	1951
Lowest innings total against	37	Cambridge	1965

Highest match aggregate	1109-19		Cambridge	1949
Lowest match aggregate	390-30		Brentwood	1939
Highest individual innings	205	G.A.Gooch	Cambridge	1980
Highest individual innings against	219*	G.H.G.Doggart	Cambridge	1949
Best bowling in an innings	9-61	K.D.Boyce	Brentwood	1966
Best bowling in an innings against	8-88	R.Roopnaraine	Cambridge	1965
Best bowling in a match	13-108	K.D.Boyce	Brentwood	1966
Best bowling in a match against	8-75	K.Farnes	Chelmsford	1933

ESSEX v OXFORD UNIVERSITY

Home		P	W	L	D	A
Leyton	1894-1932	2	1	1	-	-
Chelmsford	1925-1927	3	1	-	2	-
Colchester (Garrison)	1928	1	-	-	1	-
Westcliff	1957	1	1	-	-	-
Brentwood	1960	1	-	1	-	-
Romford	1965	1	1	-	-	-
HOME TOTAL		9	4	2	3	-
GRAND TOTAL		16	8	3	5	1

Away		P	W	L	D	A
Oxford	1898-1972	7	4	1	2	1

Highest innings total	414		Chelmsford	1927
Highest innings total against	344		Chelmsford	1925
Lowest innings total	127		Westcliff	1957
Lowest innings total against	89		Oxford	1972
Highest match aggregate	1171-32		Leyton	1932
Lowest match aggregate	476-36		Romford	1965
Highest individual innings	157	J.O'Connor	Colchester (G)	1928
Highest individual innings against	167	A.M.Crawley	Colchester (G)	1928
Best bowling in an innings	7-60	W.Mead	Oxford	1898
Best bowling in an innings against	7-60	R.Bowman	Westcliff	1957
Best bowling in a match	13-125	W.Mead	Oxford	1898
Best bowling in a match against	9-70	J.D.Martin	Romford	1965

TEST PLAYING TOURING TEAMS

ESSEX v AUSTRALIANS

Home		P	W	L	D
Leyton	1896-1930	13	2	4	7
Southend	1921-1968	8	1	7	-
Chelmsford	1934-1993	7	0	3	4
Ilford	1972	1	-	-	1
TOTAL		29	3	14	12

Highest innings total	425-6d	Southend	1964
Highest innings total against	721	Southend	1948

| Lowest innings total | 67 | | Leyton | 1930 |
| Lowest innings total against | 73 | | Leyton | 1899 |

| Highest match aggregate | 1282-28 | | Chelmsford | 1975 |
| Lowest match aggregate | 499-40 | | Southend | 1938 |

| Highest individual innings | 129 | J.W.H.T.Douglas | Leyton | 1912 |
| Highest individual innings against | 219 | W.Bardsley | Leyton | 1909 |

| Best bowling in an innings | 7-32 | H.I.Young | Leyton | 1899 |
| Best bowling in an innings against | 8-72 | D.A.Renneberg | Southend | 1968 |

| Best bowling in a match | 12-137 | C.P.Buckenham | Leyton | 1905 |
| Best bowling in a match against | 12-131 | H.Trumble | Leyton | 1899 |

ESSEX v INDIANS

Home		P	W	L	D
Leyton	1932	1	-	-	1
Brentwood	1936	1	1	-	-
Southend	1946	1	-	1	-
Ilford	1952-1959	2	-	-	2
Colchester	1971	1	1	-	-
(Garrison)					
Chelmsford	1974-1982	3	-	-	3
TOTAL		9	2	1	6

| Highest innings total | 410 | | Ilford | 1952 |
| Highest innings total against | 370-9 | | Southend | 1946 |

| Lowest innings total | 146 | | Chelmsford | 1979 |
| Lowest innings total against | 138 | | Southend | 1946 |

| Highest match aggregate | 1117-35 | | Ilford | 1952 |
| Lowest match aggregate | 791-32 | | Colchester (G) | 1971 |

| Highest individual innings | 161 | B.R.Hardie | Chelmsford | 1982 |
| Highest individual innings against | 181 | V.M.Merchant | Southend | 1946 |

| Best bowling in an innings | 6-36 | R.Smith | Ilford | 1952 |
| Best bowling in an innings against | 5-44 | H.G.Gaekwad | Ilford | 1952 |

| Best bowling in a match | 8-144 | R.Smith | Ilford | 1952 |
| Best bowling in a match against | 7-124 | V.S.Hazare | Ilford | 1952 |

ESSEX v NEW ZEALANDERS

Home		P	W	L	D
Leyton	1927-1931	2	1	1	-
Southend	1931-1949	2	-	-	2
Chelmsford	1937-1994	5	-	3	2
Ilford	1958	1	-	1	-
Westcliff	1969-1973	2	1	1	-
TOTAL		12	2	6	4

| Highest innings total | 449-8d | | Chelmsford | 1990 |
| Highest innings total against | 428-5d | | Chelmsford | 1994 |

| Lowest innings total | 113 | | Leyton | 1931 |
| Lowest innings total against | 97 | | Westcliff | 1969 |

| Highest match aggregate | 1158-32 | | Southend | 1949 |
| Lowest match aggregate | 611-40 | | Westcliff | 1969 |

| Highest individual innings | 147 | J.P.Stephenson | Chelmsford | 1990 |
| Highest individual innings against | 243 | B.Sutcliffe | Southend | 1949 |

| Best bowling in an innings | 6-49 | R.E.East | Westcliff | 1969 |
| Best bowling in an innings against | 8-41 | W.E.Merritt | Leyton | 1931 |

| Best bowling in a match | 10-160 | J.O'Connor | Leyton | 1927 |
| Best bowling in a match against | 12-130 | W.E.Merritt | Leyton | 1931 |

ESSEX v PAKISTANIS

Home		P	W	L	D
Southend	1954	1	-	-	1
Leyton	1962	1	1	-	-
Colchester	1967	1	-	-	1
(Castle Park)					
Chelmsford	1978-1992	3	-	2	1
TOTAL		6	1	2	3

| Highest innings total | 357-9d | | Chelmsford | 1992 |
| Highest innings total against | 353-6d | | Chelmsford | 1992 |

| Lowest innings total | 116 | | Colchester | 1967 |
| Lowest innings total against | 80 | | Chelmsford | 1978 |

| Highest match aggregate | 1094-28 | | Chelmsford | 1992 |
| Lowest match aggregate | 713-31 | | Leyton | 1962 |

| Highest individual innings | 141 | G.A.Gooch | Chelmsford | 1992 |
| Highest individual innings against | 153* | Salim Malik | Chelmsford | 1992 |

| Best bowling in an innings | 6-33 | N.Phillip | Chelmsford | 1978 |
| Best bowling in an innings against | 5-40 | Wasim Akram | Chelmsford | 1987 |

| Best bowling in a match | 8-108 | B.R.Knight | Leyton | 1962 |
| Best bowling in a match against | 8-152 | Wasim Akram | Chelmsford | 1992 |

ESSEX v SOUTH AFRICANS

Home		P	W	L	D
Leyton	1907-1929	4	-	3	1
Colchester	1924	1	-	1	-
(Garrison)					
Southend	1935	2	1	1	-
Ilford	1951-1960	2	-	1	1
Colchester	1955-1965	2	-	-	2
(Castle Park)					
TOTAL		11	1	6	4

Highest innings total	380	Southend	1947
Highest innings total against	503-4d	Colchester	1955

Lowest innings total	89	Leyton	1907
Lowest innings total against	155	Leyton	1907

Highest match aggregate	1172-26	Ilford	1951
Lowest match aggregate	611-28	Leyton	1907

Highest individual innings	147	R.Smith	Ilford	1951
Highest individual innings against	167	G.M.Fullerton	Ilford	1951

Best bowling in an innings	7-66	J.W.A.Stephenson	Southend	1935
Best bowling in an innings against	7-47	J.B.Plimsoll	Southend	1947

Best bowling in a match	10-110	J.W.A.Stephenson	Southend	1935
Best bowling in a match against	10-133	J.B.Plimsoll	Southend	1947

ESSEX v WEST INDIANS

Home		P	W	L	D
Leyton	1906-1933	3	1	1	1
Ilford	1923-1957	2	-	2	-
Chelmsford	1939-1991	6	-	2	4
Southend	1950-1966	3	-	1	2
TOTAL		14	1	6	7

Highest innings total	395	Leyton	1906
Highest innings total against	379	Leyton	1906

Lowest innings total	56	Southend	1963
Lowest innings total against	106	Leyton	1933

Highest match aggregate	1131-40	Leyton	1906
Lowest match aggregate	637-36	Ilford	1957

Highest individual innings	147	C.A.G.Russell	Leyton	1928
Highest individual innings against	155	S.M.Nurse	Southend	1966

Best bowling in an innings	6-31	M.S.Nichols	Leyton	1933
Best bowling in an innings against	8-32	E.A.Martindale	Leyton	1933

Best bowling in a match	9-106	T.E.Bailey	Ilford	1957
Best bowling in a match against	13-91	L.N.Constantine	Chelmsford	1939

OTHER TEAMS

ESSEX v AUSTRALIAN IMPERIAL FORCES

Home		P	W	L	D
Leyton	1919	1	-	1	-
Southend	1919	1	-	1	-
TOTAL		2	-	2	-

ESSEX v CANADIANS

Home		P	W	L	D
Clacton	1954	1	-	-	1

ESSEX v COMBINED SERVICES

Home		P	W	L	D
Leyton	1922	1	1	-	-
Chelmsford	1950	1	-	-	1
TOTAL		2	1	-	1

ESSEX v COMMONWEALTH XI

Home		P	W	L	D
Romford	1953	1	1	-	-

ESSEX v DUBLIN UNIVERSITY

Home		P	W	L	D
Brentwood	1922	1	-	-	1

ESSEX v ENGLAND A

Home		P	W	L	D	Away		P	W	L	D
Chelmsford	1993	1	1	-	-	Lord's	1992	1	-	-	1
TOTAL		2	1	-	1						

ESSEX v JAMAICA

Home		P	W	L	D
Leyton	1970	1	-	-	1

ESSEX v M.C.C.

Away		P	W	L	D
Lord's	1895-1987	10	2	3	5

Highest innings total	356		Lord's	1949
Highest innings total against	378-8d		Lord's	1949
Lowest innings total	78		Lord's	1951
Lowest innings total against	41		Lord's	1896
Highest match aggregate	1213-34		Lord's	1949
Lowest match aggregate	347-30		Lord's	1896
Highest individual innings	143	A.V.Avery	Lord's	1949
Highest individual innings against	132	N.W.Hill	Lord's	1960
Best bowling in an innings	6-23	C.J.Kortright	Lord's	1896
Best bowling in an innings against	7-36	J.C.Laker	Lord's	1951
Best bowling in a match	10-57	C.J.Kortright	Lord's	1896
Best bowling in a match against	10-108	A.E.Trott	Lord's	1897

ESSEX v T.N.PEARCE'S XI

Home		P	W	L	D
Chelmsford	1952	1	-	1	-

ESSEX v SOUTH AFRICAN FEZELA XI

Home		P	W	L	D
Chelmsford	1961	1	-	1	-
(Hoffman's)					

ESSEX v VICTORIA

Home		P	W	L	D
Chelmsford	1991	1	-	1	-

SECTION 10 - RECORDS ON EACH HOME GROUND

BRENTWOOD

Highest innings total	570-8d	v Surrey	1934
Highest innings total against	803-4d	- Kent	1934
Lowest innings total	34	v Kent	1969
Lowest innings total against	45	- Leicestershire	1957
Highest individual innings	248	J.O'Connor v Surrey	1934
Highest individual innings against	332	W.H.Ashdown - Kent	1934
Best bowling in an innings	9-61	K.D.Boyce v Cambridge Univ	1966
Best bowling in an innings against	9-62	B.L.Muncer - Glamorgan	1948
Best bowling in a match	13-108	K.D.Boyce v Cambridge Univ	1966
Best bowling in a match against	15-161	B.L.Muncer - Glamorgan	1948

CHELMSFORD - County Ground

Highest innings total	761-6d	v Leicestershire	1990
Highest innings total against	636-6d	- Northamptonshire	1990
Lowest innings total	65	v Worcestershire	1947
	65	v Worcestershire	1973
Lowest innings total against	14	- Surrey	1983
Highest individual innings	275	G.A.Gooch v Kent	1988
Highest individual innings against	244	W.R.Hammond	
		- Gloucestershire	1928
Best bowling in an innings	9-59	M.S.Nichols v Hampshire	1927
Best bowling in an innings against	8-155	C.W.L.Parker - Gloucestershire	1928
Best bowling in a match	13-117	J.K.Lever v Leicestershire	1979
Best bowling in a match against	13-91	L.N.Constantine	
		- West Indians	1939

CHELMSFORD - Hoffman's

Highest innings total	309	v Derbyshire	1961
Highest innings total against	345	- Lancashire	1959
Lowest innings total	144	v S.A. Fezela XI	1961
Lowest innings total against	153	- Derbyshire	1961
Highest individual innings	148	G.J.Smith v Derbyshire	1961
Highest individual innings against	110*	G.Pullar - Lancashire	1959
Best bowling in an innings	6-99	L.H.R.Ralph v Lancashire	1959
Best bowling in an innings against	6-82	T.Greenhough - Lancashire	1959
Best bowling in a match	8-117	L.H.R.Ralph v Lancashire	1959
Best bowling in a match against	11-171	T.Greenhough - Lancashire	1959

CLACTON

Highest innings total	593-7	v Nottinghamshire	1951
Highest innings total against	576-9d	- Nottinghamshire	1951
Lowest innings total	70	v Gloucestershire	1960
Lowest innings total against	74	- Nottinghamshire	1939
Highest individual innings	214*	A.V.Avery v Worcestershire	1948
Highest individual innings against	203	C.Milburn - Northamptonshire	1966
Best bowling in an innings	10-90	T.E.Bailey v Lancashire	1949
Best bowling in an innings against	8-64	T.W.J.Goddard	
		- Gloucestershire	1936
Best bowling in a match	15-113	K.Farnes v Glamorgan	1938
Best bowling in a match against	11-101	O.W.Herman - Hampshire	1932

COLCHESTER - Castle Park

Highest innings total	588-9d		v Northamptonshire	1937
Highest innings total against	503-4d		- South Africans	1955
Lowest innings total	44		v Northamptonshire	1986
Lowest innings total against	56		- Sussex	1957
Highest individual innings	219*	D.J.Insole	v Yorkshire	1949
Highest individual innings against	244	A.E.Fagg	- Kent	1938
Best bowling in an innings	9-77	T.P.B.Smith	v Middlesex	1947
Best bowling in an innings against	8-57	C.W.L.Parker	- Gloucestershire	1920
Best bowling in a match	16-215	T.P.B.Smith	v Middlesex	1947
Best bowling in a match against	14-94	C.T.Spencer	- Leicestershire	1959

COLCHESTER - Garrison Ground

Highest innings total	345-9d		v South Africans	1924
Highest innings total against	450-4d		- Yorkshire	1970
Lowest innings total	69		v Hampshire	1931
Lowest innings total against	67		- Glamorgan	1930
Highest individual innings	157	J.O'Connor	v Oxford University	1928
Highest individual innings against	260*	G.Boycott	- Yorkshire	1970
Best bowling in an innings	6-28	A.B.Hipkin	v Northamptonshire	1925
Best bowling in an innings against	9-26	A.E.G.Baring	- Hampshire	1931
Best bowling in a match	10-53	M.S.Nichols	v Glamorgan	1930
Best bowling in a match against	12-105	V.W.C.Jupp	- Northamptonshire	1925

HARLOW

Highest innings total	353-8d		v Cambridge Univ	1970
Highest innings total against	330-7d		- Kent	1970
Lowest innings total	127		v Kent	1970
Lowest innings total against	47		- Cambridge Univ	1970
Highest individual innings	106	B.Taylor	v Cambridge Univ	1970
Highest individual innings against	167*	M.H.Denness	- Kent	1970
Best bowling in an innings	6-22	R.E.East	v Cambridge Univ	1970
Best bowling in an innings against	6-67	J.N.Graham	- Kent	1970
Best bowling in a match	9-81	R.E.East	v Cambridge Univ	1970
Best bowling in a match against	8-130	J.N.Graham	- Kent	1970

ILFORD

Highest innings total	510-2d		v Lancashire	1992
Highest innings total against	491-8d		- Lancashire	1938
Lowest innings total	69		v Somerset	1924
Lowest innings total against	64		- Worcestershire	1982
Highest individual innings	219*	M.E.Waugh	v Lancashire	1992
Highest individual innings against	220*	D.L.Haynes	- Middlesex	1990
Best bowling in an innings	8-30	R.E.East	v Nottinghamshire	1977
Best bowling in an innings against	8-58	D.S.Atkinson	- West Indians	1957
Best bowling in a match	13-145	J.K.Lever	v Northamptonshire	1978
Best bowling in a match against	13-61	J.C.White	- Somerset	1924

LEYTON

Highest innings total	609-4d		v Derbyshire	1912
Highest innings total against	611		- Sussex	1905
Lowest innings total	30		v Yorkshire	1901
Lowest innings total against	49		- Worcestershire	1927
Highest individual innings	277	C.P.McGahey	v Derbyshire	1905
Highest individual innings against	313	H.Sutcliffe	- Yorkshire	1932
Best bowling in an innings	10-32	H.Pickett	v Leicestershire	1895
Best bowling in an innings against	9-28	W.Rhodes	- Yorkshire	1899
Best bowling in a match	15-115	W.Mead	v Leicestershire	1903
	15-115	R.E.East	v Warwickshire	1968
Best bowling in a match against	17-91	H.Verity	- Yorkshire	1933

ROMFORD

Highest innings total	396-7d		v Worcestershire	1952
	396		v Nottinghamshire	1959
Highest innings total against	409		- Worcestershire	1950
Lowest innings total	88		v Worcestershire	1962
Lowest innings total against	76		- Worcestershire	1958
Highest individual innings	180	D.J.Insole	v Nottinghamshire	1959
Highest individual innings against	163	C.C.Inman	- Leicestershire	1967
Best bowling in an innings	8-49	T.E.Bailey	v Hampshire	1957
Best bowling in an innings against	7-57	P.I.Pocock	- Surrey	1968
Best bowling in a match	14-81	T.E.Bailey	v Hampshire	1957
Best bowling in a match against	11-83	J.A.Flavell	- Worcestershire	1962

SOUTHEND

Highest innings total	503		v Hampshire	1936
Highest innings total against	721		- Australians	1948
Lowest innings total	56		v West Indians	1963
Lowest innings total against	43		- Kent	1925
Highest individual innings	205	M.S.Nichols	v Hampshire	1936
Highest individual innings against	255*	H.Sutcliffe	- Yorkshire	1924
Best bowling in an innings	9-117	T.P.B.Smith	v Nottinghamshire	1948
Best bowling in an innings against	10-53	A.P.Freeman	- Kent	1930
Best bowling in a match	12-131	G.M.Louden	v Derbyshire	1920
Best bowling in a match against	16-94	A.P.Freeman	- Kent	1930

WESTCLIFF

Highest innings total	499-8c		v Worcestershire	1976
Highest innings total against	432		- Gloucestershire	1939
Lowest innings total	63		v Derbyshire	1949
Lowest innings total against	48		- Somerset	1961
Highest individual innings	211*	T.N.Pearce	v Leicestershire	1948
Highest individual innings against	207	W.R.Hammond		
			- Gloucestershire	1939
Best bowling in an innings	8-29	T.E.Bailey	v Derbyshire	1958
Best bowling in an innings against	9-37	D.L.Underwood		
			- Kent	1966
Best bowling in a match	13-143	B.R.Knight	v Glamorgan	1960
Best bowling in a match against	15-100	H.Verity	- Yorkshire	1936

SECTION 11 - ESSEX COUNTY CRICKET CLUB FIRST-CLASS
CAREER RECORDS 1894-1994

BATTING AND FIELDING

	Seasons	M	I	NO	R	HS	Avge	100	50	Ct/St
D.L.Acfield	1966-1986	378	353	191	1259	38	7.77	-	-	120
S.J.W.Andrew	1990-1994	60	59	18	299	35	7.29	-	-	9
F.Appleyard	1946-1947	14	19	11	55	15*	6.87	-	-	6
H.A.Arkwright	1894-1895	3	6	0	35	19	5.83	-	-	2
C.T.Ashton	1921-1938	89	146	10	3193	118	23.47	3	14	72
H.Ashton	1921-1939	21	35	1	819	90	24.08	-	4	21
P.Ashton	1924	1	2	0	52	31	26.00	-	-	-
A.V.Avery	1935-1954	268	453	35	14045	224	33.60	25	65	119
G.W.Ayres	1899	12	17	1	263	83	16.43	-	1	12
J.A.Bailey	1953-1958	71	88	24	295	27*	4.60	-	-	49
T.E.Bailey	1946-1967	482	774	152	21460	205	34.50	22	119	320
R.K.Baker	1972	1	1	1	14	14*	-	-	-	2
A.E.Banfield	1921	1	2	1	0	0*	0.00	-	-	-
A.N.Barber	1925	2	4	0	46	31	11.50	-	-	2
G.Barker	1954-1971	444	797	46	21895	181*	29.15	30	112	232
J.D.Barnfather	1924	5	5	3	50	28*	25.00	-	-	1
P.L.Barrow	1922	1	1	0	0	0	0.00	-	-	-
J.F.Bawtree	1895-1896	5	9	1	96	47	12.00	-	-	5
M.J.Bear	1954-1968	322	562	44	12564	137	24.25	9	57	113
B.H.Belle	1935-1937	26	42	3	776	63	19.89	-	2	20
C.E.Benham	1904-1909	57	80	11	985	65*	14.27	-	2	31
M.Berkley	1894	2	3	1	6	5	3.00	-	-	2
F.D.Billham	1924	2	3	1	12	12*	6.00	-	-	-
D.J.P.Boden	1992-1993	3	3	0	10	5	3.33	-	-	1
J..W.Bonner	1896-1898	16	27	1	339	59	13.03	-	1	5
A.R.Border	1986-1988	40	64	12	2778	169*	53.42	10	13	44
O.R.Borradaile	1894	1	2	0	7	5	3.50	-	-	1
N.F.Borrett	1937-1946	3	4	2	33	15*	16.50	-	-	2
C.S.R.Boswell	1932-1936	30	46	8	406	69	10.68	-	1	12
K.D.Boyce	1966-1977	211	319	18	6848	147*	22.75	3	37	181
M.J.H.Boyers	1969	1	2	0	2	2	1.00	-	-	-
A.Bradfield	1922	5	7	3	7	4*	1.75	-	-	2/3
C.Bray	1927-1937	95	154	14	3474	129	24.81	5	13	54
O.C.Bristowe	1913-1914	11	16	1	249	81	16.60	-	1	2
V.C.G.Brooks	1970-1971	3	5	0	53	22	10.60	-	-	1
A.D.Brown	1988-1992	5	5	3	13	6*	6.50	-	-	13/3
G.R.R.Brown	1924-1932	23	35	10	302	38*	12.08	-	-	14
H.J.Brunwin	1937	1	1	1	2	2	-	-	-	-
C.P.Buckenham	1899-1914	258	394	63	4882	124	14.74	2	12	143
F.G.Bull	1895-1900	88	125	31	1171	41*	12.45	-	-	41
J.Burns	1894-1896	26	47	1	713	114	15.50	1	1	11
N.D.Burns	1986	2	3	0	54	29	18.00	-	-	2/2
H.J.E.Burrell	1895	2	4	0	15	10	3.75	-	-	-
R.J.Burrell	1894-1895	6	9	1	127	40	14.11	-	-	1
K.A.Butler	1989	1	1	1	10	10*	-	-	-	-
C.N.Calnan	1919-1929	4	8	0	49	24	6.12	-	-	1
P.Campbell	1911-1919	13	21	2	270	35	14.21	-	-	6
G.N.Capel-Cure	1929	1	2	0	6	6	3.00	-	-	-
N.J.O.Carbutt	1923	2	1	1	12	12*	-	-	-	-
H.A.Carpenter	1894-1920	262	466	24	13043	199	29.50	22	61	220

	Seasons	M	I	NO	R	HS	Avge	100	50	Ct/St
R.B.Carr	1960	1	1	1	7	7*	-	-	-	-
G.Carter	1921-1923	7	11	1	163	44*	16.30	-	-	3
G.R.Cass	1964-1967	45	77	11	1447	104*	21.92	1	5	27/5
B.K.Castor	1932	1	1	0	13	13	13.00	-	-	-
I.Chapman	1929	1	1	0	9	9	9.00	-	-	-
J.H.Childs	1985-1994	191	171	83	1039	43	11.80	-	-	45
H.G.Clark	1923	2	3	0	13	11	4.33	-	-	-
L.S.Clark	1946-1947	24	44	3	745	64	18.17	-	4	11
R.D.Clark	1912-1919	7	11	1	61	14	6.10	-	-	10/1
C.B.Clarke	1959-1960	18	27	14	177	39	13.61	-	-	6
D.F.Cock	1939-1946	14	20	2	355	98	19.72	-	1	5
E.C.Coleman	1912	2	3	0	10	6	3.33	-	-	1/1
E.J.Connor	1905	2	4	0	43	26	10.75	-	-	-
R.M.O.Cooke	1973-1975	40	66	5	1373	139	22.50	2	4	24
A.V.Cooper	1923	1	2	0	14	12	7.00	-	-	-
F.J.Cooper	1921-1923	10	18	1	170	52	10.00	-	1	3
W.Cooper	1905-1910	3	6	0	32	18	5.33	-	-	1
F.W.Cottam	1922	1	did not bat				-			-
P.Cousens	1950-1955	39	50	26	72	13	3.00	-	-	3
D.M.Cousins	1993-1994	5	7	1	24	11	4.00	-	-	2
H.P.Crabtree	1931-1947	24	41	1	1281	146	32.02	4	3	12
C.L.Crawley	1929	1	2	0	3	3	1.50	-	-	1
L.G.Crawley	1926-1936	56	91	4	2949	222	33.89	6	11	17
S.J.Cray	1938-1950	99	172	6	4062	163	24.46	7	16	22
J.A.Cutmore	1924-1936	342	593	36	15937	238*	28.61	15	87	121
A.G.Daer	1925-1935	100	141	42	1469	59	14.83	-	3	48
H.B.Daer	1938-1939	9	12	3	60	17	6.66	-	-	4
G.B.Davies	1912-1914	32	51	8	757	118	17.60	2	-	27
W.Davis	1920	4	6	0	26	13	4.33	-	-	2
M.H.Denness	1977-1980	83	137	9	4050	195	31.64	6	23	38
J.N.Dennis	1934-1939	22	33	3	530	53	17.66	-	1	13
H.W.de Zoete	1897	2	2	2	2	2*	-	-	-	-
W.J.Dines	1947-1949	20	30	7	431	69*	18.73	-	2	7
S.C.Dinsdale	1970	5	7	0	97	29	13.85	-	-	4
M.Diwan	1994	1	2	0	0	0	0.00	-	-	-
J.G.Dixon	1914-1922	93	148	12	2214	173	16.27	3	3	48
T.C.Dodds	1946-1959	380	663	17	18565	157	28.73	17	107	176
C.H.Douglas	1912-1919	21	27	0	326	78	12.07	-	1	4
J.W.H.T.Douglas	1901-1928	459	746	108	17915	210*	28.07	18	77	265
W.D.F.Dow	1958-1959	2	3	2	9	9*	9.00	-	-	-
A.W.Durley	1957	5	8	0	38	16	4.75	-	-	3
D.E.East	1981-1989	190	254	32	4553	134	20.50	4	17	480/53
R.E.East	1965-1984	405	513	111	7103	113	17.66	1	22	251
G.F.Eastman	1926-1929	48	66	28	265	34*	6.97	-	-	29/21
L.C.Eastman	1920-1939	442	679	49	12965	161	20.57	7	58	254
B.E.A.Edmeades	1961-1976	335	555	69	12593	163	25.91	14	61	105
G.J.Edwards	1907	2	3	0	45	21	15.00	-	-	2
H.D.E.Elliott	1913	2	4	0	3	3	0.75	-	-	1
R.E.Evans	1950-1957	17	29	0	482	79	16.62	-	3	8
V.J.Evans	1932-1937	62	96	37	469	23*	7.94	-	-	12
S.C.Eve	1949-1957	32	51	4	1041	120	22.14	1	6	17
F.L.Fane	1895-1922	292	512	30	12599	217	26.13	18	53	141
H.A.Faragher	1949-1950	6	9	2	274	85*	39.14	-	3	4
K.Farnes	1930-1939	79	94	31	590	97*	9.36	-	1	42
G.G.Farnfield	1921	12	20	1	252	41	13.26	-	-	5

	Seasons	M	I	NO	R	HS	Avge	100	50	Ct/St
W.F.O.Faviell	1908	7	12	4	104	27	13.00	-	-	4
M.G.Field-Buss	1987	2	4	1	56	34*	18.66	-	-	-
K.W.R.Fletcher	1962-1988	574	920	122	29434	228*	36.88	45	176	519
M.K.Fosh	1976-1978	14	23	0	481	66	20.91	-	4	5
N.A.Foster	1980-1993	180	200	44	3440	107*	22.05	2	10	96
B.C.Francis	1971-1973	47	84	7	2962	188*	38.46	7	16	10
H.W.F.Franklin	1921-1931	73	104	14	1757	106	19.52	2	6	36
R.C.Franklin	1924	1	2	0	1	1	0.50	-	-	1
A.G.J.Fraser	1991-1992	5	5	2	86	52*	28.66	-	1	1
A.J.Freeman	1920	1	2	1	1	1	1.00	-	-	-
E.C.Freeman	1894-1896	5	9	0	95	35	10.55	-	-	1
E.J.Freeman	1904-1912	55	91	3	1280	84	14.54	-	7	14
J.R.Freeman	1905-1928	336	577	56	14507	286	27.84	26	64	230/46
M.A.Garnham	1989-1994	130	176	37	4109	123	29.56	4	22	266/18
W.T.Garrett	1900-1903	15	25	1	516	92	21.50	-	3	4
J.S.B.Gentry	1925	1	did not bat							
P.A.Gibb	1951-1956	145	250	12	6328	141	26.58	8	25	273/63
A.L.Gibson	1895-1910	23	36	3	492	71	14.90	-	1	6
K.L.Gibson	1909-1912	36	55	6	795	75	16.22	-	2	53/9
F.W.Gilligan	1919-1929	79	108	27	1808	78*	22.32	-	5	87/33
F.H.Gillingham	1903-1928	181	307	21	9160	201	32.02	19	39	91
C.Gladwin	1981-1987	67	114	7	2953	162	27.59	1	17	31
A.K.Golding	1983	1	2	2	8	6*	-	-	-	-
G.A.Gooch	1973-1994	346	569	54	26719	275	51.88	79	129	344
C.H.Gosling	1930	2	4	0	61	33	15.25	-	-	2
R.C.Gosling	1894-1896	4	8	1	55	21*	7.85	-	-	1
L.Graham	1926	2	3	1	14	12	7.00	-	-	2
D.A.A.Gray	1947	1	1	0	6	6	6.00	-	-	-
W.J.Gray	1894	1	2	0	4	3	2.00	-	-	-
M.A.Green	1930	2	4	0	27	13	6.75	-	-	1
W.T.Greensmith	1947-1963	371	550	149	8042	138*	20.05	1	25	147
C.Griffiths	1951-1953	27	41	3	615	105	16.18	1	1	4
A.S.Grimwood	1925	4	6	0	26	15	4.33	-	-	-
T.G.Grinter	1909-1921	8	13	1	201	49*	16.75	-	-	2
W.C.Gunary	1929	1	1	0	0	0	0.00	-	-	1
S.Hadden	1912-1920	6	5	2	29	17*	9.66	-	-	5/1
H.Hailey	1894-1895	13	22	5	301	66*	17.70	-	2	5
B.R.Hardie	1973-1990	374	601	78	17945	162	34.31	27	89	346
S.N.Hare	1921	3	5	0	117	98	23.40	-	1	1
J.Harris	1905	2	3	1	0	0*	0.00	-	-	4
J.G.W.Harrold	1923-1928	11	19	3	88	17	5.50	-	-	13
R.C.Harvey	1952	1	2	2	12	12*	-	-	-	-
F.C.Hawker	1937	1	2	-	26	16	13.00	-	-	-
A.F.G.Hayzelden	1929-1931	2	3	1	5	4*	2.50	-	-	3
E.W.Hazelton	1919	1	2	0	8	8	4.00	-	-	-
A.E.Heatley	1894	1	2	1	20	13*	20.00	-	-	4
R.M.Heaven	1939	1	1	1	5	6*	-	-	-	4
P.A.Hector	1977	3	5	1	75	40	18.75	-	-	-
R.Herbert	1976-1980	6	9	1	62	14*	7.75	-	-	5
J.P.Herringshaw	1921-1922	9	14	5	94	18	10.44	-	-	7
G.F.Higgins	1894-1895	9	17	0	306	118	18.00	1	-	2
H.M.Hills	1912-1919	14	21	4	139	26	8.17	-	-	7
C.Hilton	1964	24	23	9	128	29*	9.14	-	-	12
A.B.Hipkin	1923-1931	231	326	55	4239	108	15.64	2	12	209
R.N.S.Hobbs	1961-1975	325	429	102	4069	100	12.44	2	2	222
G.W.Hockey	1928-1931	19	33	5	305	23	10.89	-	-	4

	Seasons	M	I	NO	R	HS	Avge	100	50	Ct/S
G.W.Horrex	1956-1957	7	13	0	141	41	10.84	-	-	-
R.Horsfall	1947-1955	207	349	25	9583	206	29.59	17	49	85
W.G.Hubble	1923	1	1	0	0	0	0.00	-	-	-
M.G.Hughes	1983	1	2	0	10	10	5.00	-	-	-
F.E.Hugonin	1927-1928	6	8	3	42	17	8.40	-	-	8/
A.Hurd	1958-1960	35	34	14	115	20*	5.75	-	-	5
G.C.Hurst	1962	1	2	1	0	0*	0.00	-	-	1
N.Hussain	1987-1994	120	178	23	6738	197	43.47	18	31	153
B.J.Hyam	1993	1	2	0	1	1	0.50	-	-	2
R.W.J.G.Hyndson	1919	1	2	0	7	6	3.50	-	-	-
M.C.Ilott	1988-1994	68	72	18	716	51	13.25	-	2	18
J.H.Inns	1898-1904	10	14	3	73	28	6.63	-	-	8
D.J.Insole	1947-1963	345	574	54	20113	219*	38.67	48	97	279
R.C.Irani	1994	18	29	6	965	119	41.95	2	8	6
B.L.Irvine	1968-1969	54	89	12	2674	109	34.72	1	15	4C
V.E.Jarvis	1925	2	4	0	44	37	11.00	-	-	-
C.V.Jenkinson	1922-1923	5	6	2	9	8	2.25	-	-	4
L.C.S.Jerman	1950-1951	3	2	0	8	8	4.00	-	-	2
A.S.Johnston	1894-1896	7	12	1	235	63	21.36	-	1	3
A.M.Jorden	1966-1970	60	85	20	704	59*	10.83	-	2	3(
R.C.G.Joy	1922-1928	13	16	2	142	35	10.14	-	-	1(
M.S.Kasprowicz	1994	17	24	4	326	44	16.30	-	-	9
H.D.Keigwin	1906-1907	4	6	0	69	20	11.50	-	-	1
R.P.Keigwin	1903-1919	20	32	3	455	75	15.68	-	1	2
C.J.M.Kenny	1950-1953	18	14	6	26	16	3.25	-	-	4
T.Kent	1960-1962	10	10	4	74	23*	12.33	-	-	5
I.M.King	1957	28	36	21	131	33	8.73	-	-	29
R.J.S.King	1928	1	1	0	3	3	3.00	-	-	-
B.R.Knight	1955-1966	239	399	42	8798	165	24.64	8	46	17
N.V.Knight	1991-1994	46	74	8	2454	157	37.18	7	11	59
C.J.Kortright	1894-1907	160	255	181	4182	131	17.64	2	10	16'
J.C.Laker	1962-1964	30	29	8	248	28	11.80	-	-	1
A.W.E.Lapham	1921	3	5	0	31	16	6.20	-	-	-
A.E.Lashbrooke	1908	1	2	0	9	9	4.50	-	-	-
A.B.Lavers	1937-1953	25	44	2	695	42*	16.54	-	-	(
T.P.Lawrence	1933-1935	7	14	0	133	39	9.50	-	-	2
J.M.Leiper	1950	2	4	0	50	44	12.50	-	-	2
R.J.Leiper	1981-1982	2	4	0	53	49	13.25	-	-	2
J.K.Lever	1967-1989	443	446	168	2830	91	10.17	-	1	16(
D.C.Levick	1950-1951	3	6	0	14	6	2.33	-	-	-
J.J.B.Lewis	1990-1994	45	76	12	2422	136*	37.84	4	16	2
A.W.Lilley	1978-1990	120	190	15	4495	113*	25.68	3	24	6
P J.Lindsey	1964	1	1	1	7	7*	-	-	-	-
C.G.Littlehales	1896-1904	6	10	1	109	23	12.11	-	-	4
J.Littlewood	1905	1	1	1	5	5*	-	-	-	-
G.M.Locks	1928	2	4	2	5	3*	2.50	-	-	-
G.M.Louden	1912-1927	82	125	33	844	74	9.17	-	2	5
F.A.Loveday	1921-1923	7	14	0	321	81	22.92	-	3	2
A.P.Lucas	1894-1907	98	153	21	3554	135	26.92	2	20	5
R.A.G.Luckin	1962-1963	29	46	3	735	82	17.09	-	2	2
R.V.Lynch	1954	3	3	2	7	6*	7.00	-	-	2
L.W.Lywood	1930	2	3	0	12	7	4.00	-	-	2
M.S.A.McEvoy	1976-1981	43	74	1	1371	67*	18.78	-	8	4

	Seasons	M	I	NO	R	HS	Avge	100	50	Ct/St
K.S.McEwan	1974-1985	282	458	41	18088	218	43.37	52	82	197
C.P.McGahey	1894-1921	400	685	61	19079	277	30.57	29	97	140
C.D.McIver	1902-1922	59	101	6	2544	134	26.77	4	13	47/13
M.Mackinnon	1926	3	4	0	55	31	13.75	-	-	-
S.J.Malone	1975-1978	2	did not bat							-
J.W.Marston	1923-1924	2	4	1	12	6	4.00	-	-	1
A.D.Martin	1920-1921	3	3	0	0	0	0.00	-	-	1
E.G.Martin	1928	2	4	0	25	13	6.25	-	-	1
O.Martyn	1922	1	1	0	0	0	0.00	-	-	1
W.H.J.Mayes	1914	1	2	0	2	2	1.00	-	-	-
H.Mead	1913-1914	4	8	2	19	8*	3.16	-	-	3
W.Mead	1894-1913	332	469	125	3843	119	11.17	1	5	151
G.C.Melluish	1926	4	3	1	18	16*	9.00	-	-	-
C.F.Mercer	1929	2	4	0	26	8	6.50	-	-	-
A.H.Meston	1926-1927	12	17	4	143	41	11.00	-	-	9
S.P.Meston	1907-1908	17	29	2	476	130	17.62	1	-	7
G.Miller	1987-1989	52	65	12	1094	77	20.64	-	4	58
J.Milner	1957-1961	66	117	12	2688	135	25.60	3	12	57
E.S.Missen	1921	1	2	0	20	12	10.00	-	-	-
G.F.Mitchell	1926	1	1	0	4	4	4.00	-	-	-
K.F.Moore	1961	1	1	0	2	2	2.00	-	-	2
H.M.Morris	1919-1932	240	383	29	6974	166	19.70	3	34	78
P.E.Morris	1909-1924	28	43	5	418	55*	11.00	-	1	13
W.B.Morris	1946-1950	48	78	10	1219	68	17.92	-	5	18
H.C.Mortlock	1912-1921	4	4	0	32	26	8.00	-	-	6
A.S.Moule	1921-1924	17	31	5	317	64	12.19	-	1	5
W.Naylor	1906	1	2	0	2	2	1.00	-	-	2
F.W.H.Nicholas	1912-1929	63	101	2	2255	140	22.77	1	14	41/13
M.S.Nichols	1924-1939	418	664	66	15736	205	26.31	20	78	279
G.J.Nolan	1968	1	2	0	14	11	7.00	-	-	-
G.Norman	1920	4	5	1	44	21	11.00	-	-	1
R.O.G.Norman	1932	1	2	0	20	10	10.00	-	-	-
J.O'Connor	1921-1939	516	866	76	27819	248	35.21	71	125	215/1
C.E.L.Orman	1896	2	2	0	16	12	8.00	-	-	1
H.G.P.Owen	1894-1902	133	222	17	4459	134	21.75	3	31	38
H.A.Page	1987	15	20	4	266	60	16.62	-	2	5
E.J.Palmer	1957	4	6	5	39	11*	39.00	-	-	1
H.J.Palmer	1924-1932	53	65	23	257	25*	6.11	-	-	19
L.F.Parslow	1946	1	2	0	9	5	4.50	-	-	-
C.H.Pascoe	1909	1	1	1	3	3*	-	-	-	-
R.F.T.Paterson	1946	25	40	5	680	80	19.42	-	3	12/3
J.H.Pawle	1935-1938	6	11	0	194	68	17.63	-	1	4
T.N.Pearce	1929-1950	231	376	48	11139	211*	33.96	20	55	144
R.M.Pearson	1994	3	4	0	45	20	11.25	-	-	2
P.A.Perrin	1896-1928	525	894	88	29172	343*	36.19	65	145	284
P.J.Phelan	1958-1965	154	192	70	1505	63	12.33	-	3	67
N.Phillip	1978-1985	144	201	22	3784	134	21.13	1	18	45
L.J.Phillips	1919-1922	4	5	1	38	19	9.50	-	-	-
H.G.Pickering	1938	3	6	0	62	17	10.33	-	-	-
H.Pickett	1894-1897	52	80	34	387	35	8.41	-	-	19
S.G.Plumb	1975-1977	2	3	1	68	37*	34.00	-	-	-
I.L.Pont	1985-1988	23	26	9	356	68	20.94	-	1	4
K.R.Pont	1970-1986	198	305	44	6558	125*	25.12	7	35	92
R.N.Pook	1988	1	1	0	6	6	6.00	-	-	3
D.F.Pope	1928-1934	148	248	14	6443	161	27.53	7	31	35

	Seasons	M	I	NO	R	HS	Avge	100	50	Ct/St
A.G.Powell	1932-1937	23	35	7	495	62*	17.67	-	1	30/8
H.C.Preece	1895	2	4	0	74	49	18.50	-	-	-
E.R.Presland	1962-1970	30	41	4	625	51	16.89	-	1	24
K.C.Preston	1948-1964	391	460	165	3024	70	10.25	-	2	344
E.J.Price	1948-1949	43	56	16	214	26*	5.35	-	-	24
P.J.Prichard	1984-1994	224	359	43	11498	245	36.38	23	66	146
D.R.Pringle	1978-1993	213	280	55	6325	128	28.11	5	35	115
G.C.Pritchard	1965-1966	10	11	2	19	8	2.11	-	-	3
S.Proffitt	1937	7	14	0	170	39	12.14	-	-	1
S.C.Puddefoot	1922-1923	8	8	2	101	42	16.83	-	-	2
G.R.Pullinger	1949-1950	18	20	11	53	14*	5.88	-	-	14
J.H.Purves	1960-1961	5	7	0	36	14	5.14	-	-	1
A.B.Quick	1936-1952	19	32	1	433	57	13.96	-	2	12
S.E.V.Quin	1924	1	1	0	0	0	0.00	-	-	-
M.Raison	1928-1930	17	27	2	451	57	18.04	-	1	6
L.H.R.Ralph	1953-1961	174	262	39	3763	73	16.87	-	9	143
A.H.Read	1904-1910	22	30	6	419	70	17.45	-	2	7
H.D.Read	1933-1935	32	41	15	104	17*	4.00	-	-	14
I.Redpath	1987	7	12	1	128	46	11.63	-	-	2
D.Reese	1906	8	15	2	198	70	15.23	-	1	-
W.Reeves	1897-1921	271	422	34	6451	135	16.62	3	24	115
R.J.Richards	1970	1	did not bat							-
C.S.Richardson	1914	1	1	0	15	15	15.00	-	-	1
J.V.Richardson	1924-1926	14	18	3	300	82	20.00	-	3	8
P.J.Richardson	1912	2	2	0	34	21	17.00	-	-	1
K.R.Rickards	1953	1	2	0	25	13	12.50	-	-	-
H.W.Riding	1921	1	2	0	23	16	11.50	-	-	-
G.V.N.Ridley	1922-1926	6	11	0	113	54	10.27	-	1	3
F.H.Rist	1934-1953	65	108	9	1496	62	15.11	-	3	35/5
D.C.Robinson	1908	7	12	1	148	37	13.45	-	-	12/1
D.D.J.Robinson	1993-1994	3	5	0	150	67	30.00	-	1	3
R.H.Robinson	1912	4	7	2	25	11*	5.00	-	-	9/4
R.J.Rollins	1992-1994	5	7	1	42	13	7.00	-	-	6/3
C.J.Round	1921	2	4	0	9	8	2.25	-	-	-
F.E.Rowe	1894-1895	3	5	0	32	19	6.40	-	-	1
G.W.Rowley	1926	5	7	1	53	23	8.83	-	-	-
C.A.G.Russell	1908-1930	379	628	51	23610	273	40.91	62	117	280
A.E.Russell	1898-1910	130	196	42	2025	100	13.14	1	1	163/44
T.M.Russell	1894-1905	162	246	45	3106	139	15.45	3	6	246/88
Sadiq Mohammad	1970	1	1	0	20	20	20.00	-	-	-
G.E.Sainsbury	1979-1980	3	2	2	2	2*	-	-	-	1
N.H.Saint	1920-1923	44	72	7	757	36	11.64	-	-	10
Salim Malik	1991-1993	39	63	11	2889	215	55.55	8	11	38
L.A.Savill	1953-1961	125	200	16	3919	115	21.29	4	15	50
G.J.Saville	1963-1974	124	214	29	4265	126*	23.05	2	21	101
D.Sayers	1967	1	1	1	0	0*	-	-	-	-
F.J.Scoulding	1912-1920	22	28	11	92	21	5.41	-	-	6
C.J.Searle	1947	1	1	1	5	5*	-	-	-	1/1
L.D.Sears	1925	2	4	0	18	16	4.50	-	-	-
D.J.Semmence	1962	1	2	0	33	24	16.50	-	-	-
E.H.D.Sewell	1902-1904	55	91	5	1822	107	21.18	2	11	45
A.C.H.Seymour	1988-1991	14	24	4	697	157	34.85	1	4	8
N.Shahid	1989-1994	65	97	16	2523	132	31.14	2	14	64
R.H.Sharp	1925-1928	16	25	7	169	36*	9.38	-	-	16
J.R.Sheffield	1929-1936	177	272	40	3822	108	16.47	1	15	194/54

	Seasons	M	I	NO	R	HS	Avge	100	50	Ct/St
H.R.Sherman	1967-1969	13	21	3	448	66	24.88	-	4	4
R.N.Shorter	1927-1929	23	29	11	104	21	5.77	-	-	12
I.J.Skinner	1950	13	21	7	28	7*	2.00	-	-	5
G.J.Smith	1955-1966	239	412	30	8519	148	22.30	4	44	131
G.W.O.Smith	1929-1930	10	18	3	206	39*	13.73	-	-	2
H.T.O.Smith	1929-1935	23	36	5	361	38	11.64	-	-	19
H.W.Smith	1912-1922	20	31	12	195	22	10.26	-	-	12
N.Smith	1973-1981	178	226	47	3225	126	18.01	2	8	381/47
R.Smith	1934-1956	419	646	81	11125	147	19.69	6	48	179
T.P.B.Smith	1929-1951	434	647	115	9652	163	18.14	8	32	330
W.G.Spencer	1938-1948	3	5	1	52	25	13.00	-	-	-
P.A.Spicer	1962-1963	17	29	2	526	86	19.48	-	4	4
E.E.Spinks	1926	2	3	1	2	2	1.00	-	-	1
H.Spurr	1923	1	2	0	13	9	6.50	-	-	-
E.A.W.Stanley	1950-1952	13	21	3	226	35	12.55	-	-	2
A.R.Stanyard	1960	2	3	0	47	26	15.66	-	-	-
J.P.Stephenson	1985-1994	171	293	28	9383	202*	35.40	16	51	104
J.W.A.Stephenson	1934-1939	61	93	21	1050	65	14.58	-	2	30
E.A.W.Steward	1964-1965	15	23	2	272	47	12.95	-	-	17
F.Street	1898-1899	9	11	0	246	76	22.36	-	2	4
B.T.Strutton	1914-1919	4	6	1	64	19	12.80	-	-	1
P.M.Such	1990-1994	71	62	13	509	54	10.38	-	1	26
G.Sutton	1912	1	1	0	0	0	0.00	-	-	-
C.F.Swann	1912	1	1	0	0	0	0.00	-	-	-
B.J.Swyer	1923	1	2	0	12	7	6.00	-	-	-
A.G.Taylor	1923	2	3	0	7	7	2.33	-	-	-
B.Taylor	1949-1973	539	901	69	18240	135	21.92	9	78	1040/191
J.F.Taylor	1960-1961	14	23	6	436	86	25.64	-	2	19/3
R.M.Taylor	1931-1946	206	349	21	6755	193	20.59	5	26	185
E.C.Tedder	1946	8	14	0	208	55	14.85	-	1	3
K.O.Thomas	1990	1	1	0	2	2	2.00	-	-	-
E.C.Thompson	1926-1929	44	61	17	696	45*	15.81	-	-	10
H.W.Thorn	1928	1	2	0	12	7	6.00	-	-	-
P.Toone	1912-1922	29	42	13	215	24	7.41	-	-	23
T.D.Topley	1985-1994	113	127	26	1520	66	15.04	-	4	65
G.Tosetti	1898-1905	41	63	6	1054	132*	18.49	1	3	15
E.M.O.Toulmin	1899-1912	2	2	0	1	1	0.50	-	-	2
A.F.M.Townsend	1910	1	did not bat				-			-
C.J.H.Treglown	1922-1928	34	55	3	792	77	15.23	-	5	11
B.Tremlin	1900-1919	132	193	63	1776	61	13.66	-	5	62
S.A.Trick	1905-1919	5	9	0	69	26	7.66	-	-	1
A.J.Turner	1897-1904	68	116	12	3730	124	35.86	11	13	26/2
S.Turner	1965-1986	354	503	98	9264	121	22.87	4	41	215
W.M.F.Turner	1899-1926	48	81	7	2004	172	27.08	2	12	58
P.W.Turrall	1927	1	1	0	45	45	45.00	-	-	-
E.J.Unwin	1932-1939	7	14	0	152	48	10.85	-	-	2
F.St.G.Unwin	1932-1950	52	85	8	1125	60	14.61	-	3	33
J.Valiant	1912	1	2	1	3	3	3.00	-	-	-
H.H.van Straubenzee	1938	1	1	1	4	4*	-	-	-	-
N.Vere Hodge	1936-1939	23	38	6	713	108	22.28	2	3	11
F.H.Vigar	1938-1954	256	397	62	8660	144	25.58	11	38	195
J.E.W.Waddington	1931	1	1	0	8	8	8.00	-	-	-
T.H.Wade	1929-1950	318	472	135	4972	96	14.75	-	15	413/177

	Seasons	M	I	NO	R	HS	Avge	100	50	Ct/St
H.Wagstaff	1920-1921	5	6	4	19	17*	9.50	-	-	-
K.W.Wallace	1967-1972	10	16	0	219	55	13.68	-	1	2
B.Ward	1967-1972	128	222	19	4799	164*	23.64	4	24	60
G.H.Ward	1950	1	2	0	4	2	2.00	-	-	1
B.Warsop	1931-1932	5	10	2	128	51	16.00	-	1	1
A.G.Waterman	1937-1938	10	15	1	380	103	27.14	1	1	7
D.Watkins	1949-1954	12	17	4	210	32	16.15	-	-	5
A.C.Watson	1913-1914	2	4	0	89	37	22.25	-	-	2
C.J.M.Watts	1928	8	11	0	119	41	10.81	-	-	2/2
H.P.Waugh	1919-1929	8	14	0	213	128	15.21	1	-	8
M.E.Waugh	1988-1992	65	100	17	5101	219*	61.45	16	23	78
G.H.S.West	1949-1953	2	4	0	79	55	19.75	-	1	-
L.H.West	1928	3	5	0	33	30	6.60	-	-	-
H.M.Whitcombe	1922	3	4	2	13	7*	6.50	-	-	1
P.S.Whitcombe	1922	1	2	0	9	5	4.50	-	-	-
D.R.Wilcox	1928-1947	118	186	8	5482	142	30.79	8	31	88
J.W.T.Wilcox	1964-1967	19	30	5	596	87	23.84	-	4	11
C.C.P.Williams	1954-1959	40	68	3	1518	119	23.35	1	7	23
H.R.H.Williams	1919-1920	10	12	2	67	23*	6.70	-	-	18/7
L.D.Womersley	1910	1	2	0	9	9	4.50	-	-	-
A.E.Wright	1931-1934	3	5	1	45	14	11.25	-	-	1
J.V.Wright	1962-1967	4	6	0	60	40	10.00	-	-	2
R.W.Wrightson	1965-1967	12	20	4	332	84	20.75	-	1	8
N.G.Wykes	1925-1936	30	42	3	879	162	22.53	1	2	5
H.I.Young	1898-1912	128	186	50	1413	44	10.38	-	-	59

In addition B.Stead was due to appear against Oxford University at Oxford in 1962 but did not turn up. Essex played with 10 men.

BOWLING

	Balls	Runs	Wkts	Avge	Best	5wi	10wm
D.L.Acfield	59449	23509	855	27.49	8-55	30	4
S.J.W.Andrew	9598	5457	150	36.38	7-47	3	-
F.Appleyard	2004	817	19	43.00	5-14	1	-
H.A.Arkwright	190	109	4	27.25	3-25	-	-
C.T.Ashton	5333	2923	97	30.13	7-51	3	-
P.Ashton	72	55	1	55.00	1-55	-	-
A.V.Avery	1279	627	9	69.66	1-11	-	-
G.W.Ayres	279	139	5	27.80	1-2	-	-
J.A.Bailey	10696	4553	198	22.99	7-32	11	-
T.E.Bailey	86495	35042	1593	21.99	10-90	91	10
A.E.Banfield	102	62	2	31.00	2-62	-	-
A.N.Barber	150	76	1	76.00	1-42	-	-
G.Barker	439	200	5	40.00	2-34	-	-
J.D.Barnfather	665	355	13	27.30	6-32	1	-
P.L.Barrow	72	43	1	43.00	1-21	-	-
J.F.Bawtree	105	66	2	33.00	1-16	-	-
M.J.Bear	98	53	0				
C.E.Benham	4306	2176	65	33.47	7-60	4	-
M.Berkley	138	103	7	14.71	6-50	1	-

	Balls	Runs	Wkts	Avge	Best	5wi	10wm
F.D.Billham	138	72	0				
D.J.P.Boden	336	258	3	86.00	2-118	-	-
A.R.Border	372	233	2	116.50	1-8	-	-
N.F.Borrett	96	43	0				
C.S.R.Boswell	2597	1345	36	37.36	4-22	-	-
K.D.Boyce	33471	15704	662	23.72	9-61	30	6
C.Bray	197	104	2	52.00	1-1		
O.C.Bristowe	1328	901	22	40.95	4-74	-	-
G.R.R.Brown	1930	834	30	27.80	5-55	1	-
H.J.Brunwin	24	5	1	5.00	1-5	-	-
C.P.Buckenham	43647	24629	934	26.36	8-33	72	16
F.G.Bull	16696	7923	365	21.70	5-93	29	5
J.Burns	628	310	6	51.66	3-24	-	-
H.J.E.Burrell	5	0	0				
C.N.Calnan	18	25	0				
P.Campbell	18	26	0				
G.N.Capel-Cure	66	58	2	29.00	2-58	-	-
N.J.O.Carbutt	216	202	2	101.00	2-23	-	-
H.A.Carpenter	3750	2163	46	47.02	4-57	-	-
R.B.Carr	96	62	0				
G.Carter	24	18	0				
I.Chapman	42	18	0				
J.H.Childs	34949	14427	517	27.90	8-58	29	6
L.S.Clark	30	15	0				
C.B.Clarke	2638	1353	58	23.32	7-130	3	-
E.J.Connor	252	131	2	65.50	2-21	-	-
R.M.O.Cooke	204	149	3	49.66	2-55		
F.J.Cooper	658	385	8	48.12	5-71	1	-
W.Cooper	114	69	0				
F.Cottam	60	25	0				
P.Cousens	3980	1707	44	38.79	4-63	-	-
D.M.Cousins	834	446	14	31.85	6-35	1	-
H.P.Crabtree	90	63	0				
L.G.Crawley	72	39	0				
S.J.Cray	42	40	1	40.00	1-0	-	-
J.A.Cutmore	961	687	11	62.45	2-31	-	-
A.G.Daer	13868	6183	195	31.70	6-38	3	-
H.B.Daer	570	387	11	36.18	3-21	-	-
G.B.Davies	3075	1769	68	26.01	6-51	2	-
W.Davis	84	69	1	69.00	1-67	-	-
M.H.Denness	6	0	0				
H.W.de Zoete	160	91	3	30.33	2-44		
W.J.Dines	1952	980	15	65.33	3-35	-	-
J.G.Dixon	11224	6484	206	31.47	7-61	9	2
T.C.Dodds	1759	1053	35	30.08	4-34	-	-
C.H.Douglas	445	350	6	58.33	3-46	-	-
J.W.H.T.Douglas	63317	33653	1443	23.32	9-47	93	21
W.D.F.Dow	332	171	4	42.75	4-51	-	-
D.E.East	26	17	0				
R.E.East	65017	25804	1010	25.54	8-30	49	10
L.C.Eastman	61025	26102	975	26.77	7-28	29	3
B.E.A.Edmeades	22759	9688	374	25.90	7-37	10	1
H.D.E.Elliott	138	107	1	107.00	1-67	-	-
V.J.Evans	7828	3843	129	29.79	6-47	5	1

	Balls	Runs	Wkts	Avge	Best	5wi	10wm
F.L.Fane	41	32	0				
K.Farnes	14787	7086	367	19.30	8-38	28	5
W.F.O.Faviell	30	13	0				
K.W.R.Fletcher	1577	1268	29	43.72	5-41	1	-
N.A.Foster	35823	17626	747	23.59	8-99	42	7
H.W.F.Franklin	2358	1596	36	44.33	4-40	-	-
R.C.Franklin	66	41	1	41.00	1-20	-	-
A.G.J.Fraser	237	139	3	46.33	2-37	-	-
A.J.Freeman	144	95	0				
E.C.Freeman	60	40	0				
E.J.Freeman	108	50	1	50.00	1-6	-	-
J.R.Freeman	580	365	10	36.50	3-31	-	-
M.A.Garnham	24	39	0				
W.T.Garrett	264	142	1	142.00	1-72	-	-
J.S.B.Gentry	48	20	0				
P.A.Gibb	5	4	0				
A.L.Gibson	30	16	0				
K.L.Gibson	11	9	1	9.00	1-9	-	-
F.W.Gilligan	2	6	0				
F.H.Gillingham	8	13	0				
C.Gladwin	126	71	0				
A.K.Golding	168	97	2	48.50	1-44	-	-
G.A.Gooch	13855	6368	192	33.16	7-14	3	-
D.A.A.Gray	174	63	1	63.00	1-34	-	-
W.T.Greensmith	43933	20711	720	28.76	8-59	21	2
C.Griffiths	18	22	0				
A.S.Grimwood	6	5	0				
W.C.Gunary	114	58	0				
B.R.Hardie	282	254	3	84.66	2-39	-	-
J.G.W.Harrold	180	123	3	41.00	1-15	-	-
R.C.Harvey	96	88	3	29.33	3-88	-	-
A.F.G.Hayzelden	227	110	6	18.33	3-30	-	-
E.W.Hazleton	108	77	0				
A.E.Heatley	5	10	0				
P.A.Hector	336	190	7	27.14	3-56	-	-
R.Herbert	220	148	3	49.33	3-64	-	-
J.P.Herringshaw	902	498	9	55.33	2-48	-	-
H.M.Hills	1147	738	15	49.20	5-63	1	-
C.Hilton	3783	1999	58	34.46	6-86	1	-
A.B.Hipkin	32592	13377	518	25.82	8-71	18	3
R.N.S.Hobbs	43935	19844	763	26.00	8-63	32	5
G.W.Hockey	30	20	0				
R.Horsfall	72	41	1	41.00	1-4	-	-
W.G.Hubble	106	60	2	30.00	2-3	-	-
M.G.Hughes	188	162	6	27.00	4-71	-	-
A.Hurd	4912	2221	84	26.44	6-15	5	1
N.Hussain	276	307	2	153.50	1-38	-	-
R.W.J.G.Hyndson	84	71	0				
M.C.Ilott	12819	6658	215	30.96	7-85	8	1
J.H.Inns	30	15	0				
D.J.Insole	7705	4061	119	34.12	5-22	1	-
R.C.Irani	1498	834	28	29.78	4-27	-	-
B.L.Irvine	108	70	1	70.00	1-39	-	-
V.E.Jarvis	36	23	0				

	Balls	Runs	Wkts	Avge	Best	5wi	10wm
L.C.S.Jerman	492	222	1	222.00	1-39	-	-
A.M.Jorden	6844	3501	117	29.92	4-29	-	-
R.C.G.Joy	790	398	12	33.16	3-41	-	-
M.S.Kasprowicz	3165	1869	60	31.15	7-83	3	-
H.D.Keigwin	336	179	4	44.75	1-23	-	-
R.P.Keigwin	986	639	14	45.64	4-49	-	-
C.J.M.Kenny	2493	1212	39	31.07	5-80	1	-
T.Kent	1266	561	15	37.40	4-54	-	-
I.M.King	3155	1146	34	33.70	4-25	-	-
R.J.S.King	42	20	0				
B.R.Knight	37727	17162	761	22.55	8-69	39	8
N.V.Knight	100	93	1	93.00	1-61	-	-
C.J.Kortright	16044	9036	440	20.53	8-57	35	8
J.C.Laker	5879	2367	111	21.32	7-73	7	2
A.W.E.Lapham	176	90	5	18.00	2-25	-	-
A.E.Lashbrooke	102	61	1	61.00	1-26	-	-
A.B.Lavers	960	483	13	37.15	4-68	-	-
J.M.Leiper	192	79	1	79.00	1-38	-	-
J.K.Lever	75190	34669	1473	23.53	8-37	77	11
J.J.B.Lewis	48	32	0				
A.W.Lilley	519	565	8	70.62	3-116	-	-
P.J.Lindsey	108	50	1	50.00	1-8	-	-
J.Littlewood	66	36	0				
G.M.Locks	438	227	3	75.66	2-86	-	-
G.M.Louden	18241	9066	415	21.84	8-36	33	5
A.P.Lucas	115	90	1	90.00	1-17	-	-
R.V.Lynch	258	107	4	26.75	4-64	-	-
L.W.Lywood	156	83	2	41.50	1-7	-	-
M.S.A.McEvoy	180	103	3	34.33	3-20	-	-
K.S.McEwan	277	301	4	75.25	1-0	-	-
C.P.McGahey	17871	9481	306	30.98	7-27	12	3
C.D.McIver	62	25	1	25.00	1-4	-	-
S.J.Malone	246	101	2	50.50	1-28	-	-
J.W.Marston	168	112	2	56.00	2-47	-	-
A.D.Martin	306	210	5	42.00	3-43	-	-
E.G.Martin	264	140	2	70.00	1-63	-	-
W.H.J.Mayes	84	69	0				
H.Mead	334	194	3	64.66	2-84	-	-
W.Mead	71529	28423	1472	19.30	9-40	117	30
G.C.Melluish	222	115	3	38.33	1-17	-	-
A.H.Meston	588	352	4	88.00	2-18	-	-
S.P.Meston	50	48	1	48.00	1-10	-	-
G.Miller	6032	2636	81	32.54	7-59	2	1
J.Milner	12	14	0				
G.F.Mitchell	102	45	1	45.00	1-25	-	-
K.F.Moore	174	43	4	10.75	4-21	-	-
H.M.Morris	1361	839	14	59.92	2-16	-	-
P.E.Morris	3593	1848	83	22.26	8-106	6	1
W.B.Morris	4026	1975	43	45.93	4-90	-	-
H.C.Mortlock	582	380	7	54.28	5-104	1	-
A.S.Moule	6	6	0				
M.S.Nichols	72542	34201	1608	21.26	9-32	108	22
G.Norman	18	18	0				

	Balls	Runs	Wkts	Avge	Best	5wi	10wm
J.O'Connor	38007	17523	537	32.63	7-52	17	2
H.G.P.Owen	573	321	9	35.66	2-37	-	-
H.A.Page	2042	1172	35	33.48	5-26	1	-
E.J.Palmer	432	225	7	32.14	2-35	-	-
H.J.Palmer	7138	3477	142	24.48	6-68	6	-
C.H.Pascoe	42	16	0				
R.F.T.Paterson	708	464	13	35.69	4-98	-	-
T.N.Pearce	1394	927	15	61.80	4-12	-	-
R.M.Pearson	444	226	4	56.50	1-39	-	-
P.A.Perrin	1267	740	16	46.25	3-13	-	-
P.J.Phelan	17760	8510	300	28.36	8-109	17	2
N.Phillip	20863	10638	423	25.14	6-4	18	1
L.J.Phillips	26	31	0				
H.Pickett	6154	2780	114	24.38	10-32	4	1
S.G.Plumb	84	47	2	23.50	2-47	-	-
I.L.Pont	3415	2141	65	32.93	5-73	3	-
K.R.Pont	6531	3189	96	33.21	5-17	2	-
D.F.Pope	348	272	4	68.00	1-11	-	-
E.R.Presland	1771	761	13	58.53	2-19	-	-
K.C.Preston	68718	30288	1155	26.22	7-55	37	2
E.J.Price	6189	3013	92	32.75	8-125	4	-
P.J.Prichard	289	497	2	248.50	1-28	-	-
D.R.Pringle	31801	14365	566	25.37	7-18	20	2
G.C.Pritchard	774	406	7	58.00	4-24	-	-
S.Proffitt	54	32	0				
S.C.Pudefoot	198	105	1	105.00	1-34	-	-
G.R.Pullinger	3117	1557	41	37.97	5-54	1	-
A.B.Quick	11	10	0				
S.E.V.Quin	42	13	0				
M.Raison	920	575	14	41.07	5-104	1	-
L.H.R.Ralph	24427	11053	460	24.02	7-42	19	3
A.H.Read	2162	1192	38	31.36	7-75	1	-
H.D.Read	4499	2765	131	21.10	7-35	7	1
D.Reese	258	165	6	27.50	4-55	-	-
W.Reeves	30512	16137	581	27.77	7-33	37	5
J.V.Richardson	468	253	7	36.14	2-55	-	-
P.J.Richardson	30	12	0				
F.H.Rist	25	8	1	8.00	1-8	-	-
C.J.Round	78	62	1	62.00	1-49	-	-
G.W.Rowley	60	29	0				
C.A.G.Russell	19261	7480	276	27.10	5-25	5	-
G.E.Sainsbury	480	268	8	33.50	4-85	-	-
N.H.Saint	1077	800	17	47.05	3-32	-	-
Salim Malik	2241	1265	39	32.43	5-67	1	-
L.A.Savill	12	26	1	26.00	1-26	-	-
G.J.Saville	90	59	3	19.66	2-30	-	-
D.Sayers	126	64	1	64.00	1-22	-	-
F.J.Scoulding	2465	1252	32	39.12	4-50	-	-
D.J.Semmence	48	31	0				
E.H.D.Sewell	660	388	7	55.42	2-79	-	-
A.C.H.Seymour	24	27	0				
N.Shahid	1623	1040	27	38.51	3-91	-	-
R.H.Sharp	1074	696	16	43.50	5-66	1	-
J.R.Sheffield	72	28	0				

	Balls	Runs	Wkts	Avge	Best	5wi	10wm
H.R.Sherman	42	23	0				
R.N.Shorter	1559	695	15	46.33	3-14	-	-
I.J.Skinner	1458	808	21	38.47	4-56	-	-
G.J.Smith	2206	913	33	27.66	5-39	1	-
H.T.O.Smith	3235	1618	61	26.52	6-56	3	-
H.W.Smith	1943	1055	35	30.14	5-59	1	-
R.Smith	83308	39817	1317	30.23	8-63	73	10
T.P.B.Smith	89914	42314	1610	26.28	9-77	117	27
W.G.Spencer	18	8	1	8.00	1-8	-	-
P.A.Spicer	67	55	2	27.50	2-1	-	-
E.E.Spinks	120	81	0				
E.A.W.Stanley	3	8	0				
J.P.Stephenson	7553	4296	112	38.35	6-54	3	-
J.W.A.Stephenson	8522	4156	174	23.88	8-46	10	1
F.Street	10	14	0				
B.T.Strutton	294	197	0				
P.M.Such	12989	5742	205	28.00	7-66	14	3
B.J.Swyer	78	56	0				
A.G.Taylor	114	77	1	77.00	1-40	-	-
B.Taylor	51	21	1	21.00	1-16	-	-
R.M.Taylor	4674	2933	92	31.88	7-99	3	-
K.O.Thomas	110	81	0				
E.C.Thompson	1750	938	17	55.17	2-12	-	-
H.W.Thorn	60	42	1	42.00	1-42	-	-
P.Toone	2907	1954	62	31.51	6-51	2	1
T.D.Topley	17932	9431	336	28.06	7-75	12	1
G.Tosetti	1764	891	16	55.68	3-67	-	-
E.M.O.Toulmin	150	57	2	28.50	2-16	-	-
B.Tremlin	21903	11734	452	25.96	9-126	23	4
A.J.Turner	722	438	12	36.50	3-47	-	-
S.Turner	52669	20987	810	25.90	6-26	27	1
W.M.F.Turner	276	180	3	60.00	2-12	-	-
E.J.Unwin	180	103	0				
F.St.G.Unwin	72	41	0				
J.Valiant	24	20	0				
H.H.van Sraubenzee	36	12	0				
F.H.Vigar	15188	8958	236	37.95	8-128	8	-
T.H.Wade	2712	1391	47	29.59	5-64	1	-
H.Wagstaff	198	135	2	67.50	1-19	-	-
B.Ward	148	68	5	13.60	2-5	-	-
B.Warsop	36	18	0				
A.G.Waterman	558	348	11	31.63	4-79	-	-
D.Watkins	693	421	8	52.62	2-45	-	-
C.J.M.Watts	2	4	0				
H.P.Waugh	264	135	3	45.00	1-6	-	-
M.E.Waugh	3030	1932	48	40.25	5-37	1	-
H.M.Whitcombe	240	199	1	199.00	1-34	-	-
P.S.Whitcombe	24	22	0				
D.R.Wilcox	113	117	1	117.00	1-46	-	-
C.C.P.Williams	13	5	0				
A.E.Wright	240	86	0				
N.G.Wykes	108	52	0				
H.I.Young	20155	9092	368	24.70	8-54	18	3

123